THE
CAMPAIGN THAT
WON AMERICA

The Story of Yorktown

THE
CAMPAIGN THAT
WON AMERICA

The Story of Yorktown

BURKE DAVIS

ACORN PRESS

BOOK DESIGN BY M. FRANKLIN

Library of Congress Catalog Card Number: 76-103429

Reprinted 1979 with permission of the original publisher—The Dial Press—by the Acorn Press, the publishing arm of Eastern National Park & Monument Association.

Eastern National Park & Monument Association promotes and aids the historical, scientific, and educational activities of the National Park Service. As a nonprofit cooperating association authorized by Congress, it makes interpretive material available to park visitors by sale or free distribution. It also supports research, interpretation, and conservation programs of the Service.

Produced by the Publishing Center for Cultural Resources.

Manufactured in the United States of America.

TO *Carlisle H. Humelsine*

Contents

Order of Events
of the
Yorktown Campaign
1781

APRIL: Washington sends the Marquis de Lafayette to Virginia with a small army to oppose a British invasion.

MAY 10:   Lord Charles Cornwallis, at the end of a hard campaign in the Carolinas, arrives in Virginia without orders and maneuvers against Lafayette.

AUGUST 2:   Cornwallis occupies Yorktown, under orders to hold a port for the British fleet.

AUGUST 14:   Washington, on the Hudson, learns that a large French fleet is sailing from the West Indies to Chesapeake Bay.

AUGUST 19:   French force from Newport, Rhode Island, under Count Rochambeau joins Washington's tiny army at King's Ferry on the Hudson to begin southward march. Sir Henry Clinton, British commander in New York, is deceived, fears attack on the city.

AUGUST 30:   Admiral de Grasse with large warships arrives in the Chesapeake and notifies Washington.

Washington and Rochambeau abandon deception and march openly for Virginia. Clinton fails to pursue.

Cornwallis speeds work on Yorktown fortifications.

SEPTEMBER 1:   British Admiral Thomas Graves sails from New York for the Chesapeake with fleet of nineteen ships.

Order of Events

SEPTEMBER 2–4:   French and American armies pass through Philadelphia.

SEPTEMBER 5:   British fleet driven off by de Grasse in battle off Virginia capes.

Washington receives word of de Grasse's arrival near Chester, Pennsylvania, and leads armies in celebration.

SEPTEMBER 9–12:   Washington visits Mount Vernon for first time during war, while French and American troops move southward, marching overland and sailing down the Chesapeake in small boats.

SEPTEMBER 14:   Washington and Rochambeau join Lafayette in Williamsburg, Virginia, a few miles west of Yorktown. British fleet retreats to New York.

SEPTEMBER 24:   Clinton promises Cornwallis relief by sea within a few days.

SEPTEMBER 28:   Sixteen thousand allied troops march from Williamsburg and dig in around Yorktown, hemming in the 7500-man army of Cornwallis.

OCTOBER 9:   French and American artillery open on Yorktown.

OCTOBER 14:   Parties of French and American troops storm British strong points by night, weakening Yorktown's defenses.

OCTOBER 17:   Cornwallis asks for terms of surrender.

OCTOBER 19:   British troops give up their arms, and allied victory effectively ends the war.

OCTOBER 28:   Clinton and Admiral Graves arrive off the Chesapeake with forty-four ships, discover that they are too late, and return to New York.

THE

CAMPAIGN THAT

WON AMERICA

The Story of Yorktown

THE
VANISHING ARMY

We are at the end of our tether,
and . . . now or never our deliverance must come.
                    —WASHINGTON, *9 April 1781*

The skeletons of two British soldiers, victims of some forgotten execution, hung from the wall of a ruined garden on the American side of the river. Shreds of uniforms clung to their bones and the chains which bound them were flaked with rust. The skulls stared southward into no man's land, across the narrow Harlem River to a British outpost, a redoubt from which cannon commanded the valley.

Beyond the river lay Manhattan Island, and fifteen miles away, across a vista now shimmering in heat waves, a garrison of ten thousand redcoats held New York City. It was July 6, 1781. At noon a thermometer at British Headquarters in the city stood at eighty-seven degrees.

An occasional British patrol ventured into the valley of the Harlem, and American pickets amused themselves by driving the enemy back into their lines; when reinforced parties charged them, the Americans scuttled to safety near the trussed skeletons. A faint odor of decay still hung about the place. One of the pickets was Sergeant Joseph Plumb

Martin, the twenty-year-old son of a Massachusetts minister, already a veteran of four years of war, an explosives expert in Captain David Bushnell's company of sappers and miners. Martin was near exhaustion; he had not slept the night before and had been on his feet for twenty-four hours without rest. He was coatless today. As he stood with two other sergeants, a British horseman spotted him in his white shirt and shouted, "Come over, you white-livered son of a bitch. We'll feed you."

Martin cursed them.

"We'll give you roast turkey."

The sergeant taunted the British: "Yannh, you bloody hyenas—you've had your last turkey. You won't be robbing the country again until we leave!"

Raillery between the enemies on the front lines became "quite sociable" as Martin remembered it.

One of the Englishmen shouted to ask what casualties had been caused by cannon fire from the outpost that morning. "Don't you want help? Your surgeons are a pack of buggering ignoramuses."

"You wounded a dog," Martin said. "Send your surgeons. The poor thing needs help from his own kind."

In that instant Martin narrowly missed death. "Just as I was finishing the last sentence . . . I saw the flash of a gun; I instinctively dropped, as quick as a loon could dive." The bullet struck a tree just over his head and one of his companions yelled, "They've killed him." The British shouted in triumph.

Martin jumped to his feet and turned slowly, slapping his backside to the enemy.

Two mounted French officers trotted up and one of them prodded with his riding crop at the skeletons above Martin's head. He spoke with a pronounced accent, "English or American?"

"English," Martin said.

The Frenchman attacked one of the skeletons with a savagery that fixed the macabre scene in Martin's memory: "One of the officers laid his cane several times across one of the bodies, making the dry bones rattle, at the same time exclaiming, 'Foutre l'Anglais!' "

The French and American armies had joined near the Hudson just after dawn, in sweltering heat. The Frenchmen had come down from Rhode Island—220 miles in eleven days—their bands playing, dust clouds billowing about the columns, with vast wagon trains in their wake. Among them were some of the oldest and proudest of French regiments, and except for the victims of the heat and for ten love-sick men of the Soissonnais troops who had deserted to stay with their mistresses, they were exhilarated by their escape from Newport, where they had been penned for months. As one young officer had complained, "We are vegetating at the very door of the enemy . . . we are of no possible aid to our allies."

The French had made forced marches over forbidding New England roads, preyed upon by Yankees who extorted high prices for every trifle, their strays sometimes attacked by marauding bands who murdered an occasional soldier. Medical officers forced the troops to drink vinegar with their grog in hopes of warding off malaria; almost three hundred of them came down with scurvy. Caissons and wagons broke down, horses and oxen fell in the traces. There was an occasional clash with the enemy, and once the troops were called out to fight a forest fire.

Despite everything, the soldiers were as gay as if they were off on a holiday. Inquisitive Americans thronged their camps and were welcomed with band concerts. One French diarist wrote: "Officers, soldiers and the Americans mix and dance together. It is the feast of Equality, the first fruits of the Alliance. . . . "

As they settled into the new camp, the ragged Americans gaped at the French dandies who had come to save them: infantrymen in white coats and long waistcoats, mincing along at a smart step behind sergeants who wore ostrich plumes in their caps. Each regiment bore its color on collars and lapels—sky blue, yellow, green, pink, rose, or crimson. The artillerymen wore iron gray, trimmed in red velvet. Most dazzling of all were the swaggering hussars of the Duke de Lauzun's Legion, with saddlecloths of tiger skin and tall fur hats, the officers in scarlet breeches and pale blue coats. These hard-drinking riders had long since been exiled from Newport for the safety of the citizens. Many of the Legion were Irish and German mercenaries; there were also Poles, men with huge mustaches who carried lances and curiously curved sabers.

The troops were led by a swarm of French noblemen— barons, counts and viscounts, and at least one prince—rich young adventurers lured to this forlorn revolutionary cause by the prospect of striking a blow at England, the hereditary enemy. There was the Prince de Broglie, whose father was a marshal; Count Charlus, the son of a minister of Marine; Count William Deux-Ponts, who led a German-speaking regiment from the Saar Basin; and Major General de Chastellux of the French academy, a well-known writer. There was Viscount de Noailles, from whose regiment Napoleon would rise to fame, and Captain Louis Berthier, who would become the Emperor's chief of staff; there was also Count Mathieu Dumas, who was to become a hero at Waterloo. There were many who would die in the Terror, among them Marie Antoinette's lover, the Duke de Lauzun, who would say calmly to his executioner at the guillotine, "We are both Frenchmen; we shall do our duty." And there was the handsome Swede, Count Axel Fersen, a romantic refugee from Versailles, who was also said to have been a lover of the Queen.

The French had taken the road in light marching order because of the shortage of animals, with each officer limited to 150 pounds of baggage, but they had wagons by the thousand, and infantrymen were bent under the weight of heavy packs. Young officers, who had so lately been courtiers, set an example by marching with their men. The Viscount de Noailles walked all the way. Still, hundreds of servants led strings of horses in the wake of officers. The Americans could not believe their eyes. Camp gossip had taught them to despise their allies from the army of King Louis XVI as "light, brittle, queer-shapen mechanisms, busy frizzling their hair and painting their faces," men who lived on frogs and coarse vegetables. But as a Virginia officer conceded, the French were not the fops he had expected: "Finer troops I never saw." The Americans were not long in learning that the French were much like themselves—stubborn fighters and accomplished pillagers.

These men had been long in coming. Clandestine French aid had poured into America for years—money, clothing, muskets, and barrels of the world's finest gunpowder, developed in the laboratory of Antoine Lavoisier—all smuggled in under direction of the energetic playwright Pierre Augustin Caron de Beaumarchais, secretary to Louis XVI. By 1778, due largely to the diplomatic wiles of Benjamin Franklin and the persuasion of the young Marquis de Lafayette, France had declared war on England and joined the American cause, news of which had sustained Washington's troops after the bitter winter at Valley Forge. But it was only last year that the first French troops had come, a force large enough to turn the tide of the war.

Even this new French expedition had begun badly. Little

more than half of Rochambeau's force had reached America; the British navy sealed the harbor at Brest and kept several regiments out of the war. The troops and ships in Rhode Island were soon blockaded as well—and even their welcome ashore was none too warm. The streets were empty when the French troops appeared, and doors were closed against them; Rochambeau saw "only a few sad and frightened faces in the windows." Only later did the French overcome suspicions and prejudice bred by Tory propaganda and win friends in Newport.

Count Axel Fersen was outraged by the behavior of the New Englanders who not only sold goods to the blockading British ships but robbed their new allies: "They overcharge us mercilessly; everything is enormously dear; in all the dealings we have had with them they have treated us more like enemies than friends. Their greed is unequalled, money is their God . . . "

Washington himself seemed cool and distant. The French landed in July, 1780, but it was September before Rochambeau met Washington—and the following March before the American commander appeared in Newport to welcome his allies. The Frenchmen had been unhappy and lonely in the strange city. The Duke de Lauzun wrote, "We had been ten months away from France and we had not yet received a single letter nor one penny in money," and Rochambeau reported dolefully to Paris, "Money goes, money goes. It would not be wise to send more troops until the Spring, when they can be utilized. As long as the Army is here, we consume 560,000 francs per month."

Now, despite everything, the foreign troops had joined Washington, ready for action. The French inspected George Washington's tiny army with unconcealed astonishment; most of the Americans had no uniforms and were barefoot and tousle-haired. They seemed to have no baggage; three or four men slept in each odorous tent, without so much as a mattress—they lay on branches covered with dirty blankets. Many of these troops were children, boys of twelve or thirteen, and there were hundreds of old men; all were lean and underfed. Their marching was indifferent, but their muskets shone, and the troops were cheerful and healthy and had the look of men who would not be easily overcome. The French detected something wild and untamed in their manner. Even most of the men who were in uniform were ragged, in hunting shirts or old linen jackets and short trousers worn without stockings; but they suffered less from the heat than did their splendid allies.

One American regiment caught every French eye—the Rhode Islanders, more than three-quarters of their ranks filled by Negroes. The French Commissary found them the best-uniformed and best-trained of the volunteers. Another officer, the young Count de Bourg, wrote soon after this meeting: "I cannot insist too strongly how I was surprised by the American army. It is truly incredible that troops almost naked, poorly paid, and composed of old men and children and Negroes should behave so well on the march and under fire."

A French chaplain, the Abbé Claude Robin, saw more in this camp than scarecrow soldiers and shrunken regiments: Washington was an American Gideon who concealed his numbers even from his own troops: "Now with a few soldiers he forms a Spacious Camp and spreads a large number of tents. Then again with a large number of men he reduces his tentage and his force almost vanishes." Today, the abbot noted, the camp seemed to hold only the skeleton of an army. Count Deux-Ponts took a more cynical view: "They told us at Newport that the American army had 10,000 men. It has 2500 or 3000 men, and that is not much of a lie for the Americans."

The American force was no more than two thousand: four small regiments from New York and New Jersey, the Rhode Islanders, a regiment of Canadians, a few light infantry, 225 artillerymen, a handful of engineers and sappers and miners, and one hundred cavalrymen. The French had brought four thousand in all—four infantry regiments, a battalion of artillery, and Lauzun's Legion, made up of both cavalry and infantry. The allied army spread across the hills above Manhattan from the Hudson to the Connecticut border, cutting off the enemy from the mainland. The Americans, on the left, held earthworks that stretched from Dobbs Ferry on the Hudson to the Sawmill River; the French line ran eastward, across the Bronx River and through White Plains.

The newcomers found the country barren and forbidding, its hills covered with thorns and heather, but some were fascinated by the huge tulip poplars and catalpas, under which they camped.

In the opening days of July the advance troops had skirmished with the British at the enemy's northern outposts in the first combined assault by the French and Americans, but the thrust by converging columns seemed to have failed. The alert British merely retired across the Harlem. Washington's spies in New York soon brought him better news; the attack had alarmed Sir Henry Clinton, the British commander, and he had called for reinforcements from the south. Sir Henry feared that Washington and his new ally, Count de Rochambeau, were ready to storm New York.

There was a stir in the camp in the morning when the New Jersey troops were called out, and 150 picked men were told off for escort duty, scrubbed and brushed until their sergeants were content. They were marched to Washington's headquarters at the Joseph Appleby house on the

The Vanishing Army

Dobbs Ferry-White Plains road, not far from the Hudson. The general was going out to reconnoiter the enemy position —again. It was July 18, another blistering day.

Billy Lee, the general's body servant, held two horses at the front steps in the bright sunlight, one of them Washington's favorite, the white horse. Washington came down to the horses, a spare, muscular figure well over six feet tall, with the light step of a much younger man. He weighed more than 200 pounds, and he was not fat. He wore a well-cut blue coat and buff breeches and waistcoat, and his huge boots gleamed; epaulettes were the only sign of rank. A black cockade was pinned to his hat. He was as broad in the hips as in the shoulders and was not quite fully erect; his chest was slightly hollow, the result of a lung ailment in youth. Next winter the general would be fifty years old.

His men watched him now for signs of coming combat. They watched respectfully for he did not encourage affection; the one man who dared call him George to his face had done so on a wager and had drawn an icy stare—yet his wife called him "My old man," and some of the frontiersmen in his ranks knew him as "Old Hoss." His troops kept alive the tradition that he was the strongest and most taciturn man in the army, and relished tales of the rare occasions when he had given way to laughter or profanity. They criticized him only for his rigid discipline and his harshness with deserters—they would have scoffed at the plaint of John Adams, the Massachusetts philosopher of the revolution, that Washington was "not a scholar . . . he was too illiterate, unlearned and unread."

The general spoke quietly to the dark mulatto, Billy Lee, as he approached the horse, then swung easily into the saddle. His great size became more obvious as he mounted. The hands in which he took the reins were enormous—the young Marquis de Lafayette said they were the largest he had ever seen—but for all his bulk Washington rode through the camp with striking grace and dignity. The escort trailed after him as he went with an aide to meet Rochambeau.

The general's head seemed too small for his body; a queue of graying brown hair bobbed on his neck, and the hair was brushed back from the forehead, powdered and tied in precise military fashion. Behind him rode Billy Lee, with equal grace, also in a cocked hat. Billy Lee was about the general's age; they had been together for most of their lives— for six years of the war and for a generation of hunting foxes in northern Virginia, companions who were almost like brothers.

When he met the French commander the general smiled faintly, revealing defective teeth. His expression was otherwise transformed: the blue-gray eyes glittered with sudden animation. The strong, pocked face was not handsome; the large nose was thick and the features irregular, the cheeks were sunburned, but had not lost their sallowness. There was an uncomfortable set to the broad lips; the general had wired his false teeth in place with pincers sent by his Philadelphia dentist, and had been using the cruel scraper to clean his own remaining teeth. His voice was hollow and a trifle indistinct because of the teeth.* The two commanders went out to inspect the defenses of New York.

The French marveled at Washington—a country man with

---

* Washington was beset by the dental troubles for most of his life and in later years wore a succession of weird dentures, some of them experimental. Most of these were of hippopotamus ivory, but Washington was also apparently the first man to wear the teeth of pigs, cows, elk, etc., in his dentures. He also used other human teeth. One pair of his false teeth, set in lead, weighed three pounds, and the teeth were bored and strung with coiled springs of heavy steel, held firmly within the lead base. The general could hold these crude contrivances in place only with much discomfort by use of strong facial muscles. Washington was his own dental technician and skillfully made delicate adjustments in gold wires and springs which held his teeth together.

graces that would have made him at home anywhere. One officer said, "I have never seen anyone who was more naturally and spontaneously polite. . . . He asks few questions, listens attentively, and answers in low tones and with few words." The same Frenchman had watched as Washington played ball with his aides for hours in camp, throwing as vigorously as men half his age, apparently tireless.

The Europeans were baffled by the commander, whose modesty was "very astonishing, especially to a Frenchman." He spoke of the war he directed as if he were only a spectator; he accepted no pay for his services. The Prince de Broglie, groping for an explanation to his countrymen, wrote of Washington, ". . . he preserves that polite and attentive good breeding which satisfies everybody, and that dignified reserve which offends no one. He is a foe to ostentation and to vainglory . . . He does not seem to estimate himself at his true worth."

One perceptive Frenchman noted that Washington had no single striking feature, and that one left him with a rather vague memory "of a fine man . . . a fine figure, an exterior plain and modest . . . a manly courage, an uncommon capacity for grasping the whole scope of a subject."

The Swede, Count Axel Fersen, saw something else: "A tinge of melancholy affects his whole being, which is not unbecoming; it renders him more interesting."

The stout French general who rode out with Washington to inspect the enemy lines was a remarkable soldier and the key to a unique alliance. He was Jean Baptiste Donatien de Vimeur, Count de Rochambeau, a veteran of almost forty years of warfare and a field soldier, more at home with his troops than at court or in army headquarters. The count was fifty-six, with thinning gray hair and an imposing paunch; he called himself Papa Rochambeau. He had studied for the priesthood, but turned to the army in his youth, serving in the most celebrated battles of his time under Marshal Saxe and Richelieu.

The French provided most of the troops, arms, food, and money for the final offensive of the war, but there was never a challenge to Washington's authority. Rochambeau urged the Virginian to use him as he wished; when the time came for planning strategy, the Frenchman was a wily schemer, subtly advancing his own views, but always with the amiable air of a pliant, willing ally devoted to the cause of driving the British from America.

Rochambeau had made it clear from the start that he had come to serve and not to command. He wrote Washington on his first day ashore, "The commands of the King, my master, place me under the orders of Your Excellency. I come, wholly obedient and with the zeal and the veneration which I have for you and for the remarkable talents you have displayed in sustaining a war which will always be memorable."

Toward Washington and the Americans he was unfailingly courteous and self-effacing, but his stern discipline sometimes caused turmoil in the French camp. Some of his officers found Rochambeau trying. Commissary Blanchard found that dealing with the old general required all the tact at his command: "M. de Rochambeau . . . mistrusts everyone and always believes that he sees himself surrounded by rogues and idiots. This character, combined with manners far from courteous, makes him disagreeable to everybody."

But Blanchard conceded that, for all his shortcomings, Rochambeau was an admirable commander, "a wise effective leader," and above all else an exceptional judge of military terrain, "having an excellent glance, readily becoming acquainted with a country, and understanding war perfectly." The Frenchman had little enthusiasm for an attack on New

York, and he revealed it today. He was a veteran of fourteen sieges, and he looked apprehensively across the Hudson to the enemy heights, which could be taken only in an amphibious assault by an enormous army.

The two generals made a striking contrast as they inspected British positions, the portly French professional, a scarred veteran of European wars, and the towering Virginian, a self-taught commander whose doggedness had sustained the revolution during the six dark years since 1775. Several aides and officers rode with them, among them Louis Duportail, the chief engineer, who had already been four years with Washington—he had built the defenses at Valley Forge. Interpreters made a clatter about them as they rode; Rochambeau did not speak English, and Washington spoke no French.

The party crossed to the New Jersey bank of the Hudson and rode down the river until they could look past Manhattan Island to the sea; Washington swept the island's western shore with his glass. He could discover only one British sentry along the upper flank of the enemy, a lone soldier on guard at Jeffrey's Rock, the future site of 176th Street. To the east he saw only open country, without houses or troops. Washington looked with nostalgia at the post he had lost five years before in his most humiliating defeat: "The island is totally stripped of Trees, and wood of every kind. . . ." The British had destroyed forests which had covered the hillsides in 1776, and now only waist-high bushes grew there.

The generals found no vulnerable spots along the river; a ravine adjoining the Jumel mansion near Harlem was inviting but Washington saw the tents of two Hessian camps and a drove of dragoon horses not far away. There was also a likely spot at Cox's Hill guarded by a decaying fort, but there were about one hundred tents of German riflemen within a few yards.

Washington saw hundreds of huts in the rear of McGowan's Heights, a ridge where Mt. St. Vincent's College was to be built. One of the staff told him that two battalions of British grenadiers were camped there.

The general finally turned away reluctantly. He had come here many times before, studying the defenses of Manhattan, trying to persuade Rochambeau that they might launch an attack across the water.

It was only two months since the commanders had held a conference at Wethersfield, Connecticut, to plan the war's final offensive, both aware that the French would pour no more troops, ships, and money into the American cause. Washington had written in his diary:

> Fixed with Count de Rochambeau upon plan of Campaign . . . to commence an operation against New York . . . or to extend our views to the southward as circumstances and a Naval superiority might render more necessary. . . .

Rochambeau, on returning to Newport after the conference, had found his officers opposed to the plan and in a council of war changed the pattern of the campaign. When the Duke de Lauzun carried news of this change to Washington the commander exploded. Lauzun wrote:

> It threw Washington into such a rage that he would not answer. It was only on the third day, and then out of regard for me, that he gave me an answer, a very cold one, in which he said that he held to the plan that he had signed.

Rochambeau accepted the rebuke and prepared to march as they agreed, but he continued to resist Washington's scheme to assault New York. He pressed his ally to turn the campaign toward Virginia, where a tiny American army under the Marquis de Lafayette had followed Lord Charles Cornwallis to the shores of the Chesapeake Bay.

Rochambeau wrote Admiral François Joseph Paul de Grasse, who had just arrived in the West Indies with a large fleet from France, urging him to bring five thousand fresh troops to North America:

> These people here are at the end of their resources. Washington has not half the troops he counted on; I believe, though he is hiding it, that he has not 6000 men. M. de La Fayette has not 1000 regulars with the militia to defend Virginia. . . . This is the state of affairs and the great crisis at which America finds itself. . . .

He told de Grasse that only the fleet could save the cause of the Revolution. His final plea to the Admiral put an end to Washington's hopes of attacking New York:

> The southwesterly winds and the distressed state of Virginia will probably lead you to prefer Chesapeake Bay, and it is there that we think you can render the greatest services. . . .

Rochambeau told Washington candidly what he had written to de Grasse and they began to make new plans. Washington had never closed his mind to the prospect that the war might be won in Virginia, after all. He had never conducted a siege nor directed an amphibious campaign, but his grasp of the role of sea power was firm if only intuitive. In his first letter to Rochambeau the Virginian had said, "Whatever efforts are made by the land armies, the navy must have the casting vote in the present contest." The prospect of trapping Cornwallis was seldom out of Washington's mind, even as he lingered over his plan for storming New York.

More than a month earlier, on June 13, when he learned that a powerful French fleet might come to the coast, he wrote Rochambeau, "Your Excellency will be pleased to recollect that New York was looked upon by us as the only practicable object under present circumstances; but should we be able to secure a naval superiority, we may perhaps find others more practicable and equally advisable."

Now, in late July, when Rochambeau pressed him for action, Washington agreed that if they could not storm New York they should plan "secondly for the relief of the southern states." Even as he peered through his glass at every approach to New York, the Commander's thoughts were in the South, where he had sent young Lafayette to hold off enemy raiders.

Washington wrote Lafayette in Virginia with a hint of great things to come:

> I sincerely congratulate you on the favorable turn of affairs . . . and I hope you will be enabled to maintain that superiority, which you seem to be gaining over Lord Cornwallis. . . .
>
> I shall shortly have occasion to communicate matters of very great importance to you. . . .

The French had built a pavilion for the General on the east bank of the Hudson. There, shaded from the sun, he sat for hours on August 25, watching intently while Rochambeau's regiments crossed the broad river, as if he feared that one soldier among the thousands might escape his notice. He had been given a schedule of the crossing and studied it with care as the nondescript fleet of rafts, barges, and scows bore the French across the water: the Soissonnais regiment in its crimson facings; the Saintogne with green; the Bourbonnais with black; and the Royal Deux-Ponts in blue coats trimmed with yellow. The artillery and the resplendent Legion of Lauzun had already crossed, and were camped around Haverstraw with the Americans, under the forbidding ridge which was capped by High Tor.

Washington wore his blue coat despite the heat, mopping his sweating face with a handkerchief; under his shirt, as always, he wore a miniature of his wife. French officers clustered respectfully about him, moved by the sight of the aging commander who was almost without victories in his five years of war and was now opening a new campaign with a brave show of confidence. Claude Blanchard, who sat beside him, realized that Washington was "exhausted, destitute of resources." But he detected a subtle change in his bearing today, "He seemed to see a better destiny arise." The Abbé Claude Robin sensed the general's vitality: "He never has more resources than when he seems to have no more."

The French had heard American officers scoffing at this new move of the armies, even those who did not yet know where they were bound. Colonel Alexander Hamilton, who had lately broken with the general, had been especially scornful, saying that "The Great Man" was off on a wild goose chase.

Washington's air of confidence today was in striking contrast to his earlier moods. Only a few weeks earlier, when he had already begun to plan with the French, he had been in despair: ". . . instead of having everything in readiness to take the Field, we have nothing and instead of having the prospect of a glorious offensive campaign before us, we have a bewildered and gloomy defensive one."

Among the thousands at the river crossing few besides Washington and Rochambeau sensed the boldness of the move they were now beginning; to men in the ranks it seemed much like all the weary marches that had gone before, with only defeat and death and the prospect of more marching at the end. After five years of bitter campaigning, Washington's war was today almost as it had been in 1776—

the British comfortably posted in New York and the Americans above on the Hudson, watchful but apparently impotent. The British advantage now seemed greater, if anything; the army of Cornwallis had ravaged Virginia and the Carolinas, unhampered by Lafayette's little band.

To his troops this was only King's Ferry, a back-breaking passage in the remote valley between small forts at Verplanck's Point and Stony Point, but to Washington it was a crossing from which there was no turning back. Once across, the army would begin the longest march of the war, trailing down the continent for 450 miles to join in a pincers movement that had begun thousands of miles away, with the sailing of the French fleet from Brest. The march would be almost ended before the general could know whether it had been in vain: Would Clinton come out to fight, or the French fleet reach the Chesapeake in time, or Cornwallis escape Lafayette, or would the unpaid American troops mutiny on the road?

The general had planned the crossing at this place long before. The grandeur of the setting seemed to move him strongly: "It is the best, indeed for us the only passing of the river below the Highlands. It lies at the foot of the western slope of Stony Point where there are heavy boulders of granite rock, scatterings of glaciers of long ago, long spent."

Washington had gone to great lengths to conceal exact knowledge of his move, playing upon the ignorance of his troops and the enemy's fears from the start. Six days earlier, on August 19, when the armies began their move, his pickets had cleared roads into New York, burning the barricades of fallen trees and sharpened stakes as if opening the way for an attack on the city. On the same day he had sent Colonel Moses Hazen and his Canadian regiment over the Hudson at Dobbs Ferry, to march down the Jersey shore and threaten an assault on Staten Island. He ordered his staff to tell his own troops nothing: "If we do not deceive our own men, we will never deceive the enemy." He had begun well. Count Deux-Ponts broke camp at Phillipsburg as the march began, complaining in his Journal, "We do not know the object of our march, and are in perfect ignorance whether we are going against New York, or whether we are going to Virginia to attack Lord Cornwallis." Even General Henry Knox, the artillery chief, had written his wife that he could not tell her Washington's plan: "We don't know it ourselves." He had heard all the camp rumors, but he had little faith in the army's prospects. Knox wrote, "You know what we wish, but we hope for more at present than we believe."

The movement of the armies had not begun auspiciously. On August 14, Washington had a message that de Grasse was sailing for the Chesapeake—and that his stay must be brief. The planned assault on New York was now impossible; they must turn to the south. Washington was enraged. Quartermaster General Timothy Pickering and Robert Morris, the Philadelphia financier, happened into headquarters at this moment and found Washington in a blind fury, "striding to and fro in such a state of uncontrolled excitement" that he seemed not to notice his guests.

"Resentment, indignation and despair had burst upon him," Pickering said. "His hopes were blasted, and he felt that the cause was lost and his country ruined."

Pickering and Morris quietly withdrew, and when they returned half an hour later Washington had regained control, his long face was wreathed in smiles. "I must apologize for my extraordinary appearance when you came," Washington said. "I had been hoping for so many months to carry out our plans with the French—only to have them thwarted."

His manner was composed, but Pickering saw that he was "tossing like a suppressed volcano within." Finally Washington burst out in an anguished voice, "I wish to the Lord the

French would not raise our expectations of a cooperation, or fulfil them."

Pickering and Morris had glimpsed only a moment of the long and agonizing process by which the plan of campaign had evolved. The storm had passed quickly, and Washington threw himself into the new offensive with all his energies. He put aside the doubts he had been expressing to everyone for weeks, that northern men would refuse to fight in Virginia and that half his troops would desert on the long road south. He had few enough; of the 6200 recruits he had begged the states to send, only a handful had come—80 from New York and 176 from Connecticut. Now that the only chance of victory lay in the Chesapeake, and every hour counted in the race for Yorktown, Washington moved swiftly. He completed his plan for the march before the day was over and called in Pickering, ordering him to make ready wagons, boats, arms, and supplies.

By nightfall, when he made an entry in his journal, calm had returned:

> Matters having now come to a crisis and a decisive plan to be determined on, I was obliged, from the shortness of Count de Grasse promised stay on this Coast, the apparent disinclination in their Naval Officers to force the harbour of New York and the feeble compliance of the States to my requisitions for Men . . . to give up all idea of attacking New York; and instead thereof to remove the French Troops and a detachment from the American Army . . . to Virginia.

Already, in fact, he had sent officers to arrange secretly for wagons to haul supplies to the south and had ordered the army's big guns prepared for the road. Washington looked chiefly to two generals from Massachusetts to put the army in motion—Major General Benjamin Lincoln, his second in command, and Brigadier General Henry Knox, his huge chief of artillery. Lincoln, a hero of the Saratoga campaign and the victim of the British siege of Charleston, had been chosen by seniority; Knox, a former Boston bookseller, had long since won Washington's confidence and become one of his intimates.

Knox was a genial man of almost three hundred pounds, a self-taught gunner whose formal schooling had ended when he was nine years old; he had educated himself and had made his bookshop an intellectual center of Boston. He had dabbled in publishing and importing, and on the shelves of his unique shop were scientific and musical instruments, medicines, wallpaper, and objects of art; he was constantly in debt, but was always faultlessly dressed in a handsome uniform. This unlikely candidate had become Washington's chief artilleryman at the opening of the war, and despite the scorn of the French for his gunners, Washington found him one of the most effective of his officers. It was Knox who had thought of bringing guns from Ticonderoga to Washington's armed mob during the siege of Boston, dragging them over snow-covered hills for two hundred miles so that the British could be driven from the city. Knox was known in the army as an incomparable chief of artillery, resourceful in finding guns and gunners for the impoverished army, shrewd and good-humored and skillful in the handling of officers and men; factional fights and friction were almost unknown in his ranks. Knox and his sorcerers had cadged, stolen, captured, and improvised guns and equipment to prepare for this move of the armies.

Almost incredibly, within five days after Washington read the message from de Grasse, the troops were under way, supplies being collected ahead of them. Admiral de Barras had been persuaded to sail from Rhode Island to join de Grasse in the Chesapeake, the engineer, Louis Duportail, had been sent to meet de Grasse with word of the army's march, Lafayette had been advised to watch for the fleet and prevent the escape of Cornwallis—and a little army of four thousand New Englanders under General William Heath, had been left behind to watch Sir Henry Clinton, to guard West Point and the Hudson Valley, and to further the deception of the enemy.

Heath's army lay about the crossing today, guarding the French on the fourth day of their passage, but its sentries were lax. British spies prowled the camp almost at will, noting the strength of each regiment and eavesdropping on the troops as they speculated about their destination. One woman spy got into camp and discovered Washington's quarters in a house across the river.

Washington himself crossed the stream in the early afternoon, and Claude Blanchard noted that he was deeply moved as he made the crossing from which there was no turning back, off at last on his first true offensive of the war: "He pressed my hand with much affection when he left us." Rochambeau crossed later to dine with the commander in the deserted "Treason House" of Joshua Hett Smith, high above the Hudson near Stony Point, where Benedict Arnold had met with Major André the year before.

Despite shortages of food in the army the officers dined well at headquarters. Blanchard, who had lately had dinner with the general, was astonished to see such food in camp:

The table was served in the American style and pretty abundantly: vegetables, roast beef, lamb, chickens, salad dressed with nothing but vinegar, green peas, puddings, and some pie, a kind of tart, greatly in use in England

and among the Americans, all this being put upon the table at the same time. They gave us on the same plate, beef, green peas, lamb, &c.

After dinner, the cloth was taken from the table and Washington and the officers sat for a while, drinking toasts in Madeira to the King of France and the French army and Count de Grasse. Throughout the meal Washington and his staff also drank a concoction the French regarded with suspicion, something called grum, rum mixed with water.

The commander wore his familiar expression of serenity in the last hours before the armies turned southward, but his aides were desperately busy. His new secretary, Jonathan Trumbull, Jr., had prepared copies of a circular letter to governors of the states, but Washington was holding them until the last moment to preserve secrecy. He had explained his movements, and his hopes, to the governors: ". . . should the time of the fleet's arrival prove favorable, and should the enemy under Lord Cornwallis hold their present position in Virginia . . . [we will have] the fairest opportunity to reduce the whole British force in the south."

The withholding of the letters and other deceptions baffled the staff but delighted Trumbull: "No movement perhaps was ever attended with more conjectures . . . some were indeed laughable enow'; but not one I believe penetrated the real design." The general's own moves were so unhurried that he seemed to be trying to conceal the army's designs with a show of casual unconcern. As time for the departure neared, Washington left headquarters on a leisurely ride to West Point with Rochambeau, who was eager to inspect the key fortress on the Hudson. Later, the commander visited the camp of Colonel Philip van Cortlandt's New York Regiment, at the riverside. This regiment—van Cortlandt called it proudly the army's largest and finest—had come down from the Mohawk Valley with thirty-four new boats built in Albany. The general inspected the boats with care.

They were off southward at last on August 25, the Americans leading by several hours, marching in two columns; General Lincoln, with Colonel Alexander Scammell's Light Infantry and the First New York, moved through Paramus toward Springfield. Colonel John Lamb's artillery and the little band of Sappers and Miners went through Pompton toward Chatham, trailed by the baggage under guard of the Rhode Island Regiment. The French followed on a route lying to the west, through Suffern and Pompton toward Parsippany.

Until they were on the move the troops had looked apprehensively to the rear, to the heavily guarded road from New York, but there was no sign of the enemy. Sir Henry Clinton was evidently asleep. Count Deux-Ponts was incredulous: "An enemy of any boldness or any skill would have seized an opportunity so favorable for him and so embarrassing for us. . . . I do not understand the indifference with which General Clinton considers our movements. It is to me an obscure enigma."

Baron Ludwig von Closen, who rode southward with the French column, was charmed by the scenery and by the mystery of their destination: "We found open country and a very beautiful small . . . valley. The Jerseys abound in all kinds of produce . . . it is a land of milk and honey . . . after leaving New York state, where misery is written on the brows of the inhabitants. . . ." When Closen saw that the French did not follow the road down the riverside but turned toward Suffern, he saw that their goal was not New York. He did not understand the plan of campaign, but now began to suspect: "The mask is being raised!!"

These troops had disappeared on the road south from Haverstraw on August 26, when Washington returned to the ferry and sent for Colonel van Cortlandt. The New Yorker saw that the general was obsessed by the need for secrecy: "He took me by the arm and went some distance on the road, and gave me his orders both written and verbal."

Van Cortlandt was to take all the boats and entrenching tools on his march south. Washington said, "I will send a dragoon to you every day, for your report of progress. Your moves will be of first importance—you are the rear guard of the army." The New York regiment was soon on the way, the band playing, boats and pontoons rumbling behind on huge wagons, the drovers cracking whips over teams of oxen. Tories and British spies, Washington hoped, would conclude that the boats and pontoons were to be used against Staten Island, rather than hauled to distant Virginia.

When on the same day Rochambeau's vanguard reached Pompton, Count Deux-Ponts was still puzzled. The Americans seemed to be threatening Paulus Hook and Staten Island: "I cannot make up my mind as to the object of our march. I am inclined to believe that the Americans will attack one of the two points which they are threatening, and I am quite certain that they will not act without us." A day later, in camp at Whippany, Deux-Ponts wrote with an air of excitement, "I learned, under the strictest secrecy from one of my friends, well informed, that all the maneuvers by which we threaten New York are only a feint, that Lord Cornwallis is the real object of our marches, and that we are going to direct them towards Virginia."

Others were not so sure.

Dr. James Thacher, a young surgeon with Scammell's corps, noted in his journal:

Our situation reminds me of some theatrical exhibition, where the interest and expectations of the spectators are constantly increasing, and where curiosity is wrought to the highest point. . . . Bets have run high on one side, that we were to occupy the ground marked out on the Jersey shore, to aid in the siege of New York, and on the other, that we are stealing a march on the enemy, and are actually destined to Virginia.

The armies wound down through New Jersey in the heat of the last days of August in their three columns—the French on the right passing through Morristown, Bullions Tavern, and Somerset, the baggage and artillery through Boundbrook, and the American infantry through Brunswick. They were often within sight of enemy troops. Small parties left the route to aid the deception of the enemy; some troops were fired on by the British as they made a show of building bake ovens for the French at Chatham, about four miles above Staten Island; parties went through the countryside collecting forage, as if for a long encampment; and still others built small boats, or questioned civilians everywhere between Newark and Amboy, asking for boats. One band of Hazen's Canadian regiment toiled across the dunes toward Sandy Hook under the pretext of building artillery batteries to aid the French fleet in an attack on New York. The British responded by moving thousands of troops on Staten Island, and the allied armies halted for a day. Washington pulled in his rear guard, and the French held their position at Whippany until it was clear that the enemy did not intend to come out and fight.

Everywhere, as the armies passed, people thronged to see Washington—to cheer, or stare, or hold up children for a glimpse of him. The French were becoming accustomed to the spectacle.

Count Dumas, who had ridden through Providence with the general one night, was astounded to see men, women, and children press around Washington, carrying torches in his honor, content merely with a sight of him, and ecstatic if they could touch his boots or his horse. The crowd had once halted the officers in the street. Washington turned to Dumas: "We may be beaten by the English; that is the chance of war; but here is the army that they will never conquer."

The Abbé Robin, who saw Washington followed by such processions through many towns said, "The Americans, that cool and sedate people . . . are roused, animated, and inflamed at the very mention of his name, and the first songs that sentiment or gratitude has dictated, have been to celebrate General Washington."

The troops were aroused by drums at 3:00 A.M. each day, and were marching an hour later. Field officers were baffled by the precise orders as to the route and formation of their columns. Washington concealed every move zealously; even regimental commanders were told little or nothing of the army's final destination. One of General Lincoln's orders to the artillery was typical:

> You will march through the Scotch Plains, Quibble Town, and Bound Brook. On the 30th to Princeton— 31st to Trenton, where you will meet me and further orders. You will keep these orders a perfect secret.

The troops gossiped of Washington's efforts to mislead the enemy; he had questioned an old Tory farmer about details of Staten Island and the barricades on the roads. Abruptly, with an air of concern, as if he had said too much, the general told the old man that these were idle questions and that his interest was merely in the Jersey countryside. The soldiers told stories of false dispatches from headquarters, with details of a planned attack on New York, sent out so that they would fall into the hands of the enemy.

Washington seldom spoke of his stratagems, but he later confessed:

> . . . much trouble was taken, and finesse used, to misguide and bewilder Sir Henry Clinton, in regard as to the real object, by fictitious communications as well as by making a deceptive provision of ovens, forage, and boats, in his neighborhood . . . Nor, was less pains taken to deceive our own army; for, I had always conceived, when the imposition does not completely take place at home, it would never sufficiently succeed abroad.

The American troops were grim-faced and grumbling as they camped around Chatham, and Washington feared they might mutiny when they found they were marching for Virginia. In their present mood, only money would quiet the men. The general wrote Robert Morris from Chatham:

> I must entreat you . . . to procure one month's pay in specie for the detachment . . . Part of these troops have not been paid anything for a long time past, and have on several occasions shown marks of great discontent. The service they are going upon is disagreeable to the northern regiments; but I make no doubt that a *douceur* of a little hard money would put them in proper temper.

Still, Washington was doggedly optimistic. On the same day he wrote Governor Thomas Sim Lee of Maryland, "The moment is critical, the opportunity precious, the prospects most happily favorable."

Alarming news reached headquarters late that afternoon. General David Forman, commander of the lookout post near Sandy Hook, reported, ". . . eighteen large ships of war appeared standing in from the southward to Sandy Hook this morning." Washington was deeply concerned. These new British ships, added to those already in New York harbor, would give the enemy twenty-nine big warships, enough to challenge de Grasse. Washington hurried an express to Forman, requesting more information.

When van Cortlandt reached Pompton with his slow rear guard, Washington allowed him to change his route to a better road through Parsippany, but added a firm order: the boats were to halt overnight at the junction of roads leading east to Chatham and south to Morristown, to deceive the enemy a little longer. And once he passed through Morristown, he must hurry toward Trenton—for three days more he must move with the greatest secrecy. Van Cortlandt obeyed. He had his ox teams moving at daybreak, and before darkness fell had marched twenty-four miles, instead of his usual eight or nine.

On August 28, when the American left was at Chatham and Rochambeau was at Whippany with the head of his column, Baron von Closen's suspicions as to their destination were confirmed. Washington sent an officer to ask Rochambeau to ride about fifteen miles farther after dinner so that he might dine with the commander in Princeton the next day. They were turning away southward, no longer threatening the British in New York, but moving to Princeton and Trenton. They were openly moving toward Virginia. Other signs were unmistakable. The troops were ordered to load their packs on wagons, and the pace of the march increased. They passed the last of the enemy outposts and now hurried toward Philadelphia. Dr. Thacher admired the adroitness with which Washington had hoodwinked the enemy:

Our destination can no longer be a secret. The British army under Lord Cornwallis, is unquestionably the object . . . the deception has proved completely successful . . . Major General Heath is left commander-in-chief of our army in the vicinity of New York and . . . the menacing aspect of an attack on New York will be continued till time and circumstance shall remove the delusive veil from the eyes of Sir Henry Clinton, when it will probably be too late. . . .

Closen was almost ecstatic when the news reached Rochambeau's headquarters and was given to the staff: "How happy I was when the General told me to accompany him to Philadelphia! The disguise is gradually going to be removed from our campaign."

Rochambeau and Closen rode rapidly to Princeton, where they dined with Washington the next day, August 29. The French staff rode with the commander the fifteen miles to Trenton, absorbed in the general's explanation of the movements of his battles of Trenton and Princeton, fought almost four years before. Another dispatch from General Forman was waiting at Trenton—the news from the sea was better. A more accurate count of enemy vessels revealed only twenty-two line of battle ships at New York, too few to challenge the combined French fleet. The party spent the night in the sleepy little town of Trenton on the banks of the Delaware, which still bore signs of the ravages of Hessian troops. The officers were up early the next morning, riding through pleasant Dutch farming country to Bristol, and then downstream to Red Lion Tavern, where they crossed the Delaware.

They had now put the army far behind, but Washington left careful orders for the troops, especially for van Cortlandt's lumbering rear guard with the boats. He made a laconic entry in his diary: "I set myself out for Philadelphia to arrange matters there. . . ." Even now Washington dared not hope too much.

2

A PERPLEXED
ONLOOKER

The King's birthday fell on the fourth of June, a fine day cooled by a breeze from the south, and the New York garrison burned more gunpowder in celebration than it had used in months. Artillerymen on the Battery fired a twenty-one-gun salute at noon, and an hour later the city shook to the thunder of cannon from the scores of warships and transports in the harbor. After dark the troops were turned out, British regulars, German mercenaries, and local militia companies, to form a long line in Great George Street, also known as The Broadway. The troops fired muskets in rapid succession, up and down the line, searing the night with a yellow stitching of flame almost two miles long. Other cannon saluted from across the river in Paulus Hook and the ceremony ended with three deafening cheers for George III.

It was late when the sixty thousand civilians of the fortress city went to bed. This was the sixth year that New York had celebrated George's birthday as an occupied city—and the fourth under the command of General Sir Henry Clinton, Member of Parliament and Knight of the Bath.

In the last hours of the night there was a stir on a barricaded road on the north end of Manhattan Island when a dusty rider was passed through a British outpost. The horseman was one of Clinton's scouts, Ensign John Moody, who bore a rare prize, a heavy mail pouch taken from a rebel courier near Sussex Courthouse—dispatches from Washington and Rochambeau to the Congress and Lafayette and other rebel leaders. Moody hurried it to headquarters at Beekman House, where Sir Henry himself was soon cracking the seals and reading with growing satisfaction. He sent for old General James Robertson, who now acted as governor, and for the senior German commander, General Knyphausen; they spent hours examining the papers.

Rumors spread quickly from headquarters—Ensign Moody had made one of the great captures of the war. The pouch held reports by Washington and Rochambeau on the Wethersfield conference and their plans for the coming campaign; the allied armies would combine to attack New York or, if that were impractical, they would march to Virginia. Clinton immediately called for reinforcements from the small force of Cornwallis in Virginia. Ensign Moody was given a reward of two hundred guineas. Lieutenant Frederick Mackenzie of the Royal Welsh Fusileers, an inveterate headquarters diarist, wrote, "The capture of this Mail is extremely consequential, and gives the Commander in Chief the most perfect knowledge of the designs of the Enemy."

From this day, for months afterward, Sir Henry was to remain unshaken in his conviction that he understood the enemy's intentions, a conviction disastrous to the British cause. He dismissed from his mind the possibility that it was Cornwallis, and not he, who was in danger. Clinton's careless disclosure that he had learned Washington's secrets was soon known to rebel spies in the city and then to Washington. The American scoffed at reports that the dispatches were of crucial importance, but though others began to wonder whether this had been an elaborate ruse by the rebel commander, Clinton never doubted that the captured messages were genuine.

He reasoned that the mail pouch contained dispatches Washington would not have deliberately exposed to capture —a message to Colonel Benjamin Tallmadge about American spies in New York; a letter to his nephew, Lund Washington, warning that the British might burn Mount Vernon; another to his dentist, asking for pliers to repair his false teeth—and another, quite homely one, from the unskilled hand of Martha Washington, putting questions to her housekeeper at Mount Vernon:

> M Washington will be glad to know if the Cotton for the counterpins was wove—and whitend,—how many yards was there of it, how many Counterpins will it make—she desired milly Posey to have the fine piece of linning made white how is Betty has she been spinning —all winter—is charlot done the worke I left for her To do.

The people of New York saw Sir Henry Clinton frequently, and though they knew him little, gossiped endlessly of his affairs. They smiled at sight of his bizarre drag hunts through the streets, lanes, and byways of the little city— a Hessian soldier flying ahead, dragging a bone on a rope, followed by a yelping hound, and behind, at breakneck speed, Clinton and a few redcoat horsemen, careening through fields and soaring over fences in pathetic imitation of an English foxchase.

Civilians marveled at the extravagance of his headquarters, where hundreds of guests swarmed to be wined and dined by Clinton's staff of twelve, and to join the rounds of plays, balls, drinking bouts, or concerts by an amateur orchestra, in which Sir Henry played the violin. The General's menage was a royal court in miniature; he maintained four houses and a farm, scattered about the city and Long Island, and moved between them according to his mood and the season. He was paid almost £12,000 a year in salaries and expenses and was saving at a rate to assure him of a comfortable old age, but he grumbled plaintively of his living costs. Meat was cheap, a shilling per pound, yet his butcher's bill amounted to £25 per week; his fuel bill for one winter was almost £2000, and his total expenses were £6000 to £7000 per year. "If this lasts," he said, "I shall be ruined notwithstanding the greatest economy."

Sir Henry was saved from ruin by his handsome young Irish housekeeper, Mrs. Mary Baddeley, who had presided over his teeming establishment for years, keeping a sharp eye on the thirty servants and local tradesmen: "From her care alone . . . I saved at least ten thousand dollars." Mary Baddeley interested New Yorkers above all others in Clinton's entourage. She was the daughter of an Irish country gentleman and member of the Dublin Parliament who had shocked her family by marrying a carpenter and had come with him to America after he joined the army. Her husband, promoted to captain through Clinton's influence, encouraged Mary in her liaison with the general, but she had served as housekeeper for months before becoming the mistress of the lonely, neurotic widower Clinton:

> Though she admitted me to certain liberties, I never could prevail on her to grant the last—until resentment did what . . . a warm attachment could not effect. She detected her husband in an intrigue with a common strumpet. She came to me directly—told him she would— and surrendered.

Clinton was determined to keep his mistress despite gossip and the threat of blackmail, "not only because I was really attached to her but because I was convinced that all depended on her care of my affairs." Mary was to remain intimate with Clinton until the general's death, bearing him many children.

Sir Henry's father, Admiral George Clinton, a former governor of New York, had been an ineffectual, petulant, and improvident man and a failure as a parent. The boy had been reared by his mother, who was given to violent fits of temper. When he came to America early in the war he found relations with fellow general officers difficult. He formed few lasting friendships. "I am a shy bitch," he said. But he was also complex, by turns aggressive and diffident and a trial to all, including himself.

The general was now fifty-one, a small, paunchy, quarrelsome man whose face was dominated by a hooked nose, beetling brows, and large, expressive eyes. He was not only commander in chief of royal forces in America; he was the most veteran British general in the war, and except for Washington had served longer than any general on either side. He had become a hero at Bunker Hill by leading the victorious charge on the rebels, in violation of orders.

As commander in chief he had become increasingly cautious and vacillating, as if fearful of decisions which grew more perplexing by the day. After his triumph in taking Charleston, South Carolina, by siege the year before, he had been content to conduct a war of stalemate, and though full of talk of decisive campaigns to end the war, he never launched them. Out of lifelong habit he found grievances everywhere—he was forever threatening to resign—and squabbled childishly with London authorities, the Royal Navy, and his own subordinates, usually by letter.

In this summer of 1781, when Washington and Rochambeau were presenting him with a crisis in the war, Clinton sometimes shut himself in his room for three or four days at a time, refusing to see anyone. But in other moods, as his intimates knew, Sir Henry could be fiery and heedless of consequences. He had once scolded his superior in London, Lord Germain, the Secretary of State for American affairs, whom he regarded as an incompetent meddler: "For God's sake, My Lord, if you wish me to do anything leave me to myself and let me adapt my efforts to the hourly change of circumstances. If not, tie me down to a certain point and take the risk of my want of success."

Clinton was often at odds with his staff, and only with junior subordinates was he uniformly friendly. Sir Henry especially despised the aging Governor Robertson, who was forever "smelling after every giddy girl that will let him come nigh her, and retailing amongst his female acquaintances the measures of headquarters when he can come at them." Robertson, in return, was not fond of Sir Henry: "He has not the understanding necessary for a corporal. He is as inconstant as a weathercock and knows nothing."

The military government of New York under Clinton was notorious for its rapacity—at least among the rebels. General Robertson, the Governor, was a former quartermaster and barracks master and "an accomplished thief," and Lieutenant Governor Andrew Elliott had been customs officer in a city celebrated for its smuggling; these two joined the superintendent of the court of police to victimize the public. They persuaded the elderly Adjutant General, Oliver Delancey, to relinquish control of trade in and out of the captive city, and the three of them divided the profits squeezed from traders' permits.

Civil courts had been abolished, and Robertson set up new police courts in their stead, paying large salaries to his cronies who sat on the benches. These judges, an early historian said, "did what they were ordered, behaved as submissively as spaniels."

These conspirators were said to have had many civilians murdered, confiscated estates, slaughtered cattle, filled their pockets, and fed their families on goods extorted from butchers and other merchants. Robertson diverted city, church, and college moneys into a fund intended for the relief of refugees, and paid some of his living costs from the proceeds, which Robertson and Delancey, it was said, "lavished away, and squandered upon favourites, upon little misses, upon strumpets, panderers and hangers-on; in balls, in dances, in rents, and feasts, in making walls, laying walks, illuminating trees, building music galleries, and in every other kind of dissipation that two old souls could imagine."

These were merely the complaints of civilians. Clinton was aware that his post was also riddled with military graft and corruption, but when the extravagant expenditures of his command came under investigation he said blandly, "That the expense is enormous is certain . . . that commissioners and contractors make fortunes—true. But in what war have they not done so?"

In the hands of this distraught general and his incompetent, quarrelsome staff rested the fate of the American colonies.

With a show of brisk energy and military wisdom, Sir Henry turned, in the heat of July, to meet the threat of the Americans and Frenchmen then swarming outside the walls of his garrison city.

Henry Clinton had little sleep on July 22; there was a night-long stir at Beekman House. The enemy was pressing against the lines, in strong force. The general was in the saddle by 3:00 A.M., riding out to the front at Kingsbridge, where he feared an attack. The morning was very warm, sunrise was early, and Clinton kept the troops busy. His men were puzzled; there was no sign of the enemy—the woods and fields were apparently empty—but Sir Henry pointed his telescope to the top of a nearby ridge and was rewarded when his big guns roared; hundreds of dark figures scrambled up from their hiding places and dashed for the hilltop, where they stood, looking down curiously to the redoubt from which the cannon had fired. Clinton nodded with satisfaction; the unsuspecting rebel troops had revealed the extent of their line to him. It was an old ruse he had learned in European wars. One of his admiring young officers wrote in his diary, "The success of this Strategem may teach an Officer how to act on a like occasion."

Sir Henry spent most of the day observing the enemy, who remained quietly in his front. He judged that they were about four thousand strong. They seemed to have no baggage, and he concluded that they were merely making a strong reconnaissance, driving the Tory refugees from their camps near the city and clearing the region of grain and other supplies.

Clinton wanted a glimpse of Washington but was disappointed. The Virginian had come into the open here the day before, sitting his horse so boldly within easy range that a few cannon had fired at his party and driven him away. Now, perhaps, he was watching the British from concealment, gazing up and down the lines, grim, unsmiling, and as inscrutable as ever. Despite his animosity toward Washington, Clinton clung to the idea of waging a gentleman's war against him. This week his officers urged that he send a band to kidnap the rebel leader; Sir Henry was interested, but when he was told that his agents would kill their victim if they could not carry him from his camp, Clinton shook his head. It was not his kind of war.

Word spread through the command that they had nothing to fear from the French, as the diarist Lieutenant Mackenzie reported, "The French are only formidable from their reputation and discipline; those now serving against us are young and inexperienced Soldiers . . . in a Country totally unknown to them."

There was also great jealousy between the French and Americans, deserters told the British, and Mackenzie smugly recounted tales of French soldiers, who were well fed, selling loaves of bread in the camps of the half-starved Americans: "The French soldiers are frequently knocked down, and their loaves taken from them. The French will not suffer the Rebel Soldiers to come into their encampment."

But Clinton betrayed his uneasiness at the pressure of the enemy the next day. He summoned a battalion of Hessian grenadiers to stand guard about Beekman House, and sent pontoons forward to Kingsbridge, ready for a crossing of Harlem Creek in case he must meet an assault. A deserter who came in on July 24 reported that the whole of the French and American armies had come down, nine thousand strong, with eleven pieces of artillery. There were other disturbing reports: rebel boats were now clustered up and down the Hudson, and more were being built at Albany; new gun batteries appeared on both banks of the river at Dobbs Ferry; French engineers were tracing out plans for a new fort near New York; and there were vague rumors that a large French fleet was on its way to America.

Lieutenant Mackenzie was made apprehensive by these signs of enemy activity:

We seem throughout this war to have adhered to the injudicious plan of dividing our Army into numerous detachments . . . we are not formidable in any one place

... we are now weak and dispersed at most of our posts.
Should de Grasse enter the Chesapeak ... we shall run
the risk of losing all the troops in Virginia.

Clinton was by no means blind to these dangers. He often
railed against diversion of force, of "making war by detachments," and he understood sea power. He had recently written Germain, ". . . if the Enemy remain only a few Weeks
superior at Sea, our . . . situation will become very critical."
But he found himself engulfed by other concerns. His problems with Cornwallis in the south multiplied. When the
Earl and his army had appeared in Virginia, without warning, after a costly and fruitless campaign in the Carolinas,
Clinton was shocked but lacked the firmness to restore his
authority: "My wonder at this move of Lord Cornwallis will
never cease. But he has made it, and we shall say no more
but make the best of it."

Sir Henry had waited with growing dismay as Cornwallis
and Lafayette chased each other back and forth across Virginia. Clinton was mystified by the Earl's strategy: "His first
object will of course be Lafayette . . . what his next object
will be God knows." Yet Clinton dealt gingerly with Cornwallis, and his orders to him were more suggestive than
direct, offered in bewildering number and variety—plans
and counter-plans that left Cornwallis so confused that he
was often forced to rely on his judgment. At a time when he
himself had not heard from Lord Germain for four months,
Clinton was aware that Cornwallis was bypassing him, reporting directly to Germain in London, but he did little to
halt the disintegration of command. He never forgot that
Cornwallis was his social superior, with political associations
in London much more powerful than his own, and that the
Earl remained popular with the war ministry despite his
ruinous "victories" in the Carolinas. Clinton's method, once

more, was vacillation. During the troubled summer he re-
peatedly called some of the Earl's troops to New York, re-
voked his orders, demanded them again, changed his mind
once more—sometimes sending contradictory orders on the
same day.

Clinton's struggles with his stubborn lieutenant in Virginia were hardly more trying than his travail with the Navy.
For almost two years he had been hopelessly embroiled with
Vice Admiral Marriott Arbuthnot, who was almost seventy
when he took naval command in America and seemed much
older. Arbuthnot was pompous, incompetent, and unpredict-
able, given to absurd schemes of campaign. He resisted
Clinton at every turn, now friendly, then hostile, but unco-
operative throughout.

In June, Arbuthnot and the fleet had once vanished from
New York without a word, when there was danger that the
French might appear. "I know not where our old Admiral
is gone," Clinton said, "I fear he has opened Rhode Island.
I tremble while connected with this old gentleman." When
he could no longer bear the admiral's obstinate refusal to fol-
low instructions, Clinton told London that either he or
Arbuthnot must go.

The old admiral once thought of abandoning Clinton
entirely. He wrote to Cornwallis, for whom he affected
admiration, "I most ardently wish I could be near you, who
I long to serve with; give me a hint and I will come with
the fleet to the Chesapeake."

To Clinton's relief, Arbuthnot gave up his command in
mid-July and turned over the fleet to Rear Admiral Thomas
Graves. Arbuthnot confessed that he was by now almost an
invalid, that he had lost "almost totally the sight of one eye,
and the other is but a very feeble helpmate. . . . Beside, I
have lately been seized with very odd fits . . . almost instantly
I faint, remain senseless and speechless sometimes four

hours and sometimes longer . . . with cold sweats for two or three days after. . . ."

Graves, at least, was in robust health. The new fleet commander in North American waters was about fifty-six, the son and nephew of admirals. He had entered the Navy in his childhood and had became a lieutenant at eighteen. The new naval chief was a courtly, kindly man, a brave but rather uninspired officer, capable enough in the handling of a squadron, but hardly competent to fight a fleet in one of the great crises of British naval history. Clinton found him much more amenable than Arbuthnot, but his troubles with the Navy were far from ended.

In mid-August Clinton's spies began to caution him that Washington was on the point of slipping away to Virginia, and in the last two weeks of the month these reports became a deluge. A superb British intelligence service passed on to headquarters every intention of the rebels. The warnings fell upon deaf ears. Sir Henry, still gripped by the fear that he was to be attacked, busily dug trenches, built new forts, cleared ground by tearing down farmhouses, cut down orchards, and dug a canal between rivers to surround himself by water. He also kept up a heated correspondence with Cornwallis, vexing him with the problem of reinforcements for New York.

Clinton confided to friends that he had suffered two brief attacks of temporary blindness. Mrs. Baddeley, who had now been his mistress for more than three years, was about to bear him a child; his officers, especially Benedict Arnold, badgered him to take action—any action. Relations between Sir Henry and the Navy were not improved by the tensions within the high command. Admiral Graves now made headquarters in south Brooklyn, and Clinton usually kept to Beekman House, on what was to become Fifty-second Street, near the Four Mile Post on the road north. One dispatch between the admiral and the general was mislaid for three days during this crucial period.

The Royal Chief Justice of New York, William Smith, who saw Sir Henry almost daily and found him shaken by "gusts of passion," a man "insensible of his danger," said prophetically, "I despair of Clinton. . . . He will make the apprehension of a French fleet an excuse for inactivity."

On August 16 Clinton heard more ominous rumors of a French fleet—Admiral de Grasse was said to be somewhere in America with many large warships—but he passed this to Admiral Graves with a skeptical comment: "I cannot say I credit the reports of the French fleet being upon the coast." Graves himself dismissed the report as the result of "a heated imagination."

Two days later, on August 18, Sir Henry had his first clear signal of trouble brewing on the Hudson—the enemy's troops were under marching orders. A woman spy had watched the French strike tents and move from camp, and Washington was ready to cross the Hudson the next day. The British merely took new outposts on the north of Manhattan Island, where they could meet an attack.

The day produced an unmistakable sign that the French were on the move—the young Viscount de Rochambeau, the general's son, had sent his mistress across the country to the south; she was to ride horseback to Trenton, New Jersey, to meet her lover, without the knowledge of the old general, who allowed "no kept mistresses."

Amid this flood of intelligence Clinton struggled with the dilatory Admiral Graves, urging him to prepare the fleet for an emergency. Graves responded almost petulantly: one of his ships, the *Robust,* was leaky and must go to drydock. The *Prudent* must change one mast and perhaps two; no one knew how long the repairs would require.

Word of the allied movement on the Hudson became even more insistent the next day—August 19—when rebel baggage and artillery crossed to the west bank of the river. Spies heard American troops speculating freely about their destination; the men thought they were bound for Baltimore, or the Chesapeake—and one agent had it from Commissary Blanchard himself that the goal was Philadelphia. Still Clinton did not take alarm, perhaps because his Hessians engaged his attention.

Two newly arrived German regiments and some English troops fell into an amusing squabble that threatened to become a riot. When the Germans were moved to the old campsite of the Fifty-fourth Regiment, they were delighted to find lush vegetable gardens grown by the British during the spring and summer. The English demanded that the Hessians pay for the produce, the indignant Germans refused—and the redcoats fell upon the gardens, uprooting cabbages and other vegetables. The Germans rushed to halt this plunder, and only the interference of officers averted bloodshed. The Germans settled down morosely in their devastated gardens on the outskirts of Manhattan Island, so near the enemy that they could see winding columns of French and American troops.

About this time, when Washington's men were stretched out on the roads from Dobbs Ferry to Princeton, Judge Smith visited Beekman House to demand that Clinton put a stop to the endless marching and counter-marching of the enemy. He found Clinton in no mood for action.

"It's useless," Sir Henry said, "Washington has 12,000 men, and I could barely muster 3000."

William Franklin, the Tory son of Benjamin, who was now Royal Governor of New Jersey, proclaimed his disgust with Clinton's failure: "We have only one lament, that we have not penetration to fathom the policy of his deep laid schemes. For deep laid they must be, because unintelligible."

On August 22 Sir Henry had an insistent dispatch in cipher from a spy who signed himself Squib:

> General Washington with about six thousand, including French, are on their march for this neighborhood. It is said they will go against New York, but some Circumstances induce me to believe they will go to the Chesapeake. Yet for God's sake be prepared at all points. . . .

The days slipped by as the Allied troops edged steadily toward the south; as the evidence mounted, Clinton seemed to become more inert. His spy Marquand reported on each new enemy campsite each day, but when the rebels reached Chatham and Springfield, Clinton had done no more than shift troops within his garrison, still expecting an assault on the island. On August 25 Sir Henry called Lieutenant Mackenzie into his office and enthusiastically outlined a new scheme of campaign—he would strike the French fleet in Rhode Island. Clinton pursued this vigorously for a few days, ordering troops, guns, and ships made ready, as if he had forgotten the marching enemy in New Jersey.

On August 27 Sir Henry had written Cornwallis that he was at a loss to understand Washington: "I cannot well ascertain Mr. Washington's real intentions by this move of his army." He could only surmise, he said, that the American was returning to his old winter quarters at Morristown, New Jersey.

Nothing moved Sir Henry. On August 29 he had a message that should have removed all doubt, when his spy Squib sent in a scrap of paper concealed in a button: "The Chesapeake is the Object—All in motion."

Clinton wrote Cornwallis the following day, "Mr. Washington's force still remains in the neighborhood of Chatham and I do not hear that he has yet detached to the southward." On this day Washington rode into Philadelphia.

Sir Henry now received an unexpected ally in his struggle to force the leisurely Admiral Graves into action. The newcomer was one of the most able and aggressive British admirals, Sir Samuel Hood, who had sailed up from the West Indies with sixteen line of battle ships, which he left outside the harbor off Sandy Hook so that he could sail at a moment's notice. Hood was in desperate haste, for he brought news that Admiral de Grasse and the French fleet were on the loose, the first authoritative word of this to arrive in New York.

Samuel Hood was a rarity, a British admiral who had begun as a cabin boy and fought his way upward through the ranks to command. At fifty-three he was a grizzled veteran—he had first come to American waters more than thirty years earlier. In the midst of the war, when his fighting career had apparently ended, he had been rescued from a dull post as dock yard commissioner and governor of the naval academy, promoted to rear admiral, given the ninety-gun *Barfleur* as his flagship, and made second in command in American waters. Hood was full of fight, though he protested that "I have no spirits left and can scarce keep myself upon my legs."

Hood left his fleet off Sandy Hook, had himself rowed to Long Island, and burst upon the astonished Clinton and Graves, who were conferring at Sir Henry's farm—planning their attack on the small fleet of Admiral Saint-Laurent de Barras in Rhode Island. Neither Clinton nor Graves seemed to share his alarm at the coming of de Grasse, but Hood overwhelmed Graves with his air of emergency. "You have no time to lose," Hood said. "Every moment is precious. You must leave immediately, with every ship you have ready for sea. Wait for nothing." Graves promised to leave the harbor the next day, August 29, to join Hood outside the Hook.

It was three days later, on the first of September, that Admiral Graves put an end to delays and excuses, drove the carpenters from his ships, and left New York harbor to meet Admiral Hood at sea, bound for the Chesapeake.

Two days after the fleet had disappeared off Sandy Hook, Clinton came to himself with a start—he saw for the first time the whole design of the enemy's campaign. A British frigate brought conclusive word that the fleet of de Grasse was bound for the Chesapeake, and by now the flow of news from the marching enemy columns in New Jersey was too insistent to be disregarded. Sir Henry wrote Cornwallis in cipher:

New York, Sept. 2, 1781

Mr. Washington is moving an army to the southward, with an appearance of haste; and gives out that he expects the cooperation of a considerable French armament. Your Lordship, however, may be assured that if this should be the case, I shall endeavor to reinforce your command by all means within the compass of my power; or, make every possible diversion in your favor. . . .

Clinton, now anxious to warn London of the looming danger, also wrote hastily to Germain: "Things appear to be coming fast to a crisis . . . with what I have, inadequate as it is, I will exert myself to the utmost to save Lord Cornwallis."

And now that it was too late, Clinton bestirred himself with a vigor to match Washington's; he put four thousand troops aboard ships in the harbor and loaded wagons to carry twenty days' provisions for eight thousand men. He did not know how or when these could be used, for now he had to wait for the navy to clear the way. In the end, everything depended upon the fleet; without victory at sea, Clinton was helpless.

Much later Clinton attempted to explain his fatal lapse:

I will not pay Mr. Washington's understanding so bad a compliment as to suppose he thought it necessary to deceive me . . . for he too well knew I was in no capacity to intercept his March to the Southward, whenever he pleased to make it. . . .

Tension grew in New York as the days of September passed without word from Graves. Many civilians now saw that a defeat for the navy would cost Cornwallis his army and end the rebellion. Judge William Smith said that this was "an hour of anarchy" in which the fate of the Empire was at stake: "Great events will render this week memorable to remote ages."

Events had now left Sir Henry Clinton in their wake.

3

THE GREAT SHIPS GATHER

More than fifteen hundred miles to the south of New York, crowding the harbor of San Domingo, lay the French fleet of Admiral François Joseph Paul de Grasse-Tilly, twenty tall ships of the line clustered about the flagship *Ville de Paris*, the largest warship on earth. There was uneasiness in the fleet. Tropical fevers had decimated the crews; eighteen hundred sick men had been left at Martinique. De Grasse had lately fought an inconclusive battle with the British, who were prowling through the West Indies, and the enemy might reappear at any time.

On July 23, just after dawn lit the harbor of San Domingo, a clerk on the seventy-four-gun *Intrépide* went below to draw the crew's daily ration of taffia, a robust brandy served at breakfast, carrying a lantern into the sweltering hold. As he pumped brandy from a cask the volatile liquor flashed into flame and fire raced through the ship. Men aboard nearby vessels watched as "the stern sprang into the air with a majestic rumble, a horrible sight." The doomed ship flung splinters and flaming brands in all directions, showered other ships of the fleet, and injured civilians and damaged houses ashore. Twenty sailors were drowned. There was worse to come.

A few days later the frigate *Inconstante,* under sail off the San Domingo coast, also blew up when brandy was being drawn; rescue vessels found only eighty survivors of her two-hundred-man crew clinging to wreckage in the warm sea.

The fleet had been gathering for months under de Grasse, the new commander in chief of French naval forces in America. It was under orders to strike the British on the North American coast and to cooperate with Rochambeau and Washington.

De Grasse had fought the British since his boyhood, and had once been captured and thrown into a British prison, where he spent three months under lenient jailers, making friends and studying the British navy. The Admiral came from a noble family of Provence, had been trained in both a Jesuit seminary and a celebrated school at Malta which prepared young men for combat at sea.

In the ill-fated French naval campaigns earlier in the American war, de Grasse had fought as a subordinate, and it was only a year before, in 1780, that he had been promoted to flag rank and given command of French naval forces in American waters. He was haughty and quick-tempered and noted for his severity to his captains, some of whom were cowed by his grim appearance. De Grasse tended toward corpulence and he was said to be "more sheath than sword," but he was one of the handsomest Frenchmen of his day. He was six feet two inches tall, one of the tallest men in the fleet—and it was said of him that he was "six feet six on days of battle."

There were conflicting opinions in the navy about his

ability. One of his young Swedish officers said that though the Admiral had a "brutal character," he was "a good seaman and known for his bravery, but . . . somewhat too careful."

De Grasse had joined the great French offensive in March, 1781, sailing from Brest to convoy 150 merchant ships to Martinique. He carried infantry reinforcements for Rochambeau on the long sea voyage, a nightmare for the soldiers, who were packed like sardines into the tiny ships. He drove the fleet relentlessly, towing his slower ships to increase his speed, and made a thirty-six-day passage, a remarkably swift one for the time.

De Grasse sent thirty ships to Rochambeau in Rhode Island with the reinforcements—and a message which was to change the course of the war:

> His Majesty has entrusted me with the command of the naval force destined for . . . North America. The force which I command is sufficient to fulfill the offensive plans . . . of the Allied powers to . . . secure an honorable peace . . . It will not be until the 15th of July, at the soonest, that I shall be on the coast of North America.

The British navy had reported promptly to London that the huge French fleet was sailing for America, but the Admiralty dallied, and weeks passed before the little sloop *Swallow* left England with a warning—almost a month too late. Thus, when de Grasse reached Martinique on April 28, he was unexpected. The fleet of Sir Samuel Hood was in sight but lay to the leeward where it could not block the harbor, and the French transports slipped in unmolested. De Grasse sailed out to give battle, and guns rolled across the tropic sea in a brief exchange between the vans of the fleets. Six English ships were badly damaged, but de Grasse, whose mission was to anchor safely at Martinique, did not press the attack against Hood's inferior force.

For six weeks de Grasse raided through the Indies without interference from the combined British fleet under Admiral George Rodney. He captured the island of Tobago and called at Grenada, where he took aboard cattle, wood, and water. The British often sailed within sight, as if Rodney were tempted to battle, but the fleets did not clash. De Grasse spent the early summer collecting his convoy of merchantmen for a voyage to France and on July 16 herded 150 of these ships to San Domingo. He found important mail waiting for him, brought by the frigate *Concorde,* which had slipped down from Boston, eluding British ships on her way. She also carried interesting passengers—twenty-five American pilots who were familiar with the waters of the Chesapeake Bay.

The French admiral opened the dispatch pouch in the cabin of the *Ville de Paris* to discover that the American Revolution was in its last days, that land and sea power must now be combined against the British, or the cause was lost. The decision was in his hands. Letters from Rochambeau described the desperate state of the rebellion:

> That is the state of affairs and the very grave crisis in which America . . . finds herself at this particular time. The arrival of M. Comte de Grasse would save this situation . . . It is needless to write you the important service you will render if you are able to bring here a body of troops and your ships. . . .

There was also the matter of money; Rochambeau could not pay his troops beyond the end of July. He urged de Grasse to pledge the navy's credit for money in the Indies, up to 1,200,000 livres. Most vital of all were the troops: ". . . it is of the greatest consequence that you will take on board as many troops as possible . . . four or five thousand men will not be too many. . . ."

The General described once more the ragged, underfed American army and the bankrupt government, and the military moves which might save the cause. He favored concentration in the Chesapeake. Finally, he wrote, "There, Monsieur, are the different objects that you may have in view, and the actual and sad picture of the affairs of this country. I am quite persuaded that you will bring us naval superiority, but I cannot too often repeat to you to bring also the troops and the money."

De Grasse did not hesitate. He understood the urgency for strategic concentration on the North American coast and wrote Rochambeau that he would sail for the Chesapeake, "as the point . . . from which the advantage you propose may be most certainly attained."

The Admiral astounded his captains by the audacity of his plan—he ordered the fleet to prepare to sail for the north, the entire fleet, leaving the Indies exposed. He saw that the projected new campaign was worth the risk of losing the assembled merchant ships and the rich produce of the islands. He wrote Rochambeau, "Though this whole expedition had been concerted only on your demand and without warning to the ministries of France and Spain, I believe myself authorized to take some responsibility on my own shoulders for the common cause."

He also agreed to try to raise money and bring more troops; he was sure of the infantry of the Marquis Claude Henri de Saint-Simon—the regiments of Agenais, Gatinais, and Touraine, thirty-five hundred men in all.

Within twelve days after reading the dispatches, de Grasse had the fleet ready to sail. The troops of Saint-Simon boarded the warships, and when it appeared that there was no room for their field equipment and artillery, de Grasse chartered fifteen merchant ships with his own money. All were aboard by August 3—the three infantry regiments, 100 dragoons, and

350 artillerymen with weapons and equipment. Only Rochambeau's money was missing.

De Grasse and one of his captains went ashore in San Domingo to plead with their Spanish allies for gold, 300,000 piastres. The dons were evasive, but merchants of the island at last agreed to raise the money if the French would post security for the loan. De Grasse offered as security his own plantation on San Domingo and even his chateau in France, estates whose value was far greater than the sum he sought. The San Domingan merchants accepted, but when they delayed for several days, the angry de Grasse turned to the Spanish director of customs, Señor de Salavedra, and pressed him so hard that he agreed to go to Havana to raise the money. De Grasse sent Salavedra ahead of him to Havana on the frigate *Aigrette* and on August 5 put to sea himself.

The fleet was impressive as it stood out of the harbor—twenty-eight great ships of the line, led by the 110-gun three-decker *Ville de Paris,* a gift of the people of Paris to the French nation and a monster whose sides glistened in new varnish. Her sailors had decorated her with tropical plants and vines, which were now entwined between the guns. Beyond the ships of the line were seven frigates and two cutters. The armada was a long time in winding from the harbor and disappearing to the northwest. Two more seventy-four-gun ships, *Bourgogne* and *Hector,* joined the fleet at sea two days later. Even when the news reached the British, the enemy could not believe that de Grasse had taken every fighting ship in the Indies on his new adventure; such boldness was beyond imagination. As an English admiral said not long afterward, "If the British Government had sanctioned or a British admiral had adopted such a measure, however necessary to carry out a political operation, the one would have been turned out and the other would have been hung. No wonder that they succeeded and we failed."

The French vessels laboring toward Virginia, like all warships of the day, were clumsy tub-like hulks, most of them about 170 feet long and about 47 feet in the beam; blunt, top-heavy, and difficult to maneuver, they carried an enormous weight of canvas on spars and masts which towered almost 200 feet above the water line. The overburdened masts often snapped in storms when the hemp rigging stretched— and were always vulnerable in battle. Crewmen were penned in the low space between decks, in dark and stuffy holes where disease bred; they drank water from wooden casks that was often already impure when taken aboard. The great ships were floating gun platforms, carrying from 60 to 110 guns—most of them carrying 74. The cannon were primitive, fired without locks or sights; a single broadside hurled more than half a ton of metal, but the guns were elevated by guesswork.

The French captains were dismayed as they saw where their course led them—de Grasse sailed along the northern coast of Cuba, through the dreaded Bahama Channel, which no French fleet had dared before; it was noted for its treacherous reefs and violent storms. But it was the one passage where he could hide from the British, and de Grasse sailed the coast for three days, through thunderstorms and heavy rains. One ship, the seventy-four-gun *Northumberland,* came near disaster when her helmsman turned the wheel in the wrong direction and ran her into breakers.

De Grasse soon met the *Aigrette,* which was back from Havana with good news: the people of the city had gone wild with enthusiasm and with the help of the consul and the city's bankers had raised the 1,200,000 livres within six hours; ladies had even given their diamonds to aid the cause. De Grasse divided the money between his ships and sailed northward, capturing every hostile sail in sight. One of his victims was the forty-gun *Sandwich,* from Charleston, South

Carolina, carrying the British troop commander in the South, Lord Rawdon, who now went as a prisoner to witness the final act of the war. Far to the north and east, now pulling ahead of the French, the fleet of Sir Samuel Hood was also bearing for the North American coast. Neither fleet yet realized that the race was on.

Under the Earl of Sandwich as First Lord of the Admiralty, the British Navy was poorly prepared for the test that lay a few days ahead. The coming of war had found its ships rotting at their wharves, its rolls reduced to eighteen thousand seamen, its officers demoralized by years of corrupt administration. Grafting contractors enriched themselves ashore, and pursers and commanders robbed the crews at sea. Yet Sandwich remained in office as a royal favorite; he was descended from a famous admiral whose secretary had been Samuel Pepys, and he himself had given his name to a new fashion in food when he had once spent twenty-four hours at a gaming table, eating nothing but slabs of roast beef between slices of bread.

British captains were rigidly restricted by antiquated fighting instructions. Admiral Kempenfeldt, one of the most able officers of the day, had recently complained that the French now excelled in tactics at sea, but there was no reform. The new French navy grew larger and more formidable by the month. The crews of British warships were undisciplined and often a liability in battle. The Royal Navy was manned by crews recruited from prisons and slums, or kidnapped on English city streets by press gangs and ruthlessly carried to sea. Press gangs had harried Englishmen for generations. Merchant ships returning to England after long voyages were waylaid by the navy's manhunters, and sailors within sight of their homes were abducted for the fleet. Many crews spent six or seven years at sea as virtual prisoners.

Even now, in American waters, the navy was desperate for men. A few weeks earlier, a British press gang had raided New York, seizing able-bodied men in the streets and dragging them away to serve aboard the warships. When the streets were empty, the gang invaded houses. Within six hours they had herded four hundred "seamen" to the fleet.

Lieutenant Bartholomew James, a leader of the expedition, left in his journal a vivid glimpse of an early spring morning when war came to unsuspecting households in New York:

> . . . taking the husband from the arms of his wife in bed, the searching for them when hid beneath the warm clothes, and, the better to prevent delay, taking them off naked, while the frantic partner of his bed, forgetting the delicacy of her sex, pursued us to the doors with shrieks and imprecations, and exposing their naked persons to the rude view of an unfeeling press gang.

England's greatest need in the summer of 1781 was for a fighting admiral in American waters, but the great men of the navy were elsewhere. Sir George Brydges Rodney, a sixty-one-year-old veteran of fifty years in the navy, held the command. He was a sharp-tongued tyrant, harsh with his subordinates, and a noted gambler and ladies' man who was perennially in debt.

Rodney had been a fighter, but he was now distracted by treasure. The threat of a French-American concentration in North America faded in his mind from the moment he began the sack of St. Eustatius, a tiny Dutch island of the Leeward chain where the merchant fleets of the world—British included—trafficked in smuggled goods to and from America. Rodney was dazzled by the riches of the defenseless little port, where he seized goods worth more than three million pounds sterling and remained for weeks, auctioning off his treasure. Dutch officials protested that the British "acted like robbers, searching, digging, confiscating." While Rodney dallied at St. Eustatius, he had the first word of the approach of de Grasse, but he had done no more than send the small fleet of Samuel Hood to meet him. Hood urged the capture of other Dutch islands—Curaçao and Surinam—but Rodney refused; the commander was overcome by a "bewitchment . . . not to be withstood by flesh and Blood," Hood said. "He could not bear the thought of leaving St. Eustatius . . . I dare say he would have been there to this hour had not the arrival of de Grasse obliged him to decamp."

By July 7 Rodney realized that de Grasse had come to the Indies in force, and he sent a warning to Admiral Graves in New York by the ill-fated sloop *Swallow:*

> As the enemy has at this time a fleet of twenty-eight sail of the line at Martinique, a part of which is reported to be destined for North America . . . I shall keep as good a lookout as possible on their motions. . . .

By now the Admiral's health was failing; he suffered from gout and prostate trouble, and talked of going home to consult British surgeons and take the waters at Bath. Hood lost his patience: "It is quite impossible from the unsteadiness of the commander-in-chief to know what he means three days together; one hour he says his complaints are of such a nature that he cannot possibly remain in this country, and is determined to leave the command with me; the next he says he has no thought of going home . . . If he stays much longer, his laurels may be subject to wither."

Rodney left for England on August 1, leaving Hood under

orders to sail to America. Even before the commander sailed from the Indies, his warning to Admiral Graves in New York had gone astray. The *Swallow* arrived in New York on July 27, but Graves was away, cruising off New England, and when the *Swallow* was sent after him with the messages from Rodney, she was attacked by three American privateers and driven onto a Long Island beach. Her skipper burned the *Swallow* with her dispatches, and Graves did not get Rodney's warning until mid-August, when he returned to New York and read duplicate dispatches.

The British made other attempts to warn Graves of trouble approaching; Hood sent the brig *Active* northward with word of his coming—but she was captured by Americans and taken to Philadelphia, where her imprisoned captain managed to smuggle word to Graves only a day before Hood himself arrived in New York.

British communications did not improve. On August 13, when he was far at sea on his way home, Rodney sent Graves a warning that de Grasse would come to America with at least a dozen warships and added that Hood was sailing to the rescue. This message, too, failed to arrive in time. It was carried by the slow *Pegasus,* which was twenty-six days in making New York, docking three days after the British and French fleets had met off the Chesapeake and fought to a decision.

The cause of these failures was obvious even to British subordinates who saw that the haphazard handling of messages by the navy might bring ruin. In New York Lieutenant Mackenzie complained, "I cannot help remarking how frequently we suffer by sending small vessels with the most consequential dispatches . . . the French hardly ever act in this manner; whenever they have anything of importance to communicate, it is done by means of a frigate." British admirals, Mackenzie thought, were so grasping that they kept their frigates busy seeking prize ships so that they could fatten their purses.

Finally, on August 10, Samuel Hood sailed from Antigua with sixteen ships, still unaware that the American pilots had come to de Grasse or that the French had slipped away toward Virginia. Hood's swift copper-bottomed ships took a shorter route northward and outsailed de Grasse, and on August 25, a British frigate looked into the Chesapeake and found it empty. Three days later, on August 28, Hood was in New York, and the British fleet in North America had combined.

The French fleet approached the Chesapeake near sunset on August 29, but on the advice of local pilots de Grasse anchored at sea, nine miles southeast of Cape Henry, and sent frigates ahead to scout the bay for the enemy. The three ships took the British picket line by surprise; they caught the corvette *Loyalist* and chased the frigate *Guadeloupe* up the York River. Later in the day the fleet entered, a stately line of great ships fluttering the Bourbon lilies from their masts; they came to anchor in Lynnhaven Bay, just inside the capes. Frigates moved to block the rivers York and James, and forty boatloads of Saint-Simon's infantry rowed up the James to join the army of the Marquis de Lafayette at Williamsburg.

At five o'clock in the morning of September 2, Colonel Louis Duportail, after a long and wearing horseback ride from the north, came to the beach at Hampton Roads and saw de Grasse's fleet. He was the first man from headquarters to realize that Cornwallis was trapped, and that victory was within Washington's grasp. The sight of the ships, he said, "makes me forget all the hardships I experienced." Duportail went aboard the flagship, and de Grasse read Washington's message: "We have determined to remove the whole of the

French army, and as large a detachment of the American as can be spared, to the Chesapeake, to meet your Excellency there."

Both Frenchmen wrote to Washington immediately. De Grasse said that the coming of the armies from the North had changed his plans. His first thought, he confessed, had been to join Lafayette and attack Cornwallis at once: "But because of the letter which I received from Your Excellency, and on the advice of M du Portail, I have suspended my plans until the arrival of the generals."

Duportail wrote Washington that he would join Lafayette's army the next day. He added in his quaint English:

But dear general come with the greatest expedition. let us make use of the short stay of the count de grasse here. we have no choice left I thinck, when 27 ships of the line are in chesapeake, when great americain and french forces are joined we must take cornwallis or be all dishonored. . . .

De Grasse gave these letters to Captain Amie de la Laune of the cutter *Serpent*, who sailed immediately northward up the bay under a brisk wind. About 1:00 P.M. of September 4 the *Serpent* reached Baltimore, where General Mordecai Gist of the Maryland militia took the dispatches and passed them to an express rider, ordering him to ride day and night until he found Washington. By now there was a bulky package: the letters of de Grasse and Duportail, a list of the French ships added by de la Laune, and a covering letter from Gist.

News of the arrival of the French fleet spread quickly in Baltimore. Taverns roared with toasts, militiamen fired muskets in celebration, the city was illuminated, and in the dusk the express rider left the city and galloped northward in search of Washington.

4

THE LONG MARCH

The general rode into Philadelphia at one o'clock in the afternoon of August 30, and the city greeted him as if the war were already won. A troop of militia cavalry met his party outside the capital and trotted ahead of them to City Tavern, where Washington shook hands with Congressmen, city officials, and old friends—"all the notables," as Closen said. After a round of rum punch the general rode to the home of the banker Robert Morris, where he was to stay, and Rochambeau and his staff went to the residence of the French Minister, the Chevalier de La Luzerne.

There was a flurry at the Morris house as headquarters prepared for the approach of the armies. Morris had been ordered to assemble boats for about seven thousand men, but despite his pleas to governors, agents, and watermen, the small craft he had waiting could carry no more than two thousand troops. Washington sent orders for most of the army to march overland to the northern end of the Chesapeake Bay, at Head of Elk, in Maryland. Supplies were short.

Morris had sent a blunt warning to the commissary general: "Should the operations against Cornwallis fail for want of supplies the states must thank their own negligence. If they will not exert themselves upon the present occasion, they never will."

Henry Knox, also plagued by shortages for his gunners, pressed the Board of War for help—he needed cannon, 300,000 cartridges, 20,000 flints, 1000 powder horns, artillery tools, and musket balls. After collecting all the ammunition from sparse New England stocks, the army had only twelve wagonloads of cartridges and shot and shell, a pathetic supply, but all he could wring from "the vile and water-gruel governments" of the states. Knox fumed and cursed state officials, who did not seem to realize that a war was raging. Washington agreed: "Certainly, certainly, the people have lost their ardor in attempting to secure their liberty and happiness . . ."

The public saw Washington only as the chief of a conquering army; he gave no hint of his troubles. About three o'clock, the general rode the few blocks to the State House, where Congress was in session, and went inside to pay his respects in calm, brief remarks which no one troubled to record; it had been more than six years since he had been named commander of the armies here, the lone Congressman in uniform—it was a day of which he had told Patrick Henry, in a voice choked with emotion, "Remember, Mr. Henry, what I now tell you: from the day I enter upon the command of the American Armies, I date my fall, and the ruin of my reputation."

Washington returned to the Morris house, where others had come for dinner; Rochambeau and Chastellux, President Thomas McKean of the Congress, and Generals Knox, Sullivan, and Moultrie were among them. The city celebrated during the meal. Ships at the wharves had been towed into the harbor and fired salutes while the general's dinner party drank toasts. They were long at the table, drinking: To the United States, to His Most Christian Majesty, to His Catholic Majesty, to the Allied Armies, to the speedy arrival of Admiral de Grasse. McKean, a sturdy figure in a black velvet suit, gave a toast prophesying French victory over England: "When lilies flourish, roses fade." While they drank and the guns from the Delaware shook the city, the ships of de Grasse were coming to anchor in the Chesapeake, far to the south.

The streets were illuminated at dusk, and Washington walked through the city, bowing gravely to a crowd in front of the Morris house, followed by a growing mob "eagerly pressing to see their beloved general." There were Tories in the crowd who did not cheer. One of them said, "I saw this man, great as an instrument of destruction and devastation to the property, morals and principles of the people . . . walking the street, attended by a concourse of men, women and boys who huzzaed him and broke some of my father's windows and others near us."

Rochambeau and his staff were "housed like princes" at Luzerne's house, but for Washington's aides, sleeping in the Morris house was reminiscent of life in the field. The Morris family was away for the summer, and there was a spare bed only for Washington himself; the others slept on mattresses on the floor.

At eight o'clock in the morning of September 1 a dispatch rider from the north found the headquarters. He was a courier from General Forman with ominous news: the combined British fleet, twenty ships under Graves and Hood, had left New York. Now, Washington thought, the enemy might intercept de Barras as he came south from Rhode Island. The only hope was that de Barras would slip past them and join de Grasse in the Chesapeake—if de Grasse ever came. It was almost three weeks since the French admiral had been heard from. The general's next thought was that the British might enter the Chesapeake first, bar the French and free Cornwallis from the trap. He could only wait for news from the south and keep the troops marching.

His Americans entered the city the next day, a line of march nearly two miles long led by Scammell's Light Infantry. They threaded between Sunday afternoon crowds which lined the streets to see them pass. The day was hot and dry, but windy, and the troops were covered with dirt from the streets. "We raised a dust like a smothering snow-storm," Dr. Thacher said, "blinding our eyes and covering our bodies with it; this was not a little mortifying as the ladies were viewing us from the open windows of every house as we passed."

The men marched slowly to the sound of fifes and drums, in their odd array of uniforms, many of them still barefoot or without stockings. The troops stared grimly ahead and their officers quickly diagnosed the trouble; they had not been paid in many months—some of them not at all—and they were enraged by the sight of the prosperous civilians of Philadelphia: "Great symptoms of discontent . . . appeared on their passage through the city." The men were ordered to march straight through the city without a halt. A few of Knox's field guns and caissons rolled behind each brigade, and in the rear, wagons creaked along on leaning wheels, loaded with tents, baggage, and a few women and children whom Washington had allowed to follow the troops.

The Philadelphians were shocked, as the French had been, by their first glimpse of these shambling men with lean, weathered faces, lank hair, and filthy clothing, but they quickly realized that they bore the familiar look of workmen from the waterfront or settlers on their way to the western frontier. One French onlooker said, "The plainly

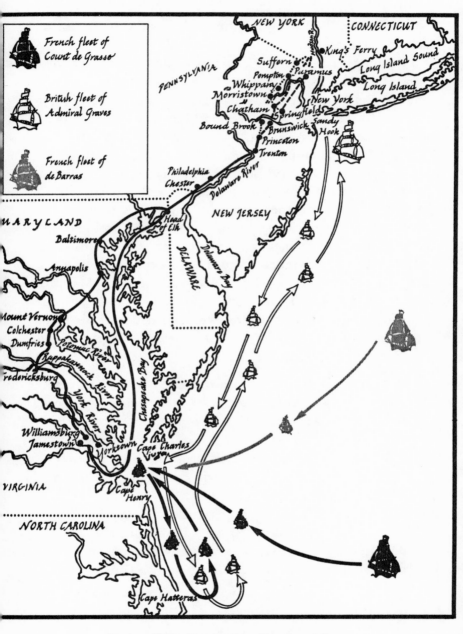

Cornwallis Is Trapped by Land and Sea

dressed American army lost no credit in the steadiness of their march and their fitness for battle."

Washington reviewed the troops as they passed, his long unsmiling face as serene as ever, almost somnolent in repose, but within he was tormented by fears: If de Grasse did not appear in the Chesapeake, the long march would have been in vain—and there was still no word from the fleet. He turned from watching his men to the business of the army. He sent pleas to Maryland and Virginia officials to gather supplies along the route of march, to furnish boats, and to improve roads for the passage of guns. He revealed his anxiety only in his longest message of the day, to Lafayette.

The Frenchman had written him that Cornwallis, who did not seem "very much alarmed," had occupied Yorktown, and Washington responded, "Nothing, my Dear Marquis, could have afforded me more satisfaction than . . . your two letters. . . ." The general wrote in detail of his plans to bring arms and clothing to Lafayette's hungry, ragged troops and then burst out:

> But, my dear Marquis, I am distressed beyond expression to know what has become of the Count de Grasse, and for fear that the English fleet, by occupying the Chesapeake . . . may frustrate all our flattering prospects . . . Should the retreat of Lord Cornwallis by water be cut off, I am persuaded you will do all in your power to prevent his escape by land. . . .
>
> You see how critically important the present moment is . . . adieu, my dear Marquis if you get any thing new from any quarter, send it I pray you, *on the spur of speed* for I am almost all impatience and anxiety. . . .

The French marched into the city on Monday. They halted just outside to change into dress uniforms and made a spectacular entry. An admiring chaplain described the parade:

... they then marched through the town, with the military music playing before them, which is always particularly pleasing to the Americans; the streets were crowded with people, and the ladies appeared at the windows in their most brilliant attire. All Philadelphia was astonished to see people who had endured the fatigues of a long journey, so ruddy and handsome, and even wondered that there could possibly be *Frenchmen* of so genteel an appearance.

When the Frenchmen had passed through the cheering crowds, they filed in single column before Washington, Rochambeau, members of Congress, and Luzerne, who stood on the balcony of the State House. The troops went past at a marching salute in honor of the Americans. Washington and Rochambeau removed their hats, and President McKean, whose black Quaker hat was set firmly on his head, turned to Rochambeau: "Should we return the salute?"

The General spoke to an interpreter: "When the troops march past the King, His Majesty always returns the salute with graciousness."

French officers smiled at the charade which followed. As each soldier passed, saluting the officials and the American flag, "the thirteen members took off their thirteen hats at each salute." McKean bowed so low to each soldier that he seemed in danger of toppling to the street.

Count Fersen saw the troops candidly: "Our army, unfortunately, is as little disciplined as the French army always is under ordinary circumstances." Rochambeau held it under control, but he seemed to know how far he could go without causing chaos: "Our chiefs are very strict, and not a day passes that there are not some two or three officers placed under arrest. I have myself seen some lamentable scenes where a whole corps of men ought to have been cashiered, but as we only number five thousand we cannot afford to lose a man. . . ." The French problems came to a crisis in Philadelphia; the troops were restless and Rochambeau doubled the guard about the camp to prevent desertion, particularly from the Deux-Ponts regiment, whose men were visited by scores of relatives now living in Pennsylvania.

Rochambeau's men camped in a meadow beside the Schuylkill, and the next day the Soissonnais regiment staged a drill at the riverside before a crowd of twenty thousand people who applauded as the troops went through their exercise, entranced by the precision and discipline of the men in spotless white broadcloth and rose silk, with pink and white plumes tossing in their hats.

To the amusement of French officers, the onlookers most admired a message-bearer, a young man in a short, tight-fitting coat and a waistcoat embroidered in silver, who carried a cane with an enormous head. This boy strode rapidly among the parading troops in rose-colored shoes, a figure of dignity and authority who, as he trotted up with his messages, appeared to be giving orders to the colonel of the regiment.

The French review opened an interlude of gaiety for ranking officers of the armies. Luzerne entertained 180 guests at his home that evening with a lavish feast, for which he borrowed thirty cooks from the French army. Other hosts besieged the officers at every meal. Joseph Reed, who had been Washington's aide early in the war and was now President of Pennsylvania, delighted French epicures with a dinner whose main dish was a ninety-pound turtle from the Delaware, which Closen found a "sumptuous, spectacular" repast: "The soup was served in an immense shell, and the fat, seasoned and peppered, had the taste of consomme."

Early on September 5, when the French rear guard had reached the city and the Americans were already camped near Wilmington, Delaware, Washington left Philadelphia; he could do no more to prepare the armies for the final march. His troops were still glum and mutinous over the prospect of going to Virginia without pay—but as he left the city the general noted cheerfully in his journal, "every thing in tolerable train here."

Rochambeau and his staff went by boat for a few miles down the Delaware to inspect Mud Island and the river forts Mifflin and Mercer, the scene of bitter fighting four years earlier; the generals were to meet at the upper end of the Chesapeake. Behind them in Philadelphia, Robert Morris began a desperate search for cash. John Laurens, a young South Carolina soldier who had been sent to Paris for aid, was in the city with news that 2,500,000 livres in silver had landed in Boston, a gift from Louis XVI, but that was weeks away, and the troops must have money immediately. Morris met with French officers at Luzerne's home, pleading for a loan of twenty thousand dollars. The French resisted: there was only forty thousand dollars left in Rochambeau's treasury, too little to pay his own soldiers. De Grasse was bringing money from the Indies, but no one knew when he would arrive. One of the Frenchmen said firmly, "We cannot make the loan in any case—the Treasurer has already left the city." Morris persisted, "I'll ride south with you until we find him. We must have money for the men, or it's all over with us." The stout banker, with his assistant, Gouverneur Morris, as translator, rode horseback with the French officers southward.

In the morning the General passed through Chester, Pennsylvania, a pleasant country village on the banks of the Delaware, and with a few officers about him was on the road about three miles south of the village, when a dusty rider galloped into sight. The horseman was the courier from Baltimore. Washington betrayed his eagerness as he opened the dispatches, and shouted boyishly when he read them: de Grasse had come. He had blocked the Chesapeake. The commander's outburst stunned his staff. It was a Washington his troops had never seen.

Count Deux-Ponts, who was watching him closely, saw the "naturally cold" manner disappear: ". . . his features, his expression, his whole carriage were changed in an instant." The General was now no longer the leader of the revolution and the hope of his country. "A child whose every wish had been granted, could not have revealed a livelier emotion," Deux-Ponts said. Count Dumas said, "I have never seen a man moved by a greater or sincerer joy."

Washington could not suppress his smiles. The messages announcing the arrival of the fleet were passed among the party. If Cornwallis remained in his vulnerable post at Yorktown, this campaign would not end, as others had, in stalemate and despair.

The General turned his horse and led the party rapidly back to Chester at a trot to give Rochambeau the news, talking with the staff all the while of his plans for Virginia—Lafayette and the troops of Saint-Simon could hold Cornwallis in place by land, and de Grasse would cut off British reinforcements by sea. They had only to hurry the armies to Yorktown to begin a siege. As the officers rode to the wharf at Chester, Rochambeau's boat came into sight, and Washington forgot himself once more. He had dismounted now, and Closen, who watched from the boat, could hardly believe his eyes: "We discerned in the distance General Washington, standing on the shore and waving his hat and a white handkerchief joyfully."

As Rochambeau came to the dock, Washington shouted the news to him, still whipping the hat and handkerchief overhead in wide circles. When the French general stepped ashore, he was astounded to be clasped in a fierce embrace by Washington, who shouted the news of de Grasse.

Word spread rapidly through the armies, which were strung out on the roads for miles. Couriers took Washington's dispatches to Congress and to Luzerne but arrived in Philadelphia when the city was already celebrating—the news had come overland from Virginia—and mobs surged through the streets, cheering the French and firing guns. One of these couriers met Robert Morris and the French officers near Chester, and when they heard the news of de Grasse, the Frenchmen hesitated no longer; Morris could have his twenty thousand dollars, on promise of repayment by October 1. Morris turned back for Philadelphia to see to the shipment of the coins, threading his way through the wagons and guns of the trailing division of the French troops.

Washington, again riding south, reached Christiana Bridge on the Delaware for breakfast on September 6 and was soon at Head of Elk, a tributary of the upper Chesapeake. He wrote a triumphant order to his army:

> It is with the highest pleasure and satisfaction that the Commander-in-chief announces to the Army the arrival of Count de Grass in the Chesapeak . . . he felicitates the army on the auspicious occasion, he anticipates the glorious events which may be expected . . . the general calls upon the gentlemen officers, the brave and faithful soldiers . . . to exert their utmost abilities in the cause of their country, to share with him . . . the difficulties, dangers, and glory of the enterprise.

The troops were more interested in Washington's broad hint that they were soon to be paid, in hard money; most of them had not seen gold or silver coins for months. The men in ranks, who had been surly and laggard, with many reported sick, responded to the incredible news. A New York officer reported, "It is extraordinary that notwithstanding the Fatigue of such a long & rapid march, there is scarcely a sick man to be found."

Washington wrote furiously from the camp on the Elk— dozens of circular letters to prominent men on the Maryland eastern shore, urging them to send boats to carry troops down the bay, and a reply to de Grasse, saying that he expected to see him "almost as soon as this will reach your hand." The general did not realize that Morris had wheedled the money from the French, and he wrote urgently once more, "Every day discovers to me the increasing necessity of some money for the troops." Lincoln's men must have a month's pay at once, or they would not move farther south. "I wish it to come on the wings of speed."

Morris had already sent the silver, and Philip Audibert, the Deputy Paymaster General, soon arrived on the Elk with his treasure, 144,000 livres. The troops were mustered, and the heads of the money kegs were knocked open, so that the men could see the silver half crowns roll upon the ground. To the soldiers, this was the climactic moment of the war. Major William Popham of a New York regiment wrote, "This day will be famous in the annals of History for being the first in which the Troops of the United States received one month's Pay in specie." Closen wrote that the sight of the money won over the mutinous troops and "raised spirits to the required level." The coins were swiftly distributed among the ranks, but even that was not enough, and Morris was called upon for more. He complained to Pennsylvania officials, "The late movements of the army have so entirely drained me of money that I have been obliged to pledge my personal credit very deeply . . . besides borrowing money from my friends and advancing . . . every shilling of my own. . . ."

The loan Morris had made from Rochambeau was accomplished by masterful sleight of hand; he would repay the French when the expected shipment of coins arrived from the north—he would use French money to repay what he had borrowed from the French. Meanwhile, Morris made elaborate plans to ship the newly-arrived treasure from Boston to Philadelphia: to save time, the thousands of coins were not counted but weighed, and an estimated fifteen hundred to two thousand crowns were packed in each strongbox, made of the toughest oak. The boxes were placed in huge one-ton chests made of thick oak planks, twenty boxes to each chest, the lids nailed down, and the chests fastened to the axles of ox carts with iron straps, which were welded by a blacksmith, so that the money could not be opened during the long journey. Four oxen and one horse drew each of the chests over the rough country roads. The treasure was to be almost two months on its journey.

Washington worked on the Elk for two days, sending off the few available boats with Lamb's artillery and siege tools, Lauzun's infantry, and the shock troops of the French regiments. The raffish fleet sailed out of sight down the Chesapeake before a wind that had freshly sprung up from the north, some of the little vessels so heavily loaded that water surged around the gunwales. The commander ordered most of the troops to follow him by land, left the rest of the embarkation to General Lincoln, and rode to the south with Rochambeau and Chastellux. They left camp early on September 8, and Washington rode so rapidly that the French soon fell behind; only Billy Lee kept pace. The general galloped much of the way, but even so, news of his approach outraced him. The city of Baltimore was waiting.

He approached the Maryland city in the late afternoon and was met by a company of militia cavalry under command of Captain Nicholas Moore, a veteran of the war's early campaigns. Artillerymen fired salutes, and Washington rode between crowds of people on the streets as he was escorted to the Fountain Inn, where he spent the night. Maryland officials appeared and read him a formal address of welcome, to which Washington responded with a rhetorical speech written by his secretary, Jonathan Trumbull. It was late when the crowd drifted away. The city was illuminated with candles and torches in Washington's honor. Rochambeau and Chastellux did not reach Baltimore until the next day, by which time the commander had gone—up before daylight, off on the punishing sixty-mile ride to Mount Vernon, alone except for his aide, David Humphreys, and Billy Lee.

Far behind him, the armies moved slowly southward. The French troops were halted at the lower crossing of the Susquehanna, where only one small scow ferried across the regiments; the officers rode upstream and waded a two-mile ford, which Closen found trying: "The view . . . was very picturesque; but the crossing, on the other hand, was diabolic." The water was less than two feet deep, but the stream was swift and full of large stones, over which the horses stumbled at each step. The wagons and artillery were also sent upstream to cross here, so that the troops camped for two or three days without tents or equipment, but there were few complaints. Count Deux-Ponts said, "We gaily make an exchange of our beds for simple bearskins." The troops finally reached Baltimore on September 12.

The vessels that had sailed from the Elk had been driven into port at Annapolis after a stormy sail of three days, and the men were glad to escape the "detestable boats" on which they had been crowded; two or three of the craft had overturned and seven men were drowned. On September 13, a messenger came back from Washington with orders that this fleet was not to leave Annapolis until further notice. The French fleet had sailed out of the lower Chesapeake a few days earlier to fight the English, and no one knew the outcome of the battle. Until the danger of the enemy sweeping up the bay was past, the flotilla must wait. The French column marching overland also delayed for two days in Annapolis, repairing shoes and uniforms, while officers fretted for fear they would be too late at Yorktown. Baron Viomenil improved morale by passing word through the ranks: "Count de Rochambeau has assured me that he will undertake nothing before we arrive." Deux-Ponts said fervently, "May he keep his word."

Washington, now far ahead of the troops, crossed the Potomac into Virginia late on Sunday, September 9, and long after nightfall he rode up the long lane to Mount Vernon with David Humphreys and Billy Lee. He had made an exhausting two-day ride to come home in the midst of the campaign; he had last been here almost six and a half years ago, on May 4, 1775, when he had ridden off to Philadelphia as a Virginia Congressman in the uniform of a retired militia colonel. There was a homecoming greeting from his wife and a new family—four of Martha's grandchildren had been born since Washington had gone to war, the children of her son, Jacky Custis.

Despite the late hour, Washington worked before he went to bed, dictating to Humphreys a letter to a county militia lieutenant asking him to turn out his troops to work on the roads—the army's guns and wagons could not pass through the mired ruts he had seen in the dusk. He carefully revised the draft made by Humphreys and had the dispatch sent out. Of his homecoming he noted in his journal only: "I reached my own Seat at Mount Vernon (distant 120 Miles from the Hd. of Elk). . . ."

That night in Philadelphia the celebration of his promising campaign had ended, and Washington's enemies were active; vandals broke into the State House and slashed the portrait of the general painted by Charles Willson Peale three years before. This was the work of "one or more volunteers in the pay of hell," an indignant newspaper said.

Early the next morning Washington's servants came to the mansion and looked "sorrowfully upon a face so changed by the storms of campaigns and the mighty cares which had burdened his mind during more than six years of absence." The general spent some time with his farm manager, and told his cooks to prepare for a feast the next day, when Rochambeau and Chastellux were to arrive; Mount Vernon's neighbors were invited.

Jonathan Trumbull, who had never been in the South, admired the plantation: "A numerous family now present. All accommodated. An elegant seat and situation, great appearance of opulence and real exhibitions of hospitality and princely entertainment." The manor house seemed less grand to the French; Chastellux thought it "simple."

Washington did not neglect the army. Dispatches went out to several Virginia militia officers, asking that roads in nearby counties be repaired, and that a carriage be sent to carry Rochambeau and Chastellux for part of the long journey to Williamsburg, where they would join Lafayette. He asked that the landings at the fords of rivers and creeks be improved. When he had reports that Lafayette's troops were dangerously short of food, he appealed to Governor Thomas Sim Lee of Maryland to send supplies down the bay. He wrote to Benjamin Lincoln, urging him to push the army, "Every day we now lose is comparatively an age . . . Hurry on then, my Dear Genl, with your Troops on the wing of Speed."

At 5:00 A.M. on September 12 servants from Mount Vernon left for nearby Fredericksburg, on the way south, to see that forage for the horses of Washington's party was ready at the roadside, and to warn a tavernkeeper that he would arrive with the French the next day. Washington, Rochambeau, and Chastellux followed soon after sunrise. Jacky Custis, the general's twenty-eight-year-old stepson, rode with them; he had pleaded with Washington to allow him a glimpse of the war of which he had yet seen nothing.

Between the villages of Colchester and Dumfries they met a courier carrying dispatches for Congress, a rider who gave them disturbing news: the French fleet had left the Chesapeake, had fought the British, and had sailed from sight. The outcome was unknown. Whatever had happened off the capes, it was too late for Washington to turn back. The officers rode swiftly toward Fredericksburg. The General's last letter to Lafayette, from Mount Vernon, was moving rapidly over the Virginia lowlands ahead of them, perhaps already in Williamsburg:

> We are thus far, my Dear Marquis, on our way to you. The Count de Rochambeau has just arrived . . . & we propose (after resting tomorrow) to be at Fredericksburg on the night of the 12th.—the 13th. we shall reach New Castle & the next day we expect the pleasure of seeing you at your encampment.
>
> Should there be any danger as we approach you, I shall be obliged if you will send a party of Horse towards New Kent Court House to meet us. . . .
>
> P.S. I hope you will keep Lord Cornwallis safe, without Provisions or Forage until we arrive. Adieu.

5

WAR IN THE BACKWOODS

The trail that led Cornwallis to Yorktown began on remote South Carolina beaches in the chill spring of 1780. Here, in an amphibious attack on the city of Charleston, South Carolina, Sir Henry Clinton launched his campaign to end the stalemated war of revolution by rolling up the colonies from the south. Cornwallis was his second in command.

Sir Henry sailed from New York in freezing weather the last of December with a fleet of ninety transports, carrying almost nine thousand troops. It was a grim voyage from the start. Men grumbled when camp followers were left behind, and they were allowed but one woman per company. The fleet barely escaped before the harbor was frozen solid; seven transports were crushed by the ice. One ship was dismasted by gales and driven across the Atlantic where it landed its cargo of miserable troops in Cornwall, to the consternation of English civilians. The expedition beat its way southward for forty days before coming to harbor. Mountainous seas had swept Clinton's baggage and horses overboard and as one soldier wrote, the troops landed "pretty much in a state of nature."

It was mid-March before Sir Henry and Cornwallis were ready for the attack on Charleston. Clinton took the city after a six-week siege and captured General Benjamin Lincoln's army of 5500 almost intact; the loss of the port and the exposure of the southern flank was one of the great American disasters of the war.

Clinton was at his best in this intricate operation, firm but cautious, planning faultlessly, enveloping the city by methodical steps. He won the admiration of his troops by his daily exposure in the front lines—but by the end of the campaign he was squabbling with his two chief lieutenants. Clinton's antagonism toward Admiral Arbuthnot was long concealed. "In appearance we were the best of friends," Clinton said, "but I am sure he is as false as hell." When he broke openly with Arbuthnot Sir Henry said, "I have determined never to serve with such an old woman."

The breach between Clinton and Cornwallis was more serious. Cornwallis might become commander in chief at any time; he held a dormant commission to succeed Clinton in case of his death or resignation, and relations between the two were delicate in this situation. On the day after Charleston fell, Cornwallis requested London to recall him, saying he would prefer to serve anywhere else in the world.

Clinton bitterly resented the Earl's attitude. "I can never be cordial with such a man," he said. He suspected Cornwallis and his secretary, Major Alexander Ross, of conspiring against him: "He will play me false, I fear; at least Ross will."

In the midst of this bickering Clinton returned to New York and left Cornwallis to complete the conquest of South Carolina, warning him against marching northward prematurely and endangering the British hold on the state. As he departed for New York Clinton said, "I leave Lord Cornwallis here with sufficient force to keep it against the world —without a superior fleet shows itself, in which case I shall despair of ever seeing peace restored to this miserable country."

Charles Cornwallis was not an inspiring figure. At forty-three he was tall and ungainly, with a heavy, plodding gait. He had a blemish in one eye, the result of a boyhood hockey injury. He had a reputation as a dull officer who fought by textbooks and seldom improvised to meet conditions in the field. But George III found him loyal, and the most able of the Whig generals who had once opposed harsh measures against the Americans.

Cornwallis came of an aristocratic family long prominent in English life; it had held the estate of Eye for three centuries. Charles had served in the army since the age of eighteen after schooling at Eton and Cambridge, had fought in major battles in Germany in his youth, and at twenty-two had taken command of a regiment. Despite his consistent Whig stand in Parliament, Cornwallis had come willingly to America in 1776 and fought bravely and well in the campaigns for Long Island and New York, often leading shock troops to victory.

It was only in the winter of seventy-six, when Washington captured his Hessians at Trenton and out-marched the Earl around Princeton, that army critics turned on Cornwallis. He had boasted that he would "bag the fox" in the New Jersey maneuvers, and when he failed, Clinton charged Cornwallis with "the most consummate ignorance I ever heard of [in] any officer above a corporal."

Before this southern campaign was old, Cornwallis would be ignoring Clinton and writing directly to London for guidance, stinging Clinton to write caustically, "As Your Lordship is now so near, it will be unneccessary for you to send your despatches to the Minister; you will therefore be so good as to send them to me in the future." In this unpromising atmosphere the two ranking British generals in America opened their fateful campaign.

British power in America was now divided more perilously than ever, with Clinton based in New York and the increasingly difficult Cornwallis seven hundred or eight hundred miles away in South Carolina. Soon after he was left in independent command, and without specific instructions, the Earl turned to the subjugation of the Carolina back country.

His campaign opened triumphantly. Cornwallis marched into the interior with a small but disciplined band of regulars to face an army of three thousand Americans led by the vainglorious Horatio Gates, the victor of Saratoga. Though Gates outnumbered the British by about fifty per cent, he was routed near the small town of Camden when green troops of his front line fled in panic, throwing away their muskets and carrying with them most of the two thousand North Carolina militia in the center. These men burst through the veteran First Maryland Brigade in the rear, throwing it into confusion; Gates' army then ran along the roads and paths toward the north.

A small band of Maryland and Delaware veterans under General Mordecai Gist and the Baron de Kalb fought the entire British army hand to hand in bayonet charges, unaware that the battle was lost and that Gates was already in flight miles to the rear. Overwhelmed at last, de Kalb and many of his men fell, their ranks were broken by Tarleton's cavalry, and resistance ended. Only about sixty Americans were left to retreat from the field in an organized body. Gates, mounted on a noted race horse, did not stop until he reached Charlotte, North Carolina, sixty miles to the north.

The American army's disastrous defeat at Camden made

Cornwallis master of South Carolina. It was only when he opened an invasion of North Carolina a few weeks later that trouble began to dog his footsteps. He advanced to Charlotte, planning to clear the rebels from that province and move into Virginia, knocking the South out of the war. He had hardly arrived in the village on the border when disaster struck. Major Patrick Ferguson, who had been plundering western South Carolina with a band of Tories and Loyal American militia, had been trapped on a remote hilltop at King's Mountain by a party of frontier riflemen.

Ferguson and his men had infuriated backwoods Carolinians by their systematic burning, looting, and murder, and the mountain men, about nine hundred strong, had tracked Ferguson's band of about a thousand to the natural fortress at King's Mountain on October 7. The Tories were brave and well trained, and skilled in the use of the bayonet, but they were quickly overcome by the backwoods hunters who swarmed up the mountain sides fighting in Indian style, hiding behind trees to fire with deadly effect, falling back before bayonet charges, only to reform and press nearer the camp.

Even when his lines were overrun Ferguson would not surrender, and when two of his men raised white flags he cut them down with his sword. The young major was shot from his horse as he tried to force his way through the Americans. A backwoods boy who inspected the body said, "Fifty rifles must have been leveled at him at the same time; seven rifle balls had passed through his body, both of his arms were broken, and his hat and clothing were literally shot to pieces." Ferguson was buried in a bloody beef hide, and many of his men were thrown into a common grave.

Hundreds of wives and children of the Tories came to the mountain the next morning to search among the dead and wounded. One young mountain boy wrote:

We proceeded to bury the dead, but it was badly done. They were thrown into convenient piles and covered with old logs, the bark of old trees, and rocks . . . the wolves became so plenty that it was dangerous for any one to be out at night, for several miles around; also the hogs in the neighborhood gathered in to the place to devour the flesh of the men. . . .

The Americans lost twenty-eight dead and sixty-two wounded in the one-hour battle. Of Ferguson's thousand, 157 were killed, 163 wounded were left on the field, and the victors marched off into the North Carolina mountains with seven hundred prisoners, several of whom were hanged. Ferguson was the only British soldier in this singular battle; the others on both sides were Americans.

This action turned the tide of the war in the South. Banastre Tarleton hurried to Cornwallis with the news, and the Earl fell back hastily to make winter quarters at Winnsboro, South Carolina. Cornwallis began to lose some of his assurance. American guerrillas, chief among them Francis Marion and Thomas Sumter, waged a kind of war he had not been taught in Europe or in the American North; they slipped through the back country at will, attacking outposts, snatching stragglers, stinging Cornwallis in hit-and-run raids.

Cornwallis was particularly resentful of American tactics, as he wrote Clinton:

They always keep at a considerable distance, and retire on our approach . . . the constant incursions of refugees, North Carolinians, back mountain men, and the perpetual rising in different parts of this province . . . keep the whole country in continual alarm, and render the assistance of regular troops everywhere necessary.

As the dreary winter of 1780 drew to a close, Cornwallis

faced a new adversary, the most able of Washington's lieutenants, the Rhode Island Quaker, General Nathanael Greene. It seemed almost too late for him to save the South, as Washington grimly told Congress, "I think I am giving you a General; but what can a General do, without men, without arms, without clothing, without stores, without provisions?" Congress made no response, and Greene rode southward through the snows, begging governors and other officials for aid. "They all promised fair," he said, "but I fear will do little." Greene was on his own.

It was December when he arrived in Charlotte, to find no more than eight hundred survivors of Gates' force fit for duty. He wrote Lafayette, who was with Washington in the North, ". . . a few ragged, half-starving troops in the wilderness, destitute of everything . . . the country is almost laid waste and the inhabitants plunder one another with little less than savage fury. We live from hand to mouth."

The troops had only three days' rations, and the nearby country was picked clean, but Greene was not one to despair. A staff officer noted that the Quaker learned more about the army's supplies and arms overnight than Gates had known during his command. Greene was a handsome, florid, stout, cheerful veteran of thirty-eight, a self-taught soldier, the son of a Quaker minister; he had been expelled from his Meeting when he joined the early revolutionary movement in New England and had fought in the major campaigns in the North. He walked with a limp from a boyhood injury and had a blemish in one eye. His troops found him remarkable, an officer who drank tea even in the wilderness and amused himself with a worn copy of Swift that was always in his saddlebags.

Greene had help from an able staff in rebuilding the tiny army: Brigadier General Daniel Morgan, an old Indian fighter who had survived Braddock's massacre and commanded riflemen in the northern campaigns; Light-horse Harry Lee, a handsome Virginia cavalryman whose Legion, mounted on fine plantation horses, was the army's crack band of raiders and scouts; Colonel William Washington, another cavalryman and cousin of the commander in chief; Colonel John Eager Howard, a wealthy young Marylander who led the remnants of two hard-bitten infantry regiments; Colonel Thaddeus Kosciusko, a Polish expert in field defenses; and Colonel Edward Carrington, a gifted forager who became quartermaster.

Greene knew that his naked and half-starved army, facing an enemy three times its strength, "will make but a poor fight . . . It is difficult to give spirits to troops that have nothing to animate them." But the Quaker was not long in discovering that these men were unlike those in Washington's ranks to the north. The people of coastal America, he said, "are sickly and but indifferent militia . . ." but "the back-country people are bold and daring in their makeup."

Greene's first move revealed a commander with a daring of his own—in the face of a greatly superior British force, he divided his small band, sending Morgan westward into South Carolina and taking the rest of the army 140 miles to the eastward, along the heights of the Pee Dee River. Cornwallis divided his own army and sent a force after Morgan.

Cornwallis ordered Colonel Banastre Tarleton to attack Greene's exposed western wing: "If Morgan is anywhere within your reach, push him to the utmost . . . No time is to be lost." Tarleton rode out with eleven hundred men and two small cannon. He told Cornwallis confidently, "I must either destroy Morgan's corps or push it before me over Broad river. . . ."

Morgan had gathered small parties of local militia, some

of them frontiersmen who had fought at King's Mountain, until his strength was about a thousand. He had few regulars in his ranks, but Morgan was an unorthodox leader who understood his men.

Morgan chose his ground at Cowpens, with a bend of Broad River five miles to his rear; it was an open hillside, free of undergrowth, exposed in front and on the flanks—an ideal battleground for British regulars. Some officers urged Morgan to move to a less exposed position, but he was adamant: "I would not have had a swamp in view of my militia on any consideration; they would have made for it, and nothing could have detained them . . . As to retreat, it was the very thing I wished to cut off all hope of . . . When men are forced to fight they sell their lives dearly. . . ."

Thomas Young, a boy volunteer in Morgan's ranks, watched the general the night before battle, shrewdly preparing his men to meet the enemy:

> He went among the volunteers, helped them with their swords, joked with them about their sweethearts, told them to keep in good spirits, and the day would be ours. And long after I laid down, he was going among the soldiers, encouraging them, and telling them, that the old wagoner would crack his whip over Ban. in the morning, as sure as they lived.
>
> "Just hold up your heads, boys, three fires," he would say, "and you are free, and then when you return to your homes, how the old folks will bless you, and the girls kiss you for your gallant conduct!" I don't believe he slept a wink that night.

Tarleton reached the field in the cold, clear dawn of January 17, 1781, put his cavalry into line and ordered a charge; he lost fifteen of the fifty men in the opening attack. When the British infantry appeared, Morgan's riflemen from

Georgia and North Carolina fired two rounds, causing casualties among British officers. The riflemen fell back by plan, to the second line, some 150 yards up the hillside where Carolina militiamen lay. When these men had fired, all fell back to the main line, held by Delaware and Maryland regulars. As these men hurried rearward, the British dragoons charged. Riflemen and cavalrymen drove them back.

Thomas Young remembered these moments all his life:

> About sunrise the British line advanced at a sort of trot, with a loud halloo. It was the most beautiful line I ever saw. When they shouted, I heard Morgan say, "They give us the British halloo, boys, give them the Indian halloo, by God!" and he galloped along the lines cheering the men and telling them not to fire until we could see the whites of their eyes. Every officer was crying, "Don't fire!" for it was a hard matter for us to keep from it. . . .
>
> The militia fired first. It was for a time, pop-pop-pop—and then a whole volley; but when the regulars fired, it seemed like one sheet of flame from right to left. Oh! it was beautiful!

A young militiaman who had fought at King's Mountain was caught up in the struggle with Tarleton's dragoons:

> Just as we got to our horses, they overtook us and began to make a few hacks at some, however without doing much injury. They, in their haste, had pretty much scattered, perhaps thinking they would have another . . . frolic, but in a few moments Colonel Washington's cavalry was among them like a whirlwind, and the poor fellows began to keel from their horses without being able to remount. The shock was so sudden and violent they could not stand it, and immediately betook them-

selves to flight. There was no time to rally, and they appeared to be as hard to stop as a drove of wild Choctaw steers, going to a Pennsylvania market.

As the American infantry was changing its position, confusion developed, and Morgan led the men rearward to form a new line. The British, who thought their enemy was fleeing, broke their ranks to charge, and the Americans turned and cut them to pieces with a volley, then charged downhill and scattered them. The Virginia cavalry joined the melee, and within a few minutes Tarleton's army had been destroyed. Morgan had lost a dozen killed and sixty wounded; British dead were 100, the wounded 229, and the uninjured prisoners 600. Tarleton escaped with a few of his horsemen.

This astounding American victory deprived Cornwallis of the light corps of his army, but he did not react cautiously, as he had after King's Mountain; instead, he plunged after Morgan on a chase that was to lead him hundreds of miles from his base, deplete his ranks, and lead him at last to Yorktown.

Morgan was on the run within two hours after the battle. He sent his prisoners ahead of him and began marching northward. Greene rode across country as soon as he learned of the victory, and their armies joined in retreat. Cornwallis was two days late in starting his pursuit, on January 19. He notified Clinton that he might advance into North Carolina—but did not write him again for three months. In his pursuit of Morgan, the Earl recklessly burned most of his wagons, all of his tents, and those provisions that could not be carried by the troops, even rum. He paid a price in the morale of his men; at least 250 men deserted at Ramsour's Mills, and others slipped away daily. It was now a race from river to river, as Cornwallis attempted to trap Greene's army; the Americans were always too quick, snatching the last of their wagons across the flood-swollen streams just as the British approached.

Though the ranks of his troops dwindled, Cornwallis led a column of thousands of slaves he had encouraged to leave their masters; they now trudged behind his wagons, consuming the Army's meager supplies. There were also hundreds of women camp followers. The Earl issued daily orders in a vain effort to control the mob:

> Great complaints having been made of negroes straggling from the line of march, plundering and using violence to the inhabitants, it is Lord Cornwallis' positive orders that no negro shall be suffered to carry arms on any pretense. . . .
>
> Lord Cornwallis has lately received the most shocking complaints of the excesses committed by the troops. He calls on the officers to put a stop to this licentiousness.

Reprimands had little effect. The Earl sometimes ordered searches of the baggage of the women, who were said to be the most inveterate looters; he forced women to witness floggings and hangings. Looting continued, and men and women wandered from the line of march daily; the Carolinians took a steady toll.

Greene fell back before the British with great skill, but his men suffered in the cold weather, struggling to keep wagons and guns moving over the crude roads, hurrying to stay ahead of the enemy until Greene was strong enough to fight.

Greene reported to Washington: "The miserable situation of the troops for want of clothing has rendered the march the most painful imaginable, with hundreds tracking the ground with bloody feet . . . Myself and my aides are almost worn out with fatigue. . . ."

Greene paused for a few days at Guilford Courthouse, in north central North Carolina, where Daniel Morgan, suffering from rheumatism and hemorrhoids, left the army for his home in Virginia, urging Greene to fight in Guilford and to use the tactics of the victory at Cowpens.

Greene crossed the Dan River with Cornwallis close behind, but the British did not follow into Virginia. After a few days, reinforced by militia, Greene turned back to Guilford Court- house and waited for battle. The armies met for two hours on March 15, in some of the most ferocious fighting of the Revo- lution. Greene now had 4400 men, most of them untrained, and Cornwallis advanced against him with about 1900 reliable veteran troops.

The Quaker had taken Morgan's advice—even to riflemen posted in the rear to kill men who fled. He placed Carolina militiamen in the front line along a rail fence, with cavalry and riflemen on the flanks. In a second line, three hundred yards behind, were Virginia militiamen, and in a third line, more than five hundred yards to the rear, were the regulars from Virginia, Maryland, and Delaware. The Carolinians broke after firing a couple of volleys, but the men on the flanks fought tenaciously. The British then charged into a deep forest to meet the Virginians, who held their position for half an hour until one wing was forced back. The Virgin- ians then retreated, some of them in disorder.

St. George Tucker, a Virginia militia officer, was stabbed in the leg with a bayonet as he tried to stop his runaway troops. He wrote his wife a version of the battle that did not get into official reports:

> The British had advanced and . . . we discovered them in our rear. This threw the militia into such confusion that . . . Holcombe's regiment and ours broke off without firing a single gun, and dispersed like a flock of sheep frightened by dogs.

The climax of the battle came in a meadow, where British

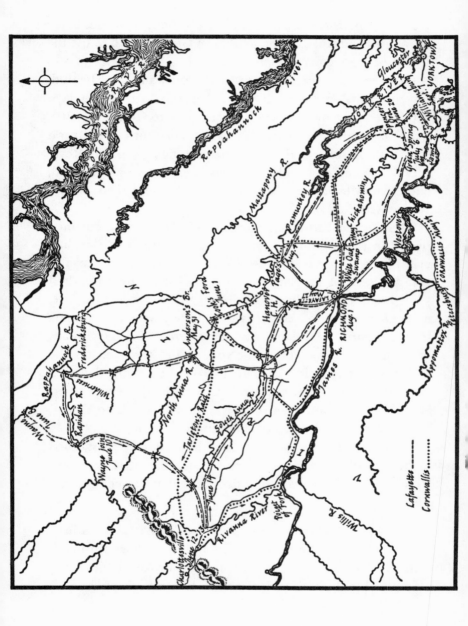

and Americans struggled over cannon hand to hand in charge and counter-charge. In the late afternoon, when he saw that he was losing the field, Cornwallis ordered his gunners to clear the meadow by firing grapeshot through the ranks of his Brigade of Guards to halt the American push. It was here that the Earl suffered most of his casualties; he lost 600 men, more than a fourth of his army, and the crack Brigade of Guards suffered most—eleven of its nineteen officers were dead or wounded, and 206 of its 462 rank and file. Exclusive of the runaway militia, Greene had lost 78 dead and 183 wounded.

Cornwallis camped on the battlefield and issued a victory proclamation calling on "all royal subjects to stand forth and take an active part in restoring good order and government"; there was no response to his plea.

The next day, the British retreated toward the seacoast. When the news of the battle reached London the Whig leader Horace Walpole said, "Lord Cornwallis has conquered his troops out of shoes and provision, and himself out of troops." And the opposition leader, Charles James Fox, said wryly, "Another such victory would ruin the British Army."

Cornwallis halted only when he reached the port of Wilmington, North Carolina, his army now reduced to one thousand effectives. Greene led his troops back into South Carolina, where he began the reduction of British posts and reclaimed the state.

The Earl revealed his state of mind to his friend General William Phillips, who was now in Virginia, first claiming a great victory and then complaining of his exhausting chase through the Carolinas, as if he had not undertaken it on his own initiative:

I have had a most difficult and dangerous campaign and was obliged to fight a battle 200 miles from any communication against an enemy seven times my number ... Here

I am, getting rid of my wounded and refitting my troops at Wilmington . . . Now, my dear friend, what is our plan? Without one we cannot succeed, and I assure you that I am quite tired of marching about the country in quest of adventure. If we mean an offensive war in America, we must abandon New York and bring our whole force into Virginia. . . .

Cornwallis had written to Germain immediately after Guilford Courthouse, but he did not write to Clinton until a month later, from Wilmington, reporting that his campaign had been a triumph. Clinton was not deceived: "His Lordship has lost an army, lost the object for which he moved it, and buried himself on the seacoast of North Carolina."

Cornwallis was soon hinting that he planned to abandon South Carolina, which had been won at such cost, and march to Virginia. He broke his long silence for the first time since plunging into North Carolina, warning Clinton indirectly of his intentions:

. . . I am very anxious to receive your Excellency's commands, being as yet totally in the darkness as to the intended operations of the summer. I cannot help expressing my wishes that the Chesapeake may become the seat of war . . . Until Virginia is in a manner subdued, our hold of the Carolinas must be difficult, if not precarious. The rivers in Virginia are advantageous to an invading army; but North Carolina is of all provinces in America the most difficult to attack.

Cornwallis marched to Virginia without orders, and when Clinton learned of it he wrote the Earl in distress:

I shall dread what may be the consequences of Your Lordship's move . . . Had it been possible for Your Lordship to have intimated the probability of your intention . . . I

should certainly have endeavored to have stopped you—
as I did then, as well as now, consider such a move as
likely to be dangerous to our interest in the southern
colonies.

It was too late for regrets. Cornwallis had already joined
the British force in tidewater Virginia, where Phillips and
Benedict Arnold had been raiding and burning, opposed only
by a weak American force under the Marquis de Lafayette.
Clinton warned his staff officers that trouble was brewing in
the Chesapeake where loss of control of the sea, even for forty-
eight hours, "may catch us in very critical movements."

Cornwallis had another critic, near at hand, who was equally
puzzled. Lafayette, whose wisdom belied his youth, studied
the Earl's tracks and his position in Virginia and said, "These
English are mad. They march through a country and think
they have conquered it."

6

THE
BOY GENERAL

In the gusty weather of mid-April a quarrelsome band of New England infantry hung about a ferry of the Susquehanna River, resisting their commander's orders to cross. They were still road-weary from a fruitless chase of British invaders in the Virginia lowlands, a countryside whose people were almost as hostile as the enemy. The New Englanders did not intend to return. Twenty-nine of them deserted in two days. They were not ordinary deserters, but the "best, finest and most experienced soldiers." Those who remained were restless. Their commander faced them sternly, and with a wisdom beyond his years.

The officer was an overgrown boy stuffed into a handsome uniform. He was red-haired, excitable, voluble, pudgy, and ungainly, with a long, pointed nose; he was already becoming bald. His face was subtly misshapen; as a Virginia officer said, "It does not appear to correspond perfectly with his person."

He was a twenty-three-year-old Major General, the Marquis de Lafayette, already legendary in the Continental Army as a kind of military foster son to Washington. It had not been long since the Queen of France had collapsed in helpless laughter at the sight of this awkward boy dancing at Versailles, but he had matured amazingly in his four years in America. For all his youth he had won Washington's trust by his tact and persistence, his strategic sense, and his gift for inspiring troops. As he played out an improbable scene with his men on the banks of the broad Susquehanna—"my Rubicon," he called it—Lafayette was opening a bizarre campaign, which was to assure his place in history.

Lafayette won over his men with an adroit use of the stick and the carrot. He hanged a captured spy at the river's edge and announced that they would march the next day—any man who chose to leave was free to return to his home, without fear of being charged with desertion. A few of them flocked to headquarters for passes—but only a few.

The young officer faced them melodramatically. He tried, as he said, "to throw a kind of infamy upon desertion"; their General was going south, if he had to go alone. The enemy would be greatly superior in numbers, but no matter. He would take with him only those who were resolved to defend their country, and die for it if necessary. Abruptly, by some miracle of his persuasion, the mood of the troops changed; the men thought of the French boy's incessant pleading with civilians, which had brought them food, clothing, and arms, and of his unassuming air as he marched and slept with them on the long roads. They saw in a new light the young foreigner who implored them to fight for their own liberty. One or two men stepped out and begged to be taken along. A sick sergeant, in tears, asked that he be carried to Virginia in a cart. Lafayette relented.

Eight deserters came back into camp and asked to be forgiven. Lafayette hanged one of them in sight of the troops, gave another a dishonorable discharge, and dismissed the rest, refusing to accept those who had asked for passes to go home. The reluctant soldiers now thought themselves disgraced unless they joined the march. The river crossing began.

Heavy winds raised whitecaps on the Susquehanna, and the wagons could not be put across on the fragile scows; only the men and their light baggage went to the Maryland shore, and wagons were seized from civilians along the route. About a thousand troops straggled at last into Baltimore, where Lafayette had preceded them, begging for aid from the Americans he had come to save.

His ragamuffin soldiers had only the wildest notions of their young commander and the world from which he had come: Marie Joseph Paul Yves Roch Gilbert du Motier, Marquis de Lafayette, heir to estates and manor houses of Auvergne—Vissac, St. Romain, Fix, Chavaniac, and many another. His marriage to fourteen-year-old Adrienne d'Ayen of the Noailles family had made him one of the wealthiest young men in France. A naive romantic, ill at ease in fashionable Versailles, Lafayette was enraptured by tales of the struggle for liberty: "The moment I heard of America, I loved her; the moment I knew she was fighting for freedom, I burned with a desire of bleeding for her"—though he told Louis XVI another story, that he was moved by "love for my country . . . the pleasure of spilling my blood for her."

He had come in 1777 in a ship he bought for the voyage—a nineteen-year-old runaway from his family, his pregnant wife, and a disapproving King, his only military experience as a captain in the barracks of a provincial regiment. The French boy had charmed a hostile Congress, offering to serve without pay and without a command of troops, and had been made a major general—an honorary one, congressmen thought. But he had charmed Washington as well, and when Lafayette was wounded at Brandywine the commander had told his surgeon, "Treat him as if he were my son, for I love him as if he were."

Now, when the cause seemed hopeless, Lafayette had been sent to halt British forays in Virginia, a theater that bore little promise of bringing the Frenchman "my one ambition, glory." In Baltimore he raised money by borrowing on his own bond, promising to repay with interest when he came into his inheritance. He bought hats and shoes and linen to be made into clothing for his men. The ladies of the city gave a ball for the marquis and his officers, and he beguiled the women into making shirts from his cloth. He kept up a barrage of correspondence with officers and civilian leaders, including Governor Jefferson of Virginia—who warned him that Virginia was near anarchy, and that he could expect scant support for his army in a state with "mild laws and a people not used to prompt obedience." Lafayette replied with an apology for "the necessity of disturbing" Virginians, but he insisted that he must take what he needed for his army: "uncommon dangers require uncommon remedies."

He now began to race for Virginia. When he could find no horses for his wagons, he pulled them with oxen. He left behind his sick, his tents, and artillery and he hurried south as if leading a carnival troupe, putting half his men in wagons while the other half walked, the laughing men exchanging places at regular intervals. He reached Richmond on April 29, just in time to prevent the British from burning the small capital; the enemy took revenge by destroying warehouses and twelve hundred hogsheads of tobacco on the south bank of the James and then retreated downstream. Lafayette then learned that Cornwallis was also coming to Virginia. The Frenchman did not yet glimpse the opportunity that lay ahead, but he was immediately alert to the danger. He wrote Washington:

> There is no fighting here, unless you have naval superiority; or, an army mounted on race-horses. Phillips' plan against Richmond has been defeated . . . It now appears

that I have business with two armies, and this is rather too much. Each is more than double, superior to me.

Washington assured Lafayette that General Anthony Wayne and his Pennsylvania troops were on their way to reinforce him; meanwhile he should avoid battle and save his army. The Frenchman moved the army's stores from Richmond and sent them westward up the James, to Point of Fork, and then reported that Richmond was not worth fighting for—a few empty houses. He also sought to control his youthful enthusiasm:

> I have been guarding against my own warmth . . . extremely cautious in my movements . . . But I am wavering between two inconveniences. Was I to fight a battle, I'll be cut to pieces, the militia dispersed, and the arms lost. Was I to decline fighting, the country would think herself given up. I am therefore determined to skarmish, but not to engage too far, and particularly to take care against their immense and excellent body of horse whom the militia fears like they would so many wild beasts. . . .

Lafayette could not conceal his growing despair:

> I am not strong enough even to get beaten. Government in this state has no energy and laws have no force . . . Our expenses were enormous, yet we can get nothing . . . the enemy can over run the country, and untill the Pennsylvanians arrive we are next to nothing.

Lafayette yearned for Washington's help in dealing with the Virginians: "There is great slowness and great carelessness in this part of the world. But the intentions are good, and the people want to be awakened. Your presence, my dear General, would do a great deal."

Instead, the marquis was joined by another striking European volunteer, Baron Frederick von Steuben, a former captain in the army of Frederick the Great, who had come to America posing as a lieutenant general and aide to the Emperor. This Prussian soldier of fortune was a spendthrift adventurer—a muscular, hard-faced, laughing, and profane man of fifty who had arrived in America in a scarlet coat gleaming with decorations, surrounded by three French aides and a pampered Italian greyhound.

He spoke no English, but as the army's first Inspector General he had transformed Washington's ranks in the terrible winter at Valley Forge, bellowing orders and swearing picturesquely in three languages until the untrained troops gained confidence and acquired the look of a professional army, disciplined and orderly.

Steuben was a thorough soldier, irascible and quick-tempered, scornful of the faint-hearted. He had quarreled bitterly with the Virginians whose militia he had come to lead; he was appalled by the state's failure to raise men to beat off a handful of invaders—and by Governor Jefferson, who complained that he was not to blame if his public disregarded his laws out of "obstinacy of spirit." Once, when Steuben rode to a country courthouse to command an expected five hundred Virginia troops, he found only five men—three of whom deserted immediately.

But when he complained that Virginians would send him no troops, the politician Benjamin Harrison retorted, "We have 600 fine men under Baron Steuben which he will not carry into action . . . his Conduct gives universal disgust . . . I believe him a good officer on the parade but the worst in every other respect in the American Army."

The Baron dismissed such critics: "I am not less tired of this State than they are of me." He added testily, "I shall always regret that circumstances induced me to undertake the defense of a country where Caesar and Hannibal would have lost their reputation, and where every farmer is a general, but where nobody wishes to be a soldier."

Steuben and Lafayette were holding a review of their combined forces in a field near Richmond when they heard that Cornwallis was coming, moving swiftly along the James. The Earl had told Sir Henry Clinton confidently, "I shall now proceed to dislodge Lafayette from Richmond, and . . . destroy any magazines or stores in the neighborhood." He did so with ease. Governor Jefferson and the Assembly fled to the west, Steuben scuttled up the James to guard the army's stores, and Lafayette marched northward, toward Fredericksburg, hoping to meet Wayne.

Clinton, in New York, thought the campaign pointless. Sir Henry hoped that the Earl would fall back to the shores of the Chesapeake, fortify a port, and save his troops for a new campaign in the fall. But Cornwallis insisted that he must destroy Virginia's few manufacturing centers and break up her government, and he advanced, burning warehouses, taking prisoners, and seizing plantation horses. Tarleton's dragoons dashed seventy miles across country in twenty-four hours, captured seven legislators in the streets of Charlottesville, and narrowly missed taking Governor Jefferson at Monticello. The Governor and a few assemblymen met in the town of Staunton, where Jefferson resigned his office and was succeeded by Thomas Nelson, Jr., the commander of Virginia's militia. Nelson was called "Junior" to distinguish him from his aged uncle, "Secretary" Thomas Nelson of Yorktown, who had served as a colonial official for many years before the war. The new Governor, a stout, energetic man who cared little for popularity, was given emergency powers by the legislature and used them courageously to promote the war. He soon pressed men into service and his commissary officers rounded up saddles, uniforms, arms, food, and shoes for Virginia troops.

Steuben retreated from the enemy raiders after hiding valuable army stores at Point of Fork on the upper James—but he left some to be captured. Lafayette continued his retreat northward, burning bridges behind him to delay pursuit. Fredericksburg was near panic as the British followed Lafayette into the neighborhood—but at the last moment the British turned back and the Frenchman prepared to follow them. Lafayette and the grateful Virginians saw it as a retreat; the Earl had merely concluded that he was too late to prevent Wayne from reinforcing Lafayette, and was turning eastward unaware of American pursuit. During this movement, on June 10, Wayne's eight hundred Pennsylvanians joined Lafayette on the South Anna River, a few miles north of Richmond.

It had been a grim march for the survivors of the once-powerful Pennsylvania Line, the sullen men herded along like prisoners, "mute as fish," their muskets empty, and their ammunition carried in heavily-guarded wagons. They had come by a circuitous route from York, Pennsylvania, driven mercilessly from dawn until darkness each day as General Wayne walked the mutinous spirit out of his little band.

Five months earlier, in the darkest hours of the Revolution, the Pennsylvania Line had mutinied, turned its guns on Wayne and his officers, and marched out of the American lines to Princeton, New Jersey, where it negotiated with Congress for back pay, food, clothing, and arms. The American cause seemed on the verge of collapse, but the men had remained loyal despite all; they hanged a few agents sent out by Sir Henry Clinton to persuade them to desert, and in the end the mutiny was put down. Wayne had dealt leniently with its leaders, the Line was disbanded, and a new force was mustered to take its place.

In May, when the new Line was in camp at York, Pennsylvania, ready to join Lafayette, Anthony Wayne found three soldiers in the guard house charged with minor offenses—and thought he detected a second mutiny. He chose a court-martial of his sternest officers and put the three soldiers and a pair of deserters on trial; all died before a firing squad, blindfolded, shot in the head at such close range that their blindfolds caught fire. Men of the firing squad wept. Guards held back the screaming women of the condemned men, and an officer felled the wife of a sergeant who ran to his body. One soldier wrote of the scene, "Even devils shrank back and stood appalled," but Wayne was not content until he had marched every man past the bodies, so that all could see the spattered blood and brains in the rye field where the five had died.

With the execution fresh in their minds the Pennsylvanians had been driven southward, in a road softened by four days of rain. The men muttered but they marched, and eventually forgot. Lafayette sent messengers into camp daily, urging speed, but the army covered only fifty miles the first five days. Wayne advanced reveille each morning, but the troops could not be hurried. Rain fell in torrents, and once held up the march a day and a half. Four men were drowned as they crossed the Potomac in leaky scows, and four cannon sank; another day was lost in taking apart and oiling the guns.

When Wayne finally joined Lafayette, the army had two thousand regulars, and three thousand Virginia militia were nearby, exclusive of Steuben's men. The Frenchman's army now outnumbered the British, and as if aware of this, Cornwallis moved rapidly eastward, bound for Williamsburg. Lafayette followed. The British campaign to conquer all of Virginia was over.

In the more populous country near Richmond the Pennsylvania troops had their first glimpse of Virginia's slave system. White women flocked from plantation houses to the roadside to watch the passing army, their faces bundled in linen against the hot sun with only their eyes visible.

Lieutenant William Feltman was fascinated by the nude Negroes who clustered about the women:

> They will have a number of blacks about them, all naked, nothing to hide their nakedness. I am surprised this does not hurt the feelings of this fair Sex to see these young boys of about Fourteen and Fifteen years Old to Attend them ... and I can Assure you It would Surprize a person to see these d——d black boys how well they are hung.

Feltman also saw naked Negroes waiting on tables in the plantation houses. The enemy left scores of Negro smallpox victims at the roadsides to infect the pursuing Americans. Lieutenant Feltman saw many of them "starving and helpless, begging of us as we passed them for God's sake to kill them, as they were in great pain and misery."

On June 22 Lafayette's army entered the village of Richmond, where smoke still curled from houses burned by the British less than twenty-four hours earlier; there was a heavy fragrance of tobacco, two thousand hogsheads of which the enemy had piled in the streets and set afire. The British had destroyed army stores—salt, harness, uniforms, food, six hundred bushels of flour, and five thousand irreplaceable muskets.

Lafayette was also troubled by reports of Steuben's loss of the army's stores at Point of Fork; he camped outside Richmond, watching Cornwallis and waiting impatiently for the Baron to join him. He hinted that Steuben had lost the stores by his cowardice; that if he had held for twenty-four hours, the Prussian might have saved them all: ". . . the militia left him. His new levies deserted. All Virginia was in an uproar against him. The enemy laughed at him, and I cannot describe to you what my surprise has been." The marquis was not sorry to see Steuben leave the army a few weeks later for Charlottesville, to recuperate from an illness.

The marquis had critics of his own. Embittered Virginians

carped against Lafayette during these days as if he were one of the enemy. A militia officer in his camp wrote, "I fear the Marquis may lose his credit. Deserters, British, cringing Dutchmen and busy little Frenchmen swarm about HdQuarters. The people do not love Frenchmen; every person they can't understand they take for a Frenchman."

Lafayette and Wayne marched swiftly out of Richmond, as if in response to criticism, almost overtaking Cornwallis. The British moved at a leisurely pace and were only a few miles ahead, to the east. Lafayette saw that Cornwallis was making political propaganda of his marches, to create the impression that the South was British territory. "When he changes his position," Lafayette wrote a friend, "I try to give his movements the appearance of a retreat. God grant that there may be an opportunity to give them the appearance of a defeat."

His officers disagreed over the effectiveness of the boy commander's strategy. Lieutenant Colonel Francis Barber wrote his wife, making light of the redcoats, ". . . we now begin to imagine ourselves a match for the enemy, and unless they receive re-enforcements they must undoubtedly retire to Portsmouth." Colonel J. F. Mercer thought Lafayette's moves "silly and misjudged," and said that his army would have been defeated and scattered if the British had been energetic, and Cornwallis could never have been trapped. In any event, the British were not being driven by Lafayette; Cornwallis was moving at his own pace and choosing his own course.

The British and American vanguards skirmished at Spencer's Ordinary, six miles west of Williamsburg, on June 26, but the main armies fell back without a general action. Only now did Cornwallis learn from prisoners that Lafayette had followed him on his one-hundred-mile retreat from the west. The Earl wrote Clinton that he planned to turn on the young Frenchman, "if I can get a favorable opportunity of striking a blow at him without loss of time."

When Lafayette's spies brought him word that Cornwallis was going to cross the James River and move to Portsmouth, the Frenchman forgot his caution and sent Wayne in pursuit. The Pennsylvanian made a twenty-four-hour forced march with five hundred men, and on July 6 arrived at Greenspring plantation near Jamestown Island, were a cavalry patrol had found the enemy rearguard. Wayne opened fire on a few British pickets in a swampy meadow, and his cavalry and riflemen skirmished with these outposts for two hours in the early afternoon.

Lafayette, who had arrived by now, studied the position carefully; he galloped to a nearby point from which he could see the situation—Cornwallis had sent his baggage southward across the river, but his troops were left behind, lying in ambush along Powhatan Creek. Cornwallis waited patiently in his hiding place until his pickets had drawn in the Americans, and the Pennsylvanians were caught in the trap before the Marquis could return. A masked British gun opened on the Americans, and Major William de Galvan charged it with a small party.

Wayne plunged recklessly to the rescue across a narrow causeway which was the only approach to the British position. With eight hundred men and three small cannon he charged the oncoming redcoats as they emerged from cover, though they outnumbered him three or four to one. A withering fire soon broke the Pennsylvanians. Lafayette galloped onto the field amid the retreating men, moving from company to company, risking his life heedlessly. Two of the Frenchman's horses were shot beneath him.

Many boys who were under fire for the first time found themselves abruptly soldiers. One of these was Ebenezer Denny, a twenty-year-old red-haired ensign from Carlisle, Pennsylvania, who found himself in command of his company when the captain was wounded. Denny was not a novice; he had been a courier at Fort Pitt on the frontier at the age of eleven. As the British moved to flank the Pennsylvanians, Denny took over his company; he felt hopelessly unequal to the task: "young and inexperienced, exhausted with hunger and fatigue, [I] had like to have disgraced myself—had eat nothing all day but a few blackberries—was faint and with difficulty kept my place; once or twice was about to throw away my arms. . . ."

Denny's company fought the British for no longer than three or four minutes, but took heavy casualties; Denny was the only unwounded officer in the unit. The artillery horses were all dead and the redcoats captured two cannon and drove the Pennsylvanians to the rear. But the company withdrew across the causeway and ran until they were out of range.

Lieutenant Feltman's company, on another part of the field, charged to within eighty yards of the British line under a heavy fire of grapeshot. Feltman was struck in the left breast by a piece of canister, but he stayed in line until the battalion fell back: "Upon our retreat I felt very faintish, but the thought of falling into the enemy's hands made me push on as hard as I possibly could for about five miles. . . ." Feltman got a horse and rode very slowly to a tavern twelve miles in the rear. Lafayette rallied the men at a house near Greenspring, where the main force of his continentals and militia came up. The Marquis had lost about 140 men, more than in all his other skirmishes, but he had saved the army, and his men had escaped the trap by fighting like wildcats. His Pennsylvanians had behaved like veterans, for all their troubled past.

The next day, July 7, Cornwallis crossed to the south bank of the James and had barely made camp when he got an insistent dispatch from Clinton, asking for reinforcements. The Earl agreed to send men to New York—but he added a prophetic warning to Clinton: there was danger in taking a defensive position in tidewater Virginia, which would pin down Cornwallis' troops in "some Acres of an unhealthy swamp, and is for ever liable to become a prey to a foreign Enemy, with temporary superiority at Sea."

By now Cornwallis had a new servant in his tent, a Negro called James who had joined the army during the river crossing. James was a spy for Lafayette, but though he reported faithfully on every move of the army as it marched eastward to Portsmouth, he could learn nothing of future British plans. As Lafayette complained, "his Lordship is so shy of his papers that my honest friend says he cannot get at them."*

Lafayette settled at Malvern Hill on the road between Richmond and Williamsburg to keep watch on the enemy. After five months of working, fighting, and marching he had cleared the invaders from Virginia north of the James, and there was praise for him on all sides. James McHenry of his staff thought that Lafayette had used "sorcery and magic" in driving Cornwallis to Portsmouth.

Washington wrote about this time:

> The command of the troops in that state cannot be in better hands than the Marquis's. He possesses uncommon military talents, is of quick and sound judgment, persevering, and enterprizing without rashness, and besides these, he is of very conciliating temper and perfectly sober, which are qualities that rarely combine in the same person. . . ."

Such praise was welcome, but Lafayette's troops were often near starvation: "I cannot conceive what our commissarys are about. It is almost an age since flour has been seen in camp . . . soap and candles are entirely out of the question. Meat is hardly eatable."

* A slave named "James Lafayette" won his freedom for this service after the war by act of the Virginia legislature.

In his quest for men Lafayette had called on Daniel Morgan, still in retirement at his home near Winchester; the victor of Cowpens complained of "the infirmities of old age," and said he was "blind as a bat" from arthritic pain, but he soon came into camp with a band of riflemen from the Shenandoah Valley. Lafayette was ecstatic at the sight of the raw-boned mountain men: "Mon Dieu! What a people are these Americans; they have reinforced me with a band of giants."

When they met Tarleton and his legion a few days later, Morgan's men beat off the dragoons. Lafayette was convinced that the marksmen from the Valley were supermen. He wrote Washington, "The riflemen ran the whole day in front of my horse without eating or resting." But it was soon over for Morgan; his pains returned after a few nights of sleeping on the ground, and he was forced to return home, to fight no more. "I am afraid I am broke down," he said. Morgan's riflemen remained in camp.

Near the end of July the spy James reported to Lafayette that the British were about to move from Portsmouth, where, he did not know. Lafayette complained that even the best intelligence from James left him to "guess at every possible whim of an enemy that flies with the wind and is not within the reach of spies or reconnoitrers."

Lafayette fretted over the Earl's intentions. "Lord Cornwallis's abilities are to me more alarming than his superiority of forces. I ever had a great opinion of him. Our papers call him a bad man, but was ever any advantage taken of him where he commanded in person? To speak plain English I am devilish affraid of him." Cornwallis continued to baffle him for several days; the transports in Hampton Roads were loaded and the wind was favorable but still the enemy did not move.

In the midst of this uncertainty the Frenchman had a cryptic message from Washington: "I shall shortly have occasion to communicate matters of very great importance to you." It was the news between the lines that was electrifying; obviously, the next move would be to the Chesapeake. Lafayette was to keep Washington informed of every move by Cornwallis.

The Marquis understood. He replied to Washington: "Should a French fleet now come in Hampton road, the British army would, I think, be ours." He wrote Luzerne more emphatically, "Mon Dieu, why haven't we a fleet here? . . . If the French army could fall from the clouds into Virginia and be supported by a squadron we should do some very good things. . . ."

About August 1, Lafayette learned that Cornwallis had begun to land his troops at Yorktown and Gloucester, and a few hours after the British had gone ashore, the marquis was reporting their moves in detail, though he apologized for his conflicting reports of the enemy: "You must not wonder my dear General that there has been a fluctuation in my intelligences. I am positive the British Councils have also been fluctuating."

He assured Washington that he would not press the enemy so closely as to risk defeat: "His Lordship plays so well that no blunder can be hoped from him to recover a bad step of ours."

The Marquis soon learned that de Grasse was approaching the bay and realized that if he could only hold Cornwallis in place, the allied concentration would bring victory. He prepared for it by sending two aides, Jean-Joseph Gimat and M. de Camus, to Cape Henry to wait for the French fleet; they were to ask de Grasse to block the mouth of the James and York rivers and to send Saint-Simon's troops to join Lafayette.

On August 25 a sudden burst of activity in the British lines alarmed Lafayette; he thought that Cornwallis had learned that the French fleet was approaching. The Marquis sent forward his little force and posted a line across the peninsula near Williamsburg, ready to challenge Cornwallis if he attempted escape. The British could break through his lines, but he was fiercely determined to fight, if necessary, to hold the Earl in Yorktown.

His ability to hold Cornwallis in the trap was uppermost in his mind, as he wrote Washington on September 1:

> I hope you will find we have taken the best precautions to lessen his Lordship's chances to escape. He has a few left but so very precarious that I hardly believe he will make the attempt. If he does he must give up Ships, Artillery, Baggage, part of the Horses, all the Negroes. He must be certain to loose the third of his Army and run the greatest risk to loose the whole without gaining that glory which he may derive from a brilliant defense.

On the same day Lafayette learned that a big fleet had sailed into the Chesapeake. For a few anxious hours he did not know whether it was French or English, but late in the night it became clear: de Grasse was in the bay with twenty-eight line of battle ships, several frigates, and three regiments of St. Simon. Cornwallis was cut off by sea. Lafayette wrote Washington with a surge of boyish emotion, "From the bottom of my heart I congratulate you upon the arrival of the French fleet . . . thanks to you, my dear General, I am in a very charming situation and find myself at the head of a Beautiful body of troops."

7

INTO THE
TRAP

Cornwallis went to Yorktown on the first of August, anchoring his small fleet in the deep water of the harbor, where the intensely blue waters of the York River narrowed to half a mile. The earl also occupied Gloucester Point on the north shore, so that his guns could contest the passage of the stream from both banks. The York was less a river than an estuary of the Chesapeake, a wide straight stream which ran some twenty miles inland above Yorktown, one of the shortest of the world's major rivers. The bay tides surged strongly through the narrows at nine miles an hour, in a channel whose depth reached ninety feet.

When the horsemen of Colonel John Simcoe's Queen's Rangers and the British Forty-third Infantry Regiment had gone ashore, the German regiments followed, the men hurrying to escape the heat in the holds of the transports. One German soldier-diarist, Johann Doehla, wrote of "such astonishing heat that it could scarcely be endured on the ships." It was little better on the land for the Anspachers, who spent the first day uncomfortably in the beach sand without tents; it was not until three days later that they made permanent camp on the plain above the town.

The village occupied by the troops was already nearly one hundred years old and the home of several leading families of the region. Almost two generations earlier, when it had flourished as the chief tobacco port of the Chesapeake, an English traveler had said, "You perceive a great air of opulence among the Inhabitants, who have some . . . Houses equal in Magnificence to many of our superb ones at St. James." It was now a sleepy town of five churches, a handsome courthouse, and some three hundred houses straggling along a yellow marl cliff; from its upper street a few fine brick dwellings looked down on the sparkling waters of the York, which flowed eastward to the Bay. A lower street, at the water's edge, was lined with wharves, warehouses, grog shops, and hovels. Many of the houses were now in ruins or had been abandoned. The village perched on the south bank of the York not far above its mouth, on the large peninsula lying between the York and the James. Westward on the peninsula lay Williamsburg, seven miles away, and some fifty miles inland was Richmond.

The British occupied the place swiftly and almost without thought of Lafayette's presence. A band of three hundred Virginia militia slipped away before them without firing a shot, and few civilians remained behind. "They had mostly gone with bag and baggage into the country beyond," a German soldier said.

Johann Doehla was strongly impressed by the natives: "The inhabitants of Virginia are of a taller and stronger stature and most of them appear fair complexioned in spite of the great heat. Towards us they were rather agreeable and showed more respect than in the other provinces; especially the Virginia women had more affection for the Germans."

One civilian who remained was Thomas Nelson—a former state official known as "Secretary" Nelson, an uncle of the rebel Governor of Virginia, a courtly old man—who gave Cornwallis a polite welcome. The Earl made headquarters in his elegant brick house at the southern end of the village. While men were still coming ashore from the ships, Cornwallis wrote Charles O'Hara, who commanded the rear guard still in Portsmouth:

Dear Charles:

After a passage of 4 days we landed here and at Gloucester without opposition. The position is bad, and of course we want more troops . . .

Cornwallis also wrote Clinton, emphasizing his reluctance to settle here, but conceding that Yorktown was ". . . the only harbour in which we can hope to be able to give effectual protection to line-of-battle ships." A few days earlier Cornwallis had written testily to Clinton, protesting the commander's criticisms of his moves in Virginia, "as unexpected as, I trust, they are undeserved." He pointed out that Clinton had not pressed him to find and occupy a deep-water port for the fleet until quite recently. In fact, Cornwallis had gone with his engineer and naval officers to Old Point Comfort, on the peninsula southeast of Yorktown, to inspect the post; he had found it "will not answer the purpose," and had notified Admiral Graves that he was occupying Yorktown and Gloucester instead. The continuing squabble in the British high command did nothing to further the work in Yorktown.

The Earl's cavalry came from Portsmouth a few days later; Tarleton's dragoons appeared on August 10, having crossed Hampton Roads in flat boats, thrown their horses into deep water to swim ashore, and moved northward across the peninsula, raiding as they went.

American spies and scouts reported every move of the enemy

almost instantly: at least three thousand slaves flocked to the village, seeking food, shelter, and freedom. There were said to be few Loyalists in the camp. A staff officer at the headquarters of the vigilant Lafayette had written a few days earlier, "Lord Cornwallis neither pushes his works with rapidity on the land or water side. Like some of the heroes in romance, he appears to despise armour and to confide in his own natural strength."

The British began fortifying on the Gloucester shore, where they built a log palisade to protect the point and a small triangular fort and a line of earthworks along the bluff. Slaves did much of the work, and the troops were not hard-pressed, but desertions began almost immediately, especially among the Germans. Four men of the Bayreuth Regiment slipped away on August 10, and others followed.

The Earl's moves were unhurried, almost languid, as if he were a victim of the heat, until the third week of August when he brought the last of his troops to Yorktown. He explained to New York that he was fortifying not because he expected an attack but only to hold open a port for the fleet; he would remain on the defensive until the hot weather had passed. His work on the lines in the heat, he told Clinton, was so demanding that he could not promise to send the reinforcements Sir Henry sought. The Earl said flatly, "I cannot at present say, whether I can spare any troops, or if any, how soon."

The arrival of the last troops from Portsmouth brought the garrison's strength to more than seven thousand. The newcomers were led by Brigadier General Charles O'Hara, who was one of Cornwallis' few intimates, a dark, handsome, courtly Irishman of forty who had been in the army since the age of twelve and was a veteran of campaigns in Germany, Africa, and Portugal. He was the illegitimate son of James O'Hara, Lord Tyrawley, was well known in London society, and was a personal friend of Horace Walpole. O'Hara was recovering from two serious wounds received at Guilford Courthouse but he was, even now, a "most perfect specimen of a soldier and a courtier of the past age."

With the coming of O'Hara and the last of his troops, Cornwallis had an impressive force of veterans to defend the posts: seven British line regiments, the two largest of about 600 men each, most of the others reduced to about 200; the Brigade of Guards, 467 men; about 600 light infantry; 400 cavalry and 200 artillerymen. There were also more than 1700 Germans and about 100 North Carolina Loyalists.

The Earl wrote Clinton after all these troops had arrived that they must work at least six weeks to build proper defenses —but he offered to send twelve hundred men to New York if Clinton thought they would be more useful in the North than in digging trenches about Yorktown.

The first chilling news came on August 29, a clear, hot day when British outposts on the beaches south of Yorktown could see far across the bay toward the capes. A picket ship, the old *Loyalist,* lay at anchor near the mouth of the channel. Her lookouts were indolently watchful; these were British waters, and no one dreamed of an enemy intrusion. The twenty-eight-gun *Guadeloupe* left Yorktown on the morning ebbtide and fell down the bay seaward with dispatches from Cornwallis; her captain was to look for the British fleet outside the capes, since the Earl expected fresh troops to help man the Yorktown defenses.

The *Guadeloupe* passed the *Loyalist* under full sail but soon began to tack skittishly and made about. Big ships, bearing in from the southeast, were making unfamiliar signals, and the *Guadeloupe* fled before them, beating back toward Yorktown. The strangers in her wake were French. The *Guadeloupe* outran them, but they shot away the masts of the *Loyalist* and towed her to an anchorage in Hampton Roads.

A great fleet came behind the French vanguard and anchored just inside Cape Henry, dozens of ships of all classes.

The *Guadeloupe* was back in Yorktown with news of her adventure the next day, and within a few hours naval officers reported more fully—there were thirty or forty enemy ships in the bay, "some of them very large."

Work on the defenses was no longer leisurely. Parties now worked day and night; Corporal Stephan Popp of the Bayreuth German regiment complained, "We hardly had time for eating. Often we had to eat raw meat."

The Earl's secretaries also felt the change. For several days they worked furiously over dispatches to Clinton in duplicate and triplicate, most of them in code. They hurried them off on dispatch boats which left daily, slipping past the French cordon. Some of the vessels were small schooners, but most were galleys and whaleboats, rowed by crews of eight or ten men through the ocean up the long coast, past Virginia, Maryland, Delaware, and New Jersey, into New York. On August 31 Cornwallis sent out the schooner *Mary* with news of the French arrival—news that Clinton was to read in New York five days later. The Earl took care to see that this news went through secretly. Among the flurry of dispatches that went north were several written in cipher on American continental bank notes, the coded numbers bearing the message: "An enemy's fleet within the Capes, between thirty and forty ships of war, mostly large."

Dispatches of the following days reported the vigorous moves of de Grasse: the French put troops ashore, anchored ships to block nearby rivers, and sent scouts everywhere.

Despite the new threat from the bay, there was no real sense of crisis at headquarters. The French fleet cut them off by sea, but it was inconceivable that the blockade would not soon be lifted. Cornwallis assured his men that the troops of Saint-Simon, who had reinforced Lafayette, were "raw and sickly," undisciplined vagabonds collected from the West Indies, "enervated by a hot climate," who would fall victim to the mild Virginia winter. But the Earl made no move to attack the French marines as they landed. Henry Clinton later said he could not account for the failure of Cornwallis "to cut up Monsieur St. Simon's three thousand enervated troops on their landing within a few miles of him . . . or placing himself between them and Lafayette's small corps."

Cornwallis could not long conceal the growing danger from his troops. On the last day of August Johann Doehla went on unloading duty in the harbor, helping to strip guns and ammunition from the ships, to strengthen the defenses on the land side, where the allied armies must attack. It was cruelly hot by day, but cool at night. Frequent thunderstorms burst over the village, and the German camp was struck by lightning several times, but the work went on.

There were more ominous signs for the Earl's force as September came in. On the first of the month four French ships sailed into the York and anchored about two miles below the town, blocking the channel. Lieutenant James, who had been scouting in the bay in a small boat, escaped under full sail just ahead of the enemy and "fled up the harbour like a scalded cock."

The next day sailors from the British fleet were moved into tents on the beach and began digging trenches facing the river to guard against naval attack. The work parties dug constantly, but there was a shortage of tools—only four hundred of the army's stock of spades, shovels, axes, and wheelbarrows could be found.

Guns were taken out of the *Charon* and put into these earthworks facing downstream. On the plain above the town facing inland across the peninsula, both soldiers and seamen were at work on the defenses.

Fever spread among the men; eight Germans died in the

hospital during the month. There were many cases of dysentery and "foul fever." "Mostly," one German said, "the nitre-bearing water is to blame." An occasional deserter escaped. Private Froelich, who tried to slip away, was caught and forced to run the gauntlet twenty-six times in two days, scampering for his life while three hundred men flailed at him. When it was over Froelich was so terribly beaten that he could not walk. The German troops were camped in a large cotton field, and as soon as the bolls burst to reveal their fluffy white "wool," the industrious Hessians made use of the crop: "We made ourselves coverlets for the beds and couches in our tents, where we slept on it, but we had little time for more than that."

The British in Yorktown heard firing at sea from outside the Capes on September 5 but did not know that Admiral Graves had come nor that a battle had been fought until three days later, when the action was dismissed as "some slight skirmish" from which the inferior British fleet was forced to withdraw.

Cornwallis wrote to Clinton of the mysterious naval gunfire, reporting that Lafayette had been reinforced by Saint-Simon's troops and that Washington was expected. The Earl would soon be surrounded, but he was almost cheerful: "I am now working very hard at the redoubts of the place. The Army is not very sickly. Provisions for six weeks. I will be very careful of it." The Earl's delusion bred optimism in New York, where the Virginia garrison was said to be "in great spirits" and, though it expected an attack, was ready to give the enemy "a proper reception."

Rumors of the approach of the allied armies swept through the garrison. One imaginative deserter told Johann Doehla that Lafayette was only a mile to the west, strongly entrenched. Lieutenant James had a premonition of a "fatal storm, ready now almost to burst on our heads."

Men in the ranks saw that the lines were tightening about them. Doehla wrote on September 11, "We get terrible provision now, putrid ships meat and wormy biscuits that have spoiled on the ships."

The lassitude that now gripped Cornwallis was in striking contrast to his bold gambles of the winter and spring. Though he had little hope of rescue from the sea, and knew that Washington was moving south and would soon besiege him in his incomplete works, Cornwallis would do nothing to help himself beyond the work on his entrenchments. He faced the difficult choice of trying to escape before Washington reinforced Lafayette or of trusting to Clinton and the navy to save him by sea—and knew that the latter was virtually impossible. If he attempted escape, he would lose much of his equipment and most of the Loyalists who were in his camp. And yet, as Banastre Tarleton insisted, inaction meant certain defeat. The cavalryman expected no help from the sea. There was, he said, "no substantial reason to believe that the British commander in chief would be able . . . to give serious assistance to the King's troops in Virginia." An attack on the enemy, Tarleton said, was the army's only chance. Tarleton's brother pointed out the danger of awaiting siege by jumping over the earthworks to show their weakness and told the Earl that it would disgrace the British army to defend these works. "In that case," the earl said, "the blame will fall upon Clinton, and not on us."

Cornwallis maintained that he had no choice and had been immobilized by Clinton's orders to occupy Yorktown; his secretary, Ross, assured the Earl that relief would come, and upon that vague hope everything rested. The Earl did briefly entertain a bold plan of escape—or at least debated it at headquarters about the middle of the month—and sent Banastre Tarleton to probe Lafayette's position in Williamsburg. A cavalry squadron drove American pickets from the road to

the west, and when the way was clear he galloped off with nine
men to study the camp of the French marquis, near the College
of William and Mary. He made a leisurely inspection and
reported to Cornwallis, urging him to strike; a surprise night
attack along the main street of Williamsburg would scatter
Lafayette's band and enable the British to escape. A woman
spy came in during the night with a complete return of Lafayette's forces, and, when Cornwallis saw this, he agreed—they
would assault Williamsburg and break the allied ring before
reinforcements could arrive.

Cornwallis was planning the time of his march when two
dispatches arrived from Clinton. There was the message of
September 2: ". . . it would seem that Mr. Washington is moving an army to the southward . . . Your Lordship . . . may be
assured that . . . I shall . . . reinforce the army under your
Command."

But there was also a reassuring dispatch of September 6:
"As . . . I can have no Doubt that Washington is moving
with, at least, 6000 French and Rebel Troops against you, I
think the best way to relieve you, is to join you as soon as
possible, with all the Force that can be spared from hence,
which is about 4000 Men. They are already embarked. . . ."

Cornwallis and Ross convinced themselves that relief was
on the way. To Tarleton's dismay, the Earl cancelled his
attack on Williamsburg—where Washington had by now arrived. Cornwallis reported to Clinton on the abandoned
scheme:

> If I had no hopes of Relief, I would rather risk an Action
> than defend my half-finished Works. But as you . . . prom-
> ise every Exertion to assist me, I do not think myself
> justifiable in putting the fate of the War on so desperate
> an Attempt.

Cornwallis turned to his defenses. Lanterns burned all night as men dug trenches, leveled ground in front of the village, and pulled down houses to give the gunners a clear field of fire inland.

Johann Doehla, who was sent into the woods west of the village with a wood-chopping crew, was surprised to see that all trees before the trenches had been cut and the roads were blocked with barricades of sharpened logs. Wagons moved in and out of the woods carrying logs for palisades.

The bustle cheered the pessimistic Lieutenant James: "Preparations on all sides going on with great expedition and life, and full of the hopes . . . of a relief by the arrival of a British fleet." But in the York, within plain sight, blockading French frigates made signals to the main fleet. In the distance beyond these frigates a straggling fleet of tiny boats was passing southward—allied soldiers bound up the James River for Williamsburg. In face of these signs of looming disaster, Cornwallis became concerned over his dwindling provisions and drove women camp followers and their children and hundreds of Negroes out of town.

On September 22 the naval forces in the river made a desperate effort to break the enemy's stranglehold on Yorktown itself. Fireships were ordered to burn the nearest vessels of the French. At midnight the fireship *Vulcan* dropped down the river with several hastily improvised attack craft in her wake, all loaded to the gunwales with sulphur, tar, and other combustibles. They went at full speed in a stiff breeze toward the French anchorage, their skeleton crews ready to set them afire and drift them against the enemy ships. In the end, it was all in vain.

Within two hours they were among the French, but one of the fireships blazed up prematurely, French drummers beat to quarters in the darkness, and the little flotilla found some of the French crews alert and waiting in the darkness. Even so, the current ran so strongly that some of the British vessels were within two cable lengths before they were seen. Lieutenant Tornquist, a Swede who was aboard a French ship, said, "It was a beautiful and devastating sight to observe five burning ships falling astern down the stream before our eyes."

The gale blew these blazing ships harmlessly past, but another one soon blazed up in the darkness and bore down on the *Vaillant*. Tornquist and his mates saved themselves by cutting their anchor line and drifting away with only their topsails unfurled. All the French ships escaped with no greater damage than running aground, though the fire was "so violent" that it was seen by the main fleet eight miles away. The blazing fireships burned all the next day, even through rain squalls that swept the bay.

Lieutenant James took the failure philosophically. It was a "sad business" he said; if his men had done their duty they would have destroyed the blockading ships. James and his party, "not much satisfied," dragged back to their tents at 6:00 A.M. with one casualty, a man burned in an explosion, but during the day they were cheered to see the French drop downstream at a more respectful distance. It was a small victory, but now the dispatch boats to New York might escape more easily by night.

As the earthworks grew about Yorktown, Cornwallis stripped the lower peninsula of food for troops and horses, raiding the farms with his cavalry for grain, meat, and fodder. He also constantly probed Lafayette's front for information of the enemy. Tarleton's horsemen scattered a small picket on the Hampton road almost daily so that the Colonel could talk with a British spy, who lived nearby. By night, boats slipped up the river from Yorktown, carrying scouts. Cornwallis thus knew every allied move by land within a few hours. Almost as soon as they had come ashore at Jamestown, the Earl learned of the final large reinforcement of troops for Washington, recently arrived in Williamsburg.

Cornwallis, by Gainsborough.　COURTESY COLONIAL WILLIAMSBURG

The Marquis de Lafayette, by C. W. Peale.

Henry Knox, by C. W. Peale.

Washington firing the first American gun at Yorktown.   COURTESY COLONIAL WILLIAMSB

General Comte de Rochambeau and staff before Yorktown. Engraving of sketch, U.S. Government Printing Office.
COURTESY COLONIAL WILLIAMSBURG

General von Steuben, by C. W. Peale.

Alexander Hamilton, by C. W. Peale.

Generals at Yorktown. A rather primitive, seldom-seen painting of Washington flanked by Lafayette on his right and Rochambeau on his left (others unidentified). Details include dead horses on beach, British ships sunk offshore, and large French ships in distance.

The Storming of Redoubt No. 10, by Eugene Lami.

Admiral de Grasse, by A. Rosenthal.

Banastre Tarleton, by Joshua Reynolds.

The Surrender of Yorktown, by John Trumbull.
Charles O'Hara and Benjamin Lincoln in center.

The Thomas Nelson House, Yorktown, a few years after the siege. Battered by allied artillery, the house still stands. A water-color by Benjamin Latrobe. COURTESY VIRGINIA STATE LIBRARY

By now, Tarleton thought, the British position in the town was formidable, and the defense line protected the most vulnerable approaches:

The face of the country, in front of this line, was cut near the center by a morass, and, excepting this break, the ground was plain and open for near two thousand yards. An excellent field artillery was placed to the greatest advantage by Captain Rochefort.

The British command seemed not to foresee that these light guns might soon be overwhelmed by a ring of some of the world's heaviest siege artillery.

It was September 24 before the besieged garrison had a call from the allied troops who cut it off by land. In the darkness before dawn a small American party which had come down from Williamsburg crept upon a few German pickets on duty near the York River, captured every man, and fell back, firing at random. As if to reassure himself, Cornwallis inspected the naval batteries along his front; the seamen went through gunnery exercises for him, and the Earl was especially pleased by the smartness of the crews of his only big guns, a lone twenty-four pounder and three eighteens. Most of these guns from the ships were commanded by lieutenants from the *Charon*, among them Lieutenant James.

On September 26 and 27 James prepared his men for battle; the tents of the navy gunners were pitched near the batteries. James noted in his diary, "The enemy momentarily expected, and the works going on as before. . . ."

Stephan Popp was less optimistic: "Day and night we are at work strengthening our lines—have little time to eat and little food, but we are getting ready to make a stout defense." Then, in a somber afterthought, the German boy added, "There are reports we are in a very bad situation."

8

DECISION
AT SEA

On September 1, after weeks of delay, the British fleet had sailed from New York for the Chesapeake—nineteen big ships of the line, a few frigates, and other smaller ships. The fleet left without a suspicion of what lay ahead; Admiral Graves believed that Washington still threatened New York and Staten Island, rather than the army in Virginia. He had no inkling that Cornwallis was in real danger, and of the French fleets he knew only that both de Barras and de Grasse were at large. Graves sailed southward "on the chance of falling in with one of the French squadrons" and because he thought the Virginia Bay a likely place for the enemy to call. He expected the Chesapeake to be empty.

Two days after the fleet left New York, when Sir Henry Clinton had begun to understand Washington's campaign plan for the first time, Graves also had unpleasant news at sea.

There was a distress signal from the seventy-four-gun *Terrible,* one of Hood's ships up from the West Indies, supposedly in fighting trim and fit for a month's cruise. Captain Clement

Finch reported that she was leaking; worse yet, he told the exasperated Graves, she had come up from the tropics with five pumps at work. Other ships, especially the *Ajax* and *Montagu*, had leaks and sprung masts, and several were short of bread and water. The fleet lay to off the New Jersey coast, wallowing for hours until emergency repairs were made, then moved south again under full sail. The *Terrible* was the worst of its cripples, but she would be able to fight.

Graves halted at the mouth of Delaware Bay to signal two of his cruisers stationed there:

"Have you seen the French?"

"No. Nothing."

He looked for other news as the fleet straggled southward along the coast in fair weather but found none; de Grasse had seen to that, snapping up every British vessel in his path as he sailed up from San Domingo.

At dawn of September 5 Graves sighted the Chesapeake capes; he had been three and a half days in sailing 240 nautical miles, a rate of less than three miles an hour. The British bore inland in the light of the rising sun, running before the wind. Within a few hours they would enter the Chesapeake channel and the following day would be in touch with Cornwallis.

The French fleet lay in Lynnhaven Bay just inside the Chesapeake, at anchor in three lines. A scouting frigate, the *Aigrette,* patrolled outside the capes, its lookouts scanning the approaches. De Grasse was not prepared for action—eighteen hundred of his best seamen and ninety officers were ashore with small boats, fetching wood and water. Three large ships blocked the York River below Yorktown, two were in the James, and three others were sailing northward up the bay to meet Washington's army.

The twenty-four remaining ships of the fleet swung in the tide on their thick hawsers; the hemp cables squeaked monotonously. The early sun glittered on the varnished sides of the towering *Ville de Paris,* on whose decks the tropical plants from San Domingo were still entwined between the guns. Breakfast smells drifted from the galleys.

At eight o'clock the distant *Aigrette* sighted sails, first ten, then twelve; the news set off a celebration in the fleet—the approaching ships must be those of de Barras coming in from Rhode Island. But the count of the strange ships rose to twenty. They were British. Pipes shrilled in the French fleet, and calls went out for the crews ashore, most of them in vain. Decks were cleared, guns made ready, nets were spread to catch spars, or men, that might fall from aloft in battle; spare cordage was stacked for repairing torn rigging, and plugs were brought up to fill shot holes in the hulls. Tropical plants went overboard or were hidden below, and sand was sprinkled to provide safe footing in action when blood ran on the shuddering decks. The French made ready and waited as the British came on.

It was 9:30 A.M. before a lookout on Graves' frigate, the *Solebay,* reported ships at anchor in the bay, at a distance of about ten miles. Captain C. H. Everitt was incredulous: "It must be the charred pines that you see—they burn them for tar and leave the trunks standing."

Everitt climbed the mast to see for himself: the French fleet was within the hook, lying defenseless at anchor. He at first counted eight ships; they must be de Barras and his weak squadron from the north.

An hour and a half later, when Graves in his flagship *London* was still eighteen miles northeast of Cape Henry, the British *Bedford* also saw the French and counted fifteen or sixteen sail. Graves called in his cruisers and other small vessels and began closing his line for battle.

De Grasse ordered his captains to slip their cables at eleven-thirty but the fleet was still held fast by the incoming tide and could not move seaward. It could only wait as the tide slowed in Hampton Roads, then hung, and, near noon, turned outward at last. Carpenters hurriedly chopped cables with axes and left them afloat on buoys above the anchors. Despite the shortage of men, the fleet maneuvered into the semblance of a line—"for a wonder," one French officer said—and began the difficult move from the lee shore around Cape Henry, to challenge the enemy. The French ships drove for the channel on the south of the ten-mile opening between the capes, just below a menacing sand bar, Middle Ground Shoal.

De Grasse ordered his swiftest ships into the lead, and after a hasty scramble those of Commodore Louis Antoine de Bougainville won the race. Bougainville was not an ordinary sea captain; he had led a long army career before coming to the navy, and it was he who had been forced to surrender Canada to the British in the Seven Years War, after the death of General Montcalm. As a sailor he was already a veteran of long voyages of discovery in the littleknown Pacific. De Grasse and Bougainville had quarreled recently, but today the commander of the advance squadron performed flawlessly. His flagship, *Auguste,* moved toward the head of the French line. Bougainville thus replaced Captain de Monteil, who usually commanded the van but was caught today to the rear of the *Ville de Paris.* When de Grasse saw that there was no flag officer with the rear of the fleet, he shouted across the water to Monteil, ordering him to command the trailing division.

Other captains struggled to keep pace. The *Souverain* and the *Citoyen* almost ran aground and consumed precious time tacking and doubling back to reach the channel, but a ragged line of battle soon began to form off the point of the cape. The van was in poor order: the *Pluton* of seventy-four guns, the *Bourgogne* of eighty guns, and the *Marseillais* and the *Diadème,* each seventy-four. These were followed by the *Réfléchi* and the *Caton,* some distance behind and a mile and a half to the leeward. Most of the fleet straggled far to the rear.

Despite the van's bad formation, the odds favored de Grasse as the fleets moved toward battle. He had five more capital ships than Graves—twenty-four to nineteen—at least four hundred more guns, and six thousand more men. His crews were well trained and reflected the new spirit of the French navy; his ships were somewhat more maneuverable because of their design—but their bottoms were not coppered as the English ships' were, and barnacles, worms, and weeds had cut the speed of the French.

At twelve-forty-five the *Ville de Paris* swept past the cape in the track of the French van, bringing with her the center and rear divisions. De Grasse had resolved to settle the struggle for control of the great bay, its harbors, and the long reaches of its rivers.

The English fleet swept in toward the capes, its nineteen ships in a line five miles long, foresails and topgallants full under a fresh breeze from north-northeast. Hood commanded the van in the *Barfleur,* Graves the center in the *London,* and Drake the rear in the *Princessa.* Fluttering signal flags ordered the captains to close up for attack, bowsprit to stern.

The captains of Bougainville's exposed and outnumbered division saw the familiar colors of British warships clearly in the noon light: yellow hulls with black stripes at the water line, blue above, with dull red decks to match the color of blood.

The English approached through foaming seas in ideal position for attack, with every advantage of wind and tide. The *Barfleur* and the *London,* which were well to the fore, each carried ninety guns; the only French ship of such power was the *Ville de Paris,* still out of range. One French officer watched the British with admiration: "They came down upon us with a following wind and an assurance which made us think they did not know our strength." But Graves did not attack; he came in parallel to the French line, waiting for de Grasse to emerge.

By twelve-forty-five, when the *Ville de Paris* had cleared Cape Henry, occasional light squalls swept the fleets, and Graves ordered a reef in his topsails. For the next hour the British sailed inland, parallel to the outward-bound French. Hood paced his quarter deck angrily, chafing with impatience to attack.

Just after 2:00 P.M., Graves saw that his leading ship, the *Alfred,* was in danger of striking Middle Ground Shoal and signaled the fleet to turn about. The ungainly square-riggers pivoted slowly, each holding its place in line but reversing course by 180 degrees, now sailing back eastward with the French, still in parallel column but with their rear ships beginning to trail to the windward. Though Graves was forced into the same larboard tack that de Grasse was following, he still had the windward position, with more freedom of movement than his adversary. It was only at this time that Graves counted the full strength of the French, and realized that he had to cope with a force far greater than the small squadron of de Barras.

Hood was now in the British rear and Drake's division had become the van, so that the English had no formidable vessels in the lead—there was no longer a ninety-gun ship with the van, and among Drake's ships were the leaky *Terrible* and *Ajax,* liabilities in battle.

The puzzled French watched as gunfire broke out among the English fleet; the *Terrible,* still working her pumps to remain buoyant, had fallen to windward. Drake signaled her to return to her place in line, and when she was slow to respond, fired three cannon shot across her bow. Captain Finch then brought her into position.

Even now, though his van was weaker than before, Graves

felt he had the French at a disadvantage: the first four or five of Bougainville's ships were far in front of the main body, and de Grasse's center still lagged. Graves hesitated once more. To the astonishment of his own officers as well as the French, he dropped sails and waited until the French had closed the gap in their line. The *London*'s log recorded the maneuver: "Brought to in order to let the Center of the Enemys Ships come a Brest of us." Hood was incredulous that Graves should allow the enemy so long to recover; from the deck of the *Barfleur* he timed the respite at an hour and a half.

Only after de Grasse had pulled his center forward to support his van, and the French fleet was in orthodox battle position, did Graves approach the enemy. He chose a dangerous method, edging downwind toward the line of de Grasse. At 2:52 P.M. the *London* flew a signal: "lead more to starboard, or toward the enemy," and repeated this less than twenty minutes later. The British captains followed the lead ship, the *Shrewsbury*, holding to their straight line but bearing obliquely toward the French, angling into fighting position. Graves' tactic brought his fleet into gun range piecemeal, denying his captains a concentration of firepower. At 4:00 P.M. Graves was content; his own line was "pretty well formed," his van ready to fight, and the French line was "very particularly extended . . . as many of their rear were not clear of Cape Henry . . . advancing very slow." He calculated that the odds were about three to two in favor of the British, with the French rear out of the range of action. The fleets drifted seaward; all gunners stood by their cannon, slow matches burning, ready to open fire. They were five or six miles from shore. Graves was now flying a white pennant from his mast, the signal for a line ahead movement.

It was only at three minutes past four, some six and a half hours after the fleets had sighted each other, that Graves ran up a blue and white checkered flag under the white pennant:

"Ships to bear down and engage close." This new signal ordered each captain to attack his opposite number in the enemy line. Graves neglected to lower his previous flag for "line ahead" until eight minutes later, and some of his captains, especially Hood, became confused by the contradictory signals. Hood chose to obey the original signal and sailed his rear division onward, "line ahead." The *London* was the tenth ship, in the precise center of the British fleet, but Graves turned her abruptly out of line southward, toward the enemy, and when her topsail bellied out, drove her upon the French at a right angle. The move was made from "a most improper distance," Hood thought, and it immediately snarled the British van.

Other captains followed the move of Graves, dangerously crowding their ships; several found the *London* between them and the enemy, so that they could not open fire. The *London* now fired several broadsides, the balls falling short and splashing into the sea. Graves ran up other signals in an attempt to restore order, further confusing his fleet.

At four-fifteen, when the vans were within musket range of each other—about 120 yards—the fleets began firing furiously. The first broadsides were the most deadly, with thirty or forty guns of each big ship fired simultaneously, tearing and splintering the wooden hulls to kill and maim men locked below, and spreading havoc on the crowded decks. The French, as usual, aimed for the rigging, to immobilize the enemy ships, and the British decks were soon covered with flapping sails, broken spars, and cables.

The seventy-four-gun *Shrewsbury* was the first victim of the French crews. Drake's leading ship opened "in a very gallant and spirited manner," but return fire from the *Pluton* raked her immediately, tearing off a leg of her veteran captain, Mark Robinson, and killing his first lieutenant and thirteen seamen.

Before it was over twelve more of the *Shrewsbury*'s men were dead and forty-eight others wounded. Her topmast was shot through in three places, her main mizzenmast riddled, and she had five shot in the hull under water. She dropped out of line late in the day and made a signal of distress. The second British ship, the *Intrepid*, sailed forward to shield the *Shrewsbury* and came under ruinous fire from the *Marseillais*. The *Intrepid* took sixty-five shot in her starboard side, nineteen of them between wind and water. Her rudder and all her boats were damaged, and her masts and rigging were so cut to pieces that she also fell out of line.

These two ships of Drake's van suffered half the British loss in dead and a third of the wounded—they had been caught in deadly diagonal fire from the French, at a moment when they could bring only their bow guns to bear. All ships of the van were damaged, but Drake's men fought furiously. His flagship, the *Princessa*, raked the *Réfléchi* with her first broadside, killing her captain, M. de Boades, and mortally wounding another officer. The *Pluton* and the *Réfléchi* and the next French ship, the *Caton*, dropped out of line under heavy fire.

The leading ships of Bougainville's division were then battered while the rest of the fleet was out of range. One French officer wrote:

> The four ships found themselves engaged with seven or eight vessels at close quarters. The *Diadème* was near Rear Admiral Drake, who set fire to her at every shot, the wadding entering her side. The English could not cut off our van . . . they contented themselves simply with cutting up that part of our fleet which kept up a distant fight.

The *Diadème* was soon out of action, "having only four 36-pounders and nine 18-pounders fit for use, and all on board killed, wounded, or burnt." Captain Chabert and his *Saint-Esprit* came to the rescue of the *Diadème*, sailing in her wake and opening a hot fire "that the gentlemen of Albion could not stand, and had to haul their wind."

By this time Bougainville had steered the *Auguste* so close to Drake's *Princessa* that their hulls almost touched; when Drake avoided him, Bougainville turned his guns upon the weakened *Terrible*, sending two shot through her sprung fore-mast and several more into her hull. The *Terrible* was already taking in about five feet of water per hour, and her pumps were giving out; her officers thought that she would sink within a few hours.

The *Auguste* also suffered, with ten men dead and fifty-eight wounded, but Bougainville kept his ship in the midst of the action. Twice the British shot away his foretop bowline, high above the deck, and the sailors who scrambled upward to make repairs were shot. When the line parted a third time, and no volunteers came forward, Bougainville held up his purse and offered it to any man who would go aloft and replace the line. A seaman immediately went up the mast and out upon a yard, shouting, "General, we do not go there for money." The man tied the line and came down safely amid enemy fire.

Bougainville's aggressiveness and bravery against Drake won praise from de Grasse: "Now that's what I call 'combat'! For a while I thought you were going to board!" The Admiral later told Washington and Rochambeau that "the laurels of the day belong to de Bougainville . . . for having led the van and having personally fought the *Terrible*."

Bougainville reported that his *Auguste* fired 684 cannon shot during the furious exchange and had taken seventy hits in the rigging and fifty-four in the hull.

Drake's *Princessa* was badly damaged, and a nearby ship, the *Alcide*, was soon in distress with "three shot through the main-mast; the mizzen topmast, topsail and gaffs shot away; boats much hurt; many shot under water which makes the ship leaky." The *Ajax* was also in distress.

The British had much the worst of the battle between the leading ships. The most serious fighting of the afternoon was between the vans, as the British angle of approach became steeper throughout the action, throwing the center and rear farther from the French line. Even so, a few of Graves' center ships fought briskly.

It was about 5:00 P.M. before the center divisions were within range and opened fire. By now the wind had shifted slightly toward east-northeast, and the British lost some of their wind advantage.

The first two vessels of the British center, the *Europe* and the *Montagu,* suffered almost as much as those of the van. The *Europe*'s rigging and masts were badly torn, gun carriages were damaged, and her hull shot full of holes, so that she leaked and strained; she had twenty-seven casualties. The *Montagu* dropped out of line during the evening; she had thirty casualties and was reported "in great danger of losing her masts, which might fall at any moment."

The next ships in line were slightly damaged—the *Royal Oak* had no casualties but was struck by seventeen shot; the flagship *London* had "one large shot through the mainmast and two in the foremast; a number of shot in the side . . . sails and rigging much cut; four men killed and eighteen wounded." The next ships in line—*Bedford, Resolution, Centaur,* and *Monarch*—had less damage, and the latter two lost no men. Only a dozen of the nineteen British ships had got into action, and only eight of these took a significant part; only fifteen French ships were heavily engaged.

At five-twenty-five, still flying a signal for "engage the enemy," Graves hauled down his flag for "line ahead." The ships of the rear were very nearly within range of the French, and at this change of signals Hood turned them southward to join the fight. A few French shot flew over the *Barfleur,* and at five minutes before six Hood opened fire from both the *Barfleur* and *Monarch,* but was too far away to cause damage.

Captain d'Ethy of the French *Citoyen,* who joined the final duel with Hood, wrote of these moments:

> At 5:45 P.M. the three-decked ship [the *Barfleur*] commanding the enemy rear came up, as well as the two ships ahead of her . . . they hove to and experimented to see whether their cannon balls would reach our ships. The enemy Admiral began by firing several shots and the other ships . . . followed suit . . . their fire became general up as far as my ship, but it did not last long . . . I had much the better of the exchange with the three-decker, for it appeared to me that nearly all of her cannon balls fell into the sea. . . .

Thirty-five minutes after Hood began his belated and ineffectual fire, the signal flag for engaging the enemy fluttered down from the *London*'s mast, the English ships ceased fire, and the battle was over. Silence fell upon the sea.

At sunset the watchful fleets, still cruising in parallel lines, were about ten miles southeast of Cape Henry, on the course they had held in the hours of battle. The French were at combat stations for the night, with lanterns glowing on the decks and gunners ready with matches burning. The English could see them clearly in the darkness. One of de Grasse's young officers wrote, "The fleet passed the night in the presence of the enemy in line of battle, the fires in all the vessels lighted."

Graves clung to the wind position, but his fleet was so battered that he no longer held the initiative. He sent two frigates to the van and rear divisions with orders for the night: hold the parallel line, within two cables' length of the ship ahead, remaining abreast of the enemy, the crews at battle stations.

At 10:00 P.M. the *Fortunée* returned with bad news—the

Shrewsbury, Intrepid, and *Montagu* could no longer sail in line, and the *Princessa* was in danger of losing her main topmast. The *Terrible* was still struggling to stay afloat, with all her decrepit pumps working, and the *Ajax* leaked almost as badly. The van was in no condition for battle until masts and rigging had been replaced, and the *London* herself needed repairs. Graves began to lose hope that he could attack the enemy once more—his original disadvantage of five ships had grown to ten or eleven with the crippling of his van.

Otherwise, casualties had been light in the brief, furious action. The British had lost 90 men dead and 246 wounded; total French casualties were 209. Graves had sixteen guns put out of action, about 1 percent of his total. The most telling factor had been the accurate high fire of French gunners, who had deprived the British fleet of speed and maneuverability.

The fleets drifted to the southeast during the clear night, under light and variable winds, always within sight of each other.

September 6 dawned calm, clear, and almost windless. Graves was not reassured by his first glimpse of the enemy: "The French had not the appearance of near so much damage as we had sustained." A few minutes later messenger frigates came to the *London* with more news of damaged ships; the *Shrewsbury* and *Intrepid* asked for help, and Graves sent Captain Colpoys, of the *Orpheus,* to take over and direct repairs to the *Shrewsbury* for the wounded Captain Robinson. Just before noon Admiral Drake was forced to leave the *Princessa* and move his flag to the *Alcide.*

Graves had no plan of action at this stage but seemed to fear that he would enrage the belligerent Hood if he did not devise some way to attack. He was exasperated over Hood's behavior during the battle, convinced that the slowness of the rear division had cost him victory. Late in the morning Graves sent Captain Everitt of the *Solebay* to the *Barfleur* with a message, asking Hood's advice: Should the fleet renew its attack on the enemy? Hood was interrupted in his cabin as he wrote a scathing memorandum on the conduct of the battle by Graves, and he dismissed Everitt with a hostile reply, "I dare say Mr. Graves will do what is right. I can *send* no opinion, but whenever Mr. Graves wishes to see me, I will wait upon him with great pleasure."

Hood had poured his scorn for Graves into his memorandum, which he called "Sentiments upon the Truly Unfortunate Day":

> Yesterday the British fleet had a rich and most plentiful harvest of glory in view, but the means to gather it were omitted in more instances than one.
>
> I may begin with observing that the enemy's van was not very closely attacked as it came out of Lynn Haven Bay, which, I think, might have been done with clear advantage, as they came out by no means in a regular and connected way. When the enemy's van was out it was greatly extended beyond the centre and rear, and might have been attacked with the whole force of the British fleet. Had such an attack been made, several of the enemy's ships must have been inevitably demolished in half an hour's action. . . .

Hood also charged that Graves should have ordered on more sail during the fight, so that the center ships could go to the rescue of the battered van. Most important, Hood wrote, if Graves had pulled down his confusing signal for "line ahead" and gone into close action, "the van of the enemy must have been cut to pieces," and Hood's ships could have engaged the enemy at proper range.

For most of the day both fleets moved slowly, as carpenters, riggers, and sailmakers repaired the ships. The lookout of the French *Citoyen* reported that five British ships were replacing topmasts—and one of them had a badly damaged mainmast. By 4:00 P.M., when the wind freshened, the most essential emergency repairs had been made.

Graves called Hood and Drake to a conference aboard the *London* in the evening, and Hood had hardly stepped aboard before he told Graves of the critique he had written during the day. The conference was stormy. Graves faced Hood with bitter queries on his behavior during the battle: "Why didn't you bear down and engage?"

"You had the signal up for the line," Hood said.

Graves turned to Drake.

"Why did *you* bear down on the enemy?"

"On account of the signal for action."

"What say you to this, Admiral Hood?" Graves said.

Sir Samuel spoke shortly, "The signal for the line was enough for me."

The squabble between the admirals could not be settled. Graves maintained that he had first flown the contradictory signals for "line ahead" and "attack" together for seven minutes "to push the ships ahead of me forward" and then, about 4:30 P.M., had run up "line ahead" once more briefly, when he found that "all the ships were not sufficiently extended." It was the second appearance of this signal that had so exasperated Hood. Graves declared that the flag had flown only five minutes this time—but Hood and one of his captains swore that they had seen it for at least an hour afterward, and that it had prevented their going into action until it was too late.

Graves was sensitive to comments on his signaling. He wrote Clinton, "Could I have sent orders by aide-de-camps at full speed, instead of using signals, which are ever dubious, we might by a united effort have made a pretty strong impression on the enemy."

The controversy was taken up outside the *London*'s cabin: Hood's friends cursed Graves and his conflicting orders, and the Admiralty and its outmoded signal books; the partisans of Graves denounced Hood for his "great dilatoriness" and "shyness."

Near the end of the day Graves sent Captain Duncan in the frigate *Medea* to scout inside the Chesapeake and carry a dispatch from Clinton to Cornwallis, but the fleet itself followed de Grasse farther to sea, still on a southeast course, still ignorant of the plight of Cornwallis at Yorktown.

The next day, September 7, was calm, but an early breeze sprang up from the south-southwest, and the French fleet began to jockey for the windward position. The fleets were about seven or eight miles apart, and the French did not approach near enough for battle. By the end of the day the fleets had moved almost one hundred miles from the mouth of the Chesapeake, and they were now in the vicinity of Cape Hatteras, North Carolina.

De Grasse made fresh gestures of friendship toward Bougainville during the day, expressing his confidence in him in messages that were in striking contrast to the squabbles between the English admirals:

Thus Monsieur . . . I beg you regard the squadron which you command as if it were a fleet attached to my own, of which you have all the discipline . . . If the wind continues and the English do not escape us tonight, we shall meet them at closer range tomorrow morning. I hope the day will be a happier one, which will permit us to go back and take those Johnnies in the Chesapeake. What a joy it will be to have the ships of de Barras united with ours! . . . I have great hopes based upon the damages to the enemy which I can see. I judge by them that they are not as well-outfitted as we are, and by the slowness of their movements that they are not as ready for Battle. . . .

The morning of September 8 was black and windy, with

thunderstorms rolling over the fleets. At eleven o'clock the *Terrible,* which was being pounded by a head sea, made a distress signal, and two ships were sent to her aid. At night the *Intrepid* lost her main topmast and expected her fore-yard to go at any minute. Graves wrote glumly, "These repeated misfortunes in sight of a superior enemy who kept us all extended and in motion, filled the mind with anxiety and put us in a position not to be envied."

By the morning of the ninth the wind again favored the English, but the fleets began to drift apart before Graves seized his opportunity. Later in the day the French saw a distant squadron that they could not identify and for a few hours gave futile chase. By now some of de Grasse's officers had become concerned for their anchorage in the Bay. Bougainville noted in his journal:

> I was very much afraid that the British might try to get to the Chesapeake . . . ahead of us. It is what we ought to have been doing since the battle: that is, our very best to get back into that bay, recover our ships, barges and boats . . . Perhaps we would also find the squadron of M. de Barras.

By nightfall, de Grasse had come to the same conclusion. He turned for the Chesapeake under full sail. His disappearance alarmed Admiral Hood, who watched de Grasse's fleet fill its sails and grumbled, "I was distressed that Mr. Graves did not carry all the sail he could also, and endeavour to get to the Chesapeake before him; it appeared to me to be a measure of the utmost importance to keep the French out, and if they did get in they should first beat us."

At dawn of September 10, when Hood saw no sign of the enemy, he wrote Graves:

> I flatter myself you will forgive the liberty I take in asking

whether you have any knowledge where the French fleet is, as we can see nothing of it from the *Barfleur.* . . .

I am inclined to think his aim is the Chesapeake . . . if he should enter the Bay . . . will he not succeed in giving most effectual succour to the rebels?

Graves responded by calling another conference aboard the *London.* Hood arrived on the flagship and to his astonishment found Graves "as ignorant as myself where the French fleet was." He again urged Graves to turn for the Chesapeake, though he feared it was too late.

Graves was delayed by the slow death of the *Terrible.* Her carpenters reported that even in a smooth sea she would take in six feet of water an hour without her pumps—and the pumps were almost useless. Chains and sprockets were rusty and decayed and became worse despite repairs. The pump cisterns were so badly shaken that they spouted water, though one man constantly caulked their cracks. Captain Finch had five guns of the lower deck thrown overboard to lighten her, and asked permission to dump upper guns and transfer water and provisions to other ships. On September 11, after her officers had signed certificates as to her hopeless condition, the admirals ordered her stripped and burned.

The last men to leave the *Terrible* opened sea cocks in her hull and started the flames, which caught quickly in the old oak; she was soon a roaring furnace. She exploded and drifted away from the fleet, the fire guttering at the waterline of the ruined hull as it pitched in a running sea. She passed from sight in the early darkness, the only vessel lost in the battle. Only then did Graves turn for the Chesapeake.

The French had sailed back within sight of Cape Henry before noon of September 10, and were stunned to see tall masts behind the headland—about twenty ships, very nearly the size of the English fleet. De Grasse made ready for battle, but a scouting frigate soon saw a familiar signal from a mast of the waiting ships: it was de Barras, who had slipped past both hostile fleets into the bay. He had sailed far south to the North Carolina coast and circled back to evade the British; his ships were the mysterious squadron de Grasse had pursued far at sea.

De Grasse settled in the bay once more, blocking the entrance and the major rivers; he now had thirty-five line of battle ships at his command. The transports of de Barras went immediately up the James, with their precious cargo of salt beef and siege guns for Washington's army.

Graves was on the way to the Chesapeake on September 13 when Captain Duncan of the *Medea* came in sight and signalled that the French were already in the Bay. Graves turned to Hood once more:

> Admiral Graves presents his compliments to Sir Samuel Hood and begs leave to acquaint that the *Medea* has just made the signal to inform him that the French fleet are at anchor . . . in the Chesapeake, and desires his opinion what to do with the fleet. . . .

Hood responded bluntly:

> Rear Admiral Sir Samuel Hood . . . is extremely concerned to find . . . that the French fleet is at anchor in the Chesapeake . . . though it is no more than what he expected . . . Sir Samuel would be very glad to send an opinion, but he really knows not what to say in the truly lamentable state we have brought ourselves.

The distraught Graves then called a final council of war, a brief, gloomy session which ended with the decision that sealed the fate of Cornwallis: because of the "position of the enemy, the present condition of the British fleet, the season of

the year so near the equinox, and the impracticability of giving any effectual succour to General Earl Cornwallis . . . it
was resolved, that the British squadron . . . should proceed
with all dispatch to New York."

For two weeks Graves limped northward with his crippled
ships, rumors of his defeat flying ahead of him. A small boat
carrying one of his dispatches to Clinton reached New York
on September 17 and docked before a crowd of three thousand
anxious civilians, who took no comfort from the grim face of
the naval officer who went ashore. The message from Graves
was sobering enough: he was on his way to refit his "shattered"
fleet; the French held the Chesapeake in such force that nothing could get past them, except for small boats sailing by night.

When Graves returned to the city at last, on September 19,
with ten of his bedraggled ships in need of major repairs, hundreds of Tory families began packing their belongings, preparing to leave the city.

Lieutenant Mackenzie wrote in his diary, "I fear the fate of
the Army in Virginia will be determined before our fleet can
get out of the harbour again. . . ."

The brief and haphazard action off the Virginia coast was
at first dismissed as indecisive. Graves described it as only "a
lively skirmish" and Hood as "a feeble action"; even Washington, who relied so heavily upon French sea power, first
spoke of it as "a partial engagement."

Sir Henry Clinton soon saw the significance of the few hours
of naval gunfire which had left Cornwallis at the mercy of the
allies: "All depended on a fleet. Sir Henry Clinton was promised one. Washington had one."

George III said stoutly, "I am not of a desponding disposi-
tion," but when he heard news of the battle of the Chesapeake
capes, he told the Earl of Sandwich, "I nearly think the empire
ruined . . . this cruel event is too recent for me to be as yet
able to say more."

9

"EVERY DOOR
IS SHUT"

Transports from the French fleet had come slowly up the James River for two days, and after midnight on September 2, began putting troops ashore on Jamestown Island, where men of the first permanent English colony in America had landed almost 175 years before. The troops were the three regiments of General Saint-Simon from the West Indies; they came ashore on the swampy island in torchlight amid clouds of mosquitoes, thirty-five hundred big men in white uniforms with pale blue cuffs and lapels. Pennsylvania officers from Lafayette's army greeted them eagerly.

Lieutenant Feltman said he had never seen "a more beautiful and agreeable sight" than these troops coming onto the beach, and Anthony Wayne thought the newcomers "the finest and best made body of men I ever beheld." Lafayette was in camp some miles away, ill of fever, and Wayne reported to him that since de Grasse had not only blocked the York and James rivers but had sent Saint-Simon's men, "every door is shut by the hard-hearted fellows against Cornwallis." Lafayette's army would now be strong enough to push closer to Yorktown, holding the enemy in their entrenchments. The Marines had landed without their tents, spent the first night miserably in a chilly dew, and suffered under a blistering sun the next day. Many of them soon came down with fever, including Saint-Simon himself.

The French troops discovered that they had also come upon hard times. Lafayette gave them all of his flour for bread and fed his own uncomplaining troops on cornmeal, but there was little enough of either, and brandy was not to be had in this country. There were no horses or wagons to move supplies. The newcomers were shocked by their first glimpses of the war's savagery. The young Swede from de Grasse's fleet, Ensign Karl Tornquist, went ashore a few miles below Jamestown, where British cavalry had been ravaging. Pastures were littered with carcasses of slain cattle and horses, and in one plantation house Tornquist and his companions came upon an unforgettable sight: "... a pregnant woman ... murdered in her bed through several bayonet stabs; the barbarians had opened each of her breasts and written above the bed canopy: 'Thou shalt never give birth to a rebel.' "

In another room of the silent house the troops found five severed human heads on the shelf of a cupboard, grim replacements for plaster figurines which lay in fragments on the floor.

With the coming of Saint-Simon's men Lafayette's force grew to 5500 regulars and 3000 militia. He now outnumbered Cornwallis, and more militiamen were on the way to his camp —but the Marquis did not lose his caution. The offer of de Grasse to send him 1800 more men for the immediate storming of Yorktown troubled Lafayette. He insisted upon waiting for Washington and Rochambeau: "The Army and Navy are in High Spirits and panting for action," he wrote the commander. "My little influence will be employed in preaching patience as our affairs cannot be spoiled unless we do spoil them ourselves." He was not so hasty as de Grasse: "Having so sure a game to play, it would be madness by the risk of an attack to give any thing to chance."

Louis Duportail, the engineer, reported to Washington that the Yorktown situation was in good hands: "Fortunately the intelligence and good sense of the Marquis must give us great confidence. I will put myself under his orders and second his views as much as I shall be able . . . but dear General come with the greatest expedition."

Lafayette's Americans marched into Williamsburg on September 4, and the marquis posted his troops with care, his pickets protected by ravines and his flanks by creeks that led to the York and the James. He wrote Washington:

> Williamsburg and its strong buildings are in our front . . . There is a line of armed Ships along James River, and a small reserve of militia. . . . Should Lord Cornwallis come out against such a position as we have everybody thinks that he cannot but repent of it.

Lafayette had recently complained of the fierce summer heat of Virginia and the prevalence of disease but said proudly, ". . . almost all my people at present have fever. I on the other hand have never felt better." As he settled in Williamsburg he was stricken once more. He struggled against his illness, saying that three hours of sleep would cure him, but he was forced to go to bed and leave his troops. He dictated a confession to Luzerne:

> I beg your pardon . . . for not writing to you personally, but by dint of acting as quartermaster and commissary, stealing salt provisions, impressing beef, and clamoring for flour I have finished awkwardly enough by giving my-

self a fever and headache. . . . Perhaps I am dying of old
age since two days ago I rang out my twenty-fourth
birthday.

His most insistent worry was that Cornwallis might elude
him before the trap was sprung: "Lord Cornwallis has still
one way to escape. He may land at West Point and cross James
River some miles below Point of Fork . . . to prevent even a
possibility I would wish some ships were above York." Anthony Wayne was another of Lafayette's concerns. The handsome Pennsylvanian was riding cross-country to join Lafayette
when he failed to hear a challenge by a young American sentry
who fired, wounding Wayne painfully in the leg. Surgeons put
the general to bed where he was to lie for several days, cursing
his luck and vowing to have the sentry shot.

The small city occupied by the army had served as the capital of Virginia since the end of the seventeenth century, and
only the year before had war driven the government to Richmond. Many soldiers were anxious to see this small hotbed
of rebellion, and some, like Lieutenant Feltman, enjoyed its
quiet charm, wide streets and greens, taverns, billiard tables,
and gracious hosts. There were other views of the village.

An American chaplain wrote:

There are about 300 houses in this town, some of which
are very good, but the greater number are very mean. The
College is about 130 feet in length and 40 in breadth.
Two handsome wings . . . have been added to this building. This College is three stories high; and has a large
library . . . The capitol, or state-house, in which the Assembly used to meet, and the palace in which the Govern-
or resided, are both very grand buildings. . . .

Lieutenant Colonel St. George Tucker of the Virginia militia, who had been a student at William and Mary, found the

town much changed. He wrote his wife, "Among the plagues the British left in Williamsburg, that of Flies is inconceivable. It is impossible to eat, drink, sleep, write, sit still or even walk about in peace."

The college, which had been closed by the war, was used as a hospital by the French, who soon erected an enormous common privy against the front of the building—a three–story scaffolding of rough boards, which amazed Dr. James Tilton, a visiting American physician: "doors opened upon each floor of the hospital; and all manner of filth and excremen-titious matters were dropped and thrown down this common sewer, into the pit below. This sink of nastiness perfumed the whole house . . . and all the air within the wards."

Lafayette was well enough to stay on horseback a few min-utes on September 9, and he rode out to review his troops at their camp near the college. Soon afterward an officer arrived from the north with word that Washington was probably on his way to Williamsburg, but even this failed to cheer Lafay-ette. Depressed by his fever and overcome by the accumulated cares of his lonely four-month campaign to hold Cornwallis in check, and the hardly less strenuous effort to wrest food, clothing, and arms from the Virginians, he wrote to Governor Nelson on September 11:

> I could wish to sleep tonight but I fear it will be impossi-ble with the prospect which is before us tomorrow. There is not one grain of flour in camp either for the American or French army. What we are to do I know not . . . Has your Excellency any hopes for tomorrow? I am distressed in the extreme, in a thousand ways, and without the power of offering either myself or the soldiers the small-est relief.

Relief was only two days away. Abruptly, almost incredibly, the remote village became the focus of the allied war effort, and Lafayette was alone no longer. Nelson came into camp with his Virginia militia. Wayne returned in a carriage, hobbling from his wound but spoiling for action. The Pennsylvanian caused a stir by demanding a court-martial of the sentry who had shot him, but the court ruled that the boy had only done his duty. Steuben came down from the mountains, his gout miraculously cured by the promise of combat. Finally, on September 14, the commander in chief arrived in Williamsburg, and the war in Virginia was transformed.

At four o'clock in the afternoon a band of mud-spattered horsemen came in from the northwest with Washington at their head—they had ridden from Mount Vernon in two and a half days, at a brisk pace that had left officers strung out for miles in the rear. Rochambeau and Adjutant General Edward Hand and a few saddle-sore aides had hung on gamely all the way, marvelling at the durability of the general and Billy Lee, the old foxhunters. Washington rode through the camp of the Virginia militia at the edge of town without halting, but he observed military etiquette by dismounting at the French camp near the college to wait until Saint-Simon's men prepared their welcome. News of his coming spread swiftly through the village.

St. George Tucker, who had met Washington many years before, rode past at this time, and to his surprise the general called him by name, shook hands, and introduced him to Rochambeau. They were interrupted by horsemen galloping toward them—Lafayette, Governor Nelson, and Saint-Simon. Tucker never forgot this reunion of Lafayette and Washington:

> . . . at this moment we saw the Marquis, riding in at full speed from the town, and as he approached General Washington, threw his bridle on the horse's neck, opened both his arms as wide as he could reach, and caught the

General round his body, hugged him as close as it was possible, and absolutely kissed him from ear to ear once or twice. . . .

The pale young Frenchman chattered excitedly, telling Washington of the enemy position and his own troops. Washington broke in anxiously to ask if he had heard from de Grasse. Lafayette shook his head. There had been no news for eight days, since the two fleets had disappeared to sea after their brief battle. The commander was introduced to Saint-Simon and other officers, greeted Governor Nelson, and turned to review the army.

The French troops, who had been taken by surprise by the general, were now hurriedly falling into line on either side of the road. They stood at rigid attention but rolled their eyes in their eagerness to see the general of whom they had heard so much. Saint-Simon escorted Washington through the regiments in an informal review, and the general then rode back to the American camp where Lafayette's officers had drawn up the troops for inspection—the ragged light infantry that had criss-crossed Virginia in the marathon chase of Cornwallis, and Wayne's Pennsylvanians, whose mutiny and disgrace now seemed so long ago. Without these hungry and fever-ridden veterans, Washington knew, there could have been no great concentration before Yorktown. The general bowed gravely as field pieces roared in a twenty-one-gun salute.

Washington was escorted into the town, past the College of William and Mary where he had won his surveyor's license at seventeen, and down the sandy, winding main street he had known for most of his life. Everything was familiar to him here. A mile from the college, at the far end of the street, was the old Capitol, now abandoned, where he had served as a Virginia Burgess for twenty years. He passed Bruton Parish Church, in whose box pews he had sat so often—one of the last times on a day in 1774 when he had joined other Virginia leaders in a day of fasting and prayer to protest the closing of the port of Boston by the British. He turned past the weathered pink brick wall of Bruton down Palace Green, beneath a row of catalpa trees, and saw the Governor's Palace, little changed since he had first seen it more than thirty years before. He halted just beyond the church, before the home of his friend George Wythe, who had gone with the general to Congress and had signed the Declaration of Independence. Washington made headquarters in Wythe's house where for two weeks he was to direct final preparations for the siege of Yorktown. Rochambeau's headquarters were in a handsome frame house on an adjacent green, the home of the widowed Mrs. Peyton Randolph, whose husband had been the first president of Congress.

The commanders went to Saint-Simon's quarters where there was a reception for the officers of the army. Washington stood inside a doorway, flanked by Wayne and Hand, who presented men the general did not know personally. Washington and Rochambeau saluted, shook hands, and spoke briefly with each officer, until the whole corps had passed by. Later the commanders dined with senior officers, and despite the poverty of the armies, Saint-Simon's cooks served a lavish meal, complete with fine wines. A French band played popular tunes, including the quartet from Grétry's opera *Lucille*, whose theme—the happiness of a family at the arrival of its father—was interpreted as a tribute to Washington. The dinner ended at ten o'clock or later, and, as the Pennsylvania colonel Richard Butler said, the officers separated "after mutual congratulations and the greatest expressions of joy."

Washington was ill at ease as he retired, distressed over his failure to hear from de Grasse; if the Admiral had been defeated by the British fleet, the long marches and all else would have been in vain, and victory would be as far away as ever.

News from the fleet arrived late in the night. It came first to a picket line of Pennsylvania troops commanded by Lieutenant Feltman; a French officer stumbled in after midnight with a packet of letters from de Grasse, asking for men to guide him to Lafayette's quarters. Washington soon had the news in the Wythe House: De Grasse was back in the bay after fighting off the British fleet and damaging several enemy ships. He had captured two frigates—and most important of all, Admiral de Barras and his fleet had arrived from Rhode Island with siege artillery and salted meat for the armies. Washington slept content; the ring about Cornwallis was complete, or almost.

Washington reported de Grasse's victory to Congress, but added that the army's supplies were dangerously low; despite his best efforts to improve supply, he was not optimistic that his army, so near victory, would be well armed and well fed: "How far I shall succeed in my endeavours time must discover." The commander then turned to final details of the move against the enemy.

He wrote urgently to General Lincoln, who commanded the troops coming south: "Every day we now lose is comparatively an age. As soon as it is in our power with safety, we ought to take our position near the enemy. Hurry on, then, my dear Sir, with your troops on the wings of speed. . . ." Cornwallis, he wrote, was steadily improving his defenses, and each day's delay would cost more allied lives. He ordered Lincoln to land his regiments at College Landing on the James River, only two miles out of Williamsburg.

He sent Axel Fersen northward to order the boats on the upper Chesapeake to sail immediately. He sent Brigadier General George Weedon and a force of militia to watch the British outpost at Gloucester and prevent Cornwallis from escaping over the river. He ordered picket boats to guard the York River by night, so that the Earl could not escape upstream. He sent for General Arthur St. Clair and the newly enlisted troops of the Pennsylvania Line, so that the army would have overwhelming superiority during the siege.

On September 15 he wrote de Grasse requesting an interview aboard his flagship—he must convince the admiral that he should remain in the Chesapeake until Cornwallis had been taken, whatever the French plans for later operations. If the fleet left before the British surrendered, all would be lost.

Washington congratulated the army in general orders for the day as if victory had already been won. He dined with officers at Lafayette's quarters, and the next morning, September 16, he rode toward Yorktown with a few aides to reconnoiter the British lines; he learned little of the defenses of Cornwallis. He reviewed General Nelson's Virginia militia, and when he saw that some were in rags sent a plea to Richmond for uniforms. Washington dealt methodically with many other problems of the army.

He quickly resolved the matter of Baron von Steuben and his controversy with Virginians. Washington felt that the Baron had wrangled with state officials "from the warmth of his temper" and thought there should be no inquiry until the campaign was over. Since the Prussian was the army's most experienced officer in siege warfare, he asked his advice on the investment of Yorktown and reinstated him as inspector general of the army.

Steuben began at once to discipline the army for its final test. Ensign Ebenezer Denny of the Pennsylvanians, who had so lately fought in his first battle at Greenspring, once saw Steuben soon after dawn, on horseback with a couple of aides, waiting for men to come to drill. The Baron drove the troops hard for two hours, until they were ready for a public appearance. Denny had never seen American troops like these: "The guards are told off; officers take their posts, wheel by platoons to the right; fine corps of music . . . strikes up; the whole march off, saluting the Baron and field officer of the day as they pass."

But Steuben was by now a pauper. He had lost three horses during his year in Virginia and had bought others at inflated prices; his uniforms and camp equipment were in tatters. He had drawn $220,000 in inflated Continental currency, but it was worth no more than 150 guineas, he estimated. He asked Washington for a month's pay, in coin, but there was none. Steuben was forced to sell some of his silver spoons in camp in order to feed one of his aides, who was ill. He spent some of his last dollars entertaining French and American officers— "a great dinner," Claude Blanchard remembered with gratitude. The French commissary had been in need of a respite.

Blanchard had arrived in Williamsburg after a stormy voyage up the James in a tiny boat, chilled and soaked, stranded on numerous sandbars by an inept guide, and left in darkness at an unknown landing six or eight miles from the village. He had slept on the floor of a deserted house and finally made his way into Williamsburg to take over the task of feeding the troops. For days he had been the most harassed man in the armies:

> From this day, I set to work, although without a piece of paper or an employee or a bag of flour at my disposal; I was completely overwhelmed . . . my work was doubled; I caused ovens to be constructed, but I was in want of tools and I had to run about much and negotiate to obtain even a hammer . . . everybody applied to me for bread, vehicles and all possible necessaries. I was alone and had not a single employee to assist me.

After a week of frantic scurrying about, Claude Blanchard fell ill "of fatigue" and went to bed. Two men of his commissary staff finally arrived from the North, and he gave them orders from bed. His troubles had only begun.

Several French generals appeared, followed by ox carts loaded with silver, the tremendously heavy treasure brought from Havana by Admiral de Grasse. Blanchard was ordered to keep watch over the money. He saw the chests safely dragged into the house and sank back into his bed, "more oppressed than drowsy." Suddenly, the floor of the adjoining room caved in and 800,000 silver livres crashed into the cellar, followed by Blanchard's servant who slid down a beam and fell atop the hoard. Men labored for hours to recover the heavy boxes of coins which had been brought so far to aid the American cause.

De Grasse sent a boat for the army commanders, the *Queen Charlotte,* a sleek cutter captured from the English, and on September 17, Washington, Rochambeau, Henry Knox, and a few aides sailed down the James under a brisk breeze. By the morning of September 18, Washington and his party were in the broad waters of Hampton Roads and soon saw the thirty-two line of battle ships of de Grasse and de Barras, a fleet larger than Washington had ever seen—row after row of enormous ships riding at anchor, an impressive and reassuring sight. The party went aboard the *Ville de Paris* to meet de Grasse.

A story of the greeting between the commanding officers soon became one of the army's favorites and a part of Washington legend: the towering de Grasse embraced the taller Washington, kissed him on both cheeks and cried, "My dear little General!" The American officers roared with laughter, and the fat Knox shook in helpless mirth. The officers went into the admiral's cabin and conferred through interpreters; the conversation closely followed a list of written questions brought by Washington and answered forthrightly by de Grasse:

How long could the fleet remain here?

"The Instructions of Count de Grasse fix his departure to the 15th of October . . . But having already taken much upon himself, he will also engage to stay to the end of October."

Could the fleet remain to help in the siege of Yorktown, even if Saint-Simon's troops had to leave under a small convoy?

". . . as my Vessels will not depart before the 1st of November, you may count upon those Troops to that period, for the Reduction of York."

Could de Grasse send ships up the York, above Yorktown, to improve communications and shut in Cornwallis more completely?

"The thing is not impossible . . . but I suspend my definitive answer until I can reconnoitre . . . I shall certainly do every thing in my power." Washington was satisfied. De Grasse had agreed to stay two weeks longer than he had planned. Within forty days, with the aid of the fleet, the armies should be able to take Yorktown and force the surrender of Cornwallis. The general turned to lesser matters—requests for more men, cannon, and powder, and for the use of the fleet to blockade the Carolinas ports, Wilmington and Charleston. De Grasse offered the men, but only for the storming of Yorktown; he could spare some cannon, but little powder; his ships were not suited to the blockading of ports.

Afterward, de Grasse entertained his guests at dinner, took them below decks to inspect his flagship, and summoned the captains of his fleet, who came by barge to meet the American commander. Near sunset, the party left the *Ville de Paris* and was rowed to the *Queen Charlotte*. The guns of the flagship fired a salute, and the crews of the fleet manned the yards and tops in Washington's honor; the rigging of the ships was black with rows of men as far as the Americans could see.

The officers had hardly boarded the *Queen Charlotte* when a cold wind rose, blowing strongly toward the sea. The vessel made little headway up the river, but a few hours later the wind died and the officers were becalmed. Later, when a fresh breeze drove her onward, the *Charlotte* went hard aground, and Washington and his companions spent the night of September 19 on a sandbar. The next morning they were transferred to a frigate, the *Andromaque,* and after breakfast aboard Washington and Rochambeau began sailing upriver through choppy waters. They were hardly under way when they came upon the *Queen Charlotte,* which was afloat once more. Washington's party returned to the smaller craft and the commander went to his cabin to write letters and dispatches, but the rocking of the boat drove him from his desk; the *Queen* was forced to anchor near shore to ride out the storm.

On the morning of September 21, with the wind still raging, Washington insisted that the captain get under way, but after an hour or so of battering by the waves, he gave up. The *Queen Charlotte* again anchored inshore and the officers tossed miserably aboard during the dark day; Washington's one consolation was the sight of scores of flatboats, schooners, and scows at anchor in Hampton Roads, the fleet bearing his troops and guns from the North also waiting for the storm to pass so that they could sail up to Williamsburg.

September 22 dawned gray and windy, but Washington's patience was at an end. He left the *Queen Charlotte* for a small open boat and was laboriously rowed the thirty miles up the James, the craft hugging the shore to escape the full force of the wind. Near noon, cold and wet, the general's party entered College Creek and rode into Williamsburg. Six hours aboard the *Ville de Paris* with de Grasse had taken Washington from the armies for four and a half days. He was relieved to find that the enemy had hardly stirred in his absence; except for an attempted fire raid against a few French ships, the British had remained quietly in Yorktown.

Williamsburg had been filling with troops during the week;

General Lincoln and his staff had arrived from the North and Lieutenant Colonel John Laurens, the South Carolinian, had returned from his mission to Paris. Ammunition and supplies were accumulating at docks along the James, chiefly at Carter's Grove, the home of the Burwell family; they arrived, Trumbull noted, "in much better condition and with much less loss than could have been expected. Happy circumstance!"

Washington's hopes rose. He wrote to Heath in the North, "Lord Cornwallis is incessantly at work on his fortifications, and is probably preparing to defend himself to the last extremity; a little time will probably decide his fate; with the blessing of Heaven, I feel it will be favorable to the interests of America."

There was only one disturbing note as the armies prepared to move on Yorktown. A courier from the North had arrived in camp the day of Washington's return, with news of British naval reinforcements—Admiral Robert Digby had arrived with more warships, their number vaguely reported as from three to ten. Washington was not alarmed. The coming of Digby, he said, could not "have any influence on our operations while there are thirty-six French ships of the line in the Bay." But the commander hurried a report to de Grasse by a special courier, Baron von Closen.

The Baron went aboard the *Ville de Paris,* to discover that the news of Digby's arrival "alarmed and disquieted these excitable gentlemen of the navy, who think only of cruises and battles, and do not like to oblige or to cooperate with land troops." Naval officers urged de Grasse to leave the bay so that the English would not again catch him at the mercy of the tide. Closen returned rapidly to headquarters with a message from the admiral. Washington heard the dispatch translated with dismay. The enemy in American waters was now nearly his equal in strength, de Grasse wrote, and he must have his fleet ready to fight. He would leave his anchorage and cruise outside the capes, and contrary winds might prevent his return.

Washington and his officers were stunned by the final words of the admiral's dispatch:

> I will sail with my forces towards New York . . . If the enemy do not come out, it is evident because they dare not. We shall then consider what course to pursue. In the meantime you will push Cornwallis vigorously, and we will act in concert, each on his own side.
>
> I shall set sail as soon as the wind permits.

Washington's distress at his abandonment by the navy was made clear in the strong protest he wrote immediately:

> I am unable to describe the painful anxiety under which I have labored since the reception of your letter . . . the attempt upon York under the protection of your shipping, is as certain of success, as a superior force . . . can render any military operation . . . the capture of the British army is so important in itself . . . that it must greatly tend to bring an end to the war . . . If you quit the Bay . . . The consequence will be the disgrace of abandoning a design on which are founded the fairest hopes of the allied forces, after a prodigious expense, fatigue, and exertions . . . your leaving the Bay ruins the cause to all intents and purposes. Consider the good of the common cause. . . .

Washington argued that the report of a large force under Digby might be "absolutely false," and that in any event the British fleet could not defeat de Grasse in the Chesapeake.

The General sent his dispatch by Lafayette, who was now recovered from his fever, and asked him to plead with the admiral to hold his fleet in place. The weary Closen accompanied Lafayette, complaining that "the weather was devilish, the sea was rough, and I . . . had two hours of tossing in a bitch of an open launch, where I was pretty well soaked by the oarsmen."

While he awaited a reply from de Grasse, Washington sent reinforcements to General George Weedon, who commanded militia on the north bank of the York near Gloucester Point, and persuaded Rochambeau to send Lauzun and his Legion there to face the horsemen of Banastre Tarleton. He supervised the brigading of troops still arriving daily from the North and prepared to move heavy artillery from the wharves. He also distributed food and supplies, which now came in more plentifully from farmers on Virgina's eastern shore—who refused Continental currency and demanded payment in French silver. Preparatory marching orders were issued to the army's vanguard, as if the general were confident that the mercurial French admiral would reconsider and hold his position.

On September 27 Washington had his reply from de Grasse, an almost casual dispatch describing a naval council of war in which the admiral's officers had overruled him: ". . . the plans I had suggested for getting underway, while the most brilliant and glorious, did not appear to fulfil the aims we had in view." The fleet would not leave the bay. Cornwallis was still surrounded.

Washington drew up his order of battle and directed the army to be ready to march at dawn. His officers intended that the troops should look the part of conquerors, and that the Americans should not be embarrassed by the stylish French, whatever the sacrifice. The orders read to one brigade said sternly:

. . . every officer will be anxious to have his men look as neat and respectable as possible.

The Commissary will issue 12 lbs. of flour to each regiment, for the purpose of powdering their hair; the men will take care to be well shaven.

The armies were ready for the last march of the campaign.

10

"THE LIBERTIES OF AMERICA...ARE IN OUR HANDS"

The troops moved out of Williamsburg at daybreak over sandy woodland roads toward Yorktown, seven miles to the east. It was 5:00 A.M., September 28, little more than a month since Washington had slipped away from Henry Clinton in New York to begin the race for Virginia. The day was already warm when the column moved off, the Americans in front, following their pickets on a worn road that lay ankle-deep in sand. By noon, the hot gray powder burned the feet of the troops and rose about them in choking clouds. They saw no sign of the enemy on the march.

Today the men had no eyes for the somber beauty of the flat country—the narrow road masked by thickets of bayberry, catbrier, and holly; pine and hardwood forests seen through shimmering heat waves; melancholy vistas of sluggish tidal creeks flowing to the York where enormous herons flapped away over the marshes at the approach of the troops. Shaggy black cedars and giant cypress towered above the lush waterside undergrowth. There were frequent clearings, unkempt

fields of tobacco, cotton, and corn, long since ravaged by passing armies. It was the country of the first colonists; across the
wide river was the legendary site where, by John Smith's tale,
Pocahontas had saved the Captain's life.

The troops were impressed by the strength of the army when
they saw it stretched out on the road; Lieutenant Feltman of
the Pennsylvanians estimated the Continentals at fifteen thousand and found the militia beyond his counting. There were
few who did not march—a guard of two hundred remained in
Williamsburg with the stores and the sick and wounded men.
Claude Blanchard stayed behind in the village, where he and
one helper worked at a frenzied pace to care for three hundred
sick and wounded. Blanchard complained that though he had
only ten officers among the three hundred, these were harder
to please than all the rest. At the head of the French column
moving toward Yorktown was a fugitive from the hospital, the
Marquis de Saint-Simon, who was ill with malaria but rode in
a litter, determined to lead his troops into the siege lines. One
of Saint-Simon's engineers took heart at sight of the motley
band of Americans marching in front:

> Six regiments of regulars, disciplined, hardened, and in
> condition to fight in the line . . . twenty-five hundred
> militiamen of the country; and five hundred riflemen or
> mountaineers . . . these last two troops are not in uniform,
> they wear baggy breeches with or without shoes . . . good
> marksmen for skirmishing in the woods, but not for fight-
> ing in the line. . . .

The army halted for two or three hours at noon, and despite
the heat scores of cooking fires sprang up at the roadside. The
latest of Washington's orders, a grim one, was read to the
troops: if the British came out to meet them, they were to
settle the matter with cold steel in hand to hand fighting; the
allies would use the bayonet.

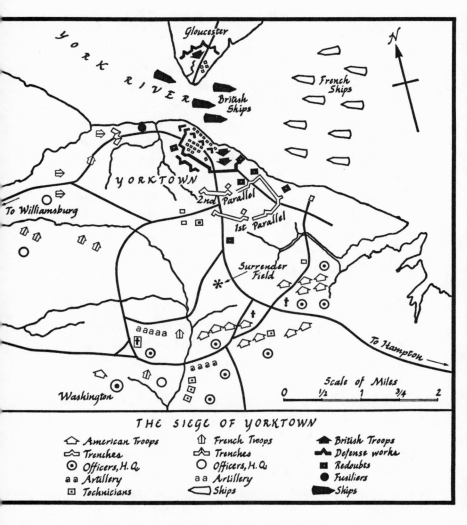

The Trap: Washington Encircles Yorktown

The column divided soon after the march was resumed, the French moving to the left, on the more direct road to Yorktown, and the Americans to the right. It was about three o'clock when the French came within sight of Yorktown and met the first enemy troops, a few pickets who fell back quietly. The French moved into position at the edge of a woodland and along creek banks without exposing themselves, anchoring their left on the high bank of the York upstream from the town. Their line ran inland to their right until it met the American position at the edge of a marsh.

On the far right, to the south of the town, the Americans were halted before a swamp where bridges had been burned. As the troops waited in the open, several platoons of green-coated enemy horsemen rode out as if to charge, but a few rounds of grapeshot turned them back. The allied army waited in the late afternoon.

Washington reconnoitered as if he were impatient for a look at the enemy. He rode out in the American front on his new horse Nelson, a light sorrel, sixteen hands high, with white face and legs. The General studied the British right with his telescope.

The landscape was not strange to him—the town was built on land which had belonged to Nicholas Martiau,* the first of his American ancestors, and the General had been here often. He had gambled on cockfights in Yorktown in his youth.

Washington saw that Cornwallis had thrown up forbidding fortifications, his flanks anchored on the river bank both above and below the town with small forts—redoubts guarded by bristling rows of sharpened logs. The redoubt on the left, at the river bank, was a large work whose guns covered the French front. On the French end of the line some British warships were anchored close inshore where their guns could

* An early Huguenot settler, also an ancestor of Queen Elizabeth II of England.

sweep the crossing of Yorktown Creek and its deep ravine. Beyond this line lay the town's inner ring of defenses, even more imposing, commanded by seven redoubts with at least half a dozen gun batteries.

In the center of the British position, the land rose above the flanking creeks which seeped down to the York. The obvious approach to the town's defenses was here, across a barren, sandy plain sparsely covered with sedges and browning grass and bear-paw cactus. On the right the plain fell away in a sheer bluff to the riverside, forty feet below. Looking northward across the York, Washington saw the British outpost on Gloucester Point—a log palisade and a few white tents. Downstream, where the river's mouth widened between marshy headlands, he could see almost into the Chesapeake; a few of de Grasse's ships rode there at anchor.

His reconnaissance convinced Washington that the enemy could be blasted into submission, and he ordered the heavy guns moved up, especially the eighty pieces of French siege artillery brought down from Rhode Island by Admiral de Barras—battering cannon and enormous mortars. Some of these had already been put ashore at Trebell's Landing on the James, in the rear of the army, and dragged painfully through swampy soil at the landing; they must now be hauled to the front over six miles of sandy road.

The army spent the first night in the open in the crudest of encampments. The headquarters tents had not come up, and Washington slept under a mulberry tree. The night was quiet except for the sound of the axes of work parties rebuilding bridges across the marsh; the troops settled uncomfortably. There was a night-long search for drinking water. Sergeant Martin of the Sappers and Miners waded through ponds where the Army's horses were watered and brought up his buckets "thick with mud and filth . . . and full of frogs." The men drank this water because they could not stomach the foul-smelling springs, which "tasted like copperas water . . . that had been standing in iron or copper vessels."

There was one consolation. The woods were full of hogs, and Martin and his companions ran down a few of the fatter ones; the aroma of roasting pork soon drifted across the woods and fields. Men in the Pennsylvania camp were busy during the night taking prisoners, dozens of British deserters who had straggled out from the town. The army was cheerful despite the hardships of the open camp, and men detected an air of optimism at headquarters. Dr. Thacher noted in his diary an "unbounded confidence in our . . . commanders," and forecast a British surrender. The troops lay on their arms all night.

Men in the British trenches were shaken by the sight of allied troops settling into position about them. One soldier wrote, ". . . the whole camp was in alarm . . . Tents were hastily removed and all the baggage taken into the town."

Lieutenant James was astounded by the enemy's strength and put his gunners to work immediately:

At noon the enemy appeared in front of our works, in force about 26,000, extending from right to left of our lines; and a number of them advancing to reconnoitre a ravine in front of my battery. I opened a fire on them until they dispersed.

Many of the British were fiercely defiant. Captain Samuel Graham of a Highland regiment overheard an aging Scot lieutenant mutter to himself as he drew his sword and glared out at the enemy, "Come on, Maister Washington, I'm uncommon glad to see you; I've been offered money for my commission, but I could na think of gangin home without a sight of you. Come on."

The American army changed position at seven o'clock the next morning, crossing the marsh in its front and moving to the right. British gunners opened on the exposed infantry, and one man's leg was mangled by a cannon ball. Surgeon Thacher amputated the leg while the fully conscious soldier screamed in agony. A few more British cannon fired during the day, but no one was hit.

The infantry lay in the heat while Washington and his officers reconnoitered the enemy works once more; the general was nettled by de Grasse's refusal to send ships through the narrows above Yorktown to aid in the siege, and he spent most of the day puzzling out a plan of attack without the support of the French fleet in the river. The French admiral had problems of his own, as he explained to Washington:

> I am impatient as your Excellency can be that the Wind will not permit Vessels . . . to ascend the York River. The Sea is not like the Land . . . and we have not yet found out a method of sailing against the Wind. But I assure your Excellency that the moment it can be done it shall be done, be it by day or night if the pilots will undertake it.

The difficulties of the fleet were not to be solved. Unfavorable winds kept its ships out of the York until it was too late to aid Washington.

It was 4:00 P.M. before the infantry settled into their new camp east of Beaver Dam Creek near Yorktown, and each brigade dug a short trench to protect its outposts. The American riflemen exchanged a few shots with the Hessian Jagers, who were sniping with their short rifles from the trenches.

The two headquarters tents were pitched during the day, the worn canvas shelters in which Washington had lived since taking command of the army outside Boston more than five years before. The General slept on a hard cot in the inner chamber of his smaller tent—the business of the army was conducted in the dining tent, so large that forty or fifty officers could be entertained at dinner. The weather-beaten gray tents stood well beyond enemy cannon range, near the center of Washington's position; as always, they were surrounded by picked veterans of his Life Guard, who screened visitors with care.

Sentries posted in the allied rear were on special alert after nightfall, since the orders of the day had included a stern warning against straying from the camp:

> Our ungenerous enemy having, as usual, propagated the smallpox in this part of the country, the Commander-in-chief forbids . . . any communication, with the houses or inhabitants in the neighborhood, or borrowing any utensils from them.

The pickets failed to detect a large-scale movement of the British from their front during the night—a surprising withdrawal from the outer lines.

Banastre Tarleton noted only that the armies regarded each other with "cautious attention," but in the Hessian trenches Johann Doehla realized at once that serious fighting was at hand. At ten o'clock in the morning a young German picket was shot nearby and died soon afterward. Doehla helped to bury him in the warm sand. At noon another private was wounded by a rifleman on the same post, and Doehla held the writhing boy while the ball was cut from between his shoulder blades. Four others were wounded at this position during the day—and more than thirty British and German soldiers in the outer works were hit.

Late in the day a party of French infantry and cavalry advanced to attack Tarleton's troops, who fell back under the cover of an artillery battery. Lieutenant James and his sailors drove off the French with seven rounds of eighteen-pound shot.

Just after dark a dispatch boat rowed into Yorktown harbor with a message from Clinton—a fleet of twenty-three ships was being sent from New York to rescue the garrison: "At a meeting of the General and Flag Officers held this day; it is determined, that above 5000 men . . . shall be embarked . . . in a few days to relieve you. . . ."

Cornwallis was urged to be on the alert: a British fleet would sail to the entrance of the Chesapeake and fire its guns. If all was well in Yorktown, Cornwallis was to signal with columns of smoke. Cornwallis reacted unexpectedly to this new promise of relief from the north. His reply to Clinton opened cheerfully:

> Sir, I have ventured these last two days to look General Washington's whole force in the face in the position on the outside of my works . . . there was but one wish throughout the whole army, which was, that the enemy would advance.

But then the Earl announced his surrender of the outer works:

> I have this morning received your letter of the 24th, which has given me the greatest satisfaction. I shall retire this night within the works, and have no doubt, if relief arrives at any reasonable time, York and Gloucester will be both in possession of his majesty's troops.

Tarleton thought the Earl had given a premature order for abandonment of his strong outer line, since it could not be assaulted by the allies until they had brought up their heavy guns. "Time would have been gained by holding and disputing the ground inch by inch," Tarleton said. To give it up was to "coop the troops up in the unfinished works" and hasten the surrender of the British army.

The troops pulled back from the outer line at one o'clock in the morning, "all in silence," as Corporal Popp said, "because the enemy always came nearer." The British were now confined to Yorktown itself.

As they retreated Johann Doehla saw eight Germans slip away to desert to the enemy; three of them were from his own regiment.

One of the first Americans to discover that the British had pulled back from their outer line was Colonel Alexander Scammell, the field officer of the day. Some of his pickets had learned the truth just after dawn, when they found an empty redoubt near the road to Williamsburg. Scammell rode forward with a few men to inspect the deserted outpost. It cost him his life.

The New Hampshire colonel saw a patrol of horsemen on the misty plain; Americans, he thought, but as he inspected the empty works the cavalrymen—they were Tarleton's dragoons—surrounded him and made him prisoner. Scammell's men escaped but were still nearby when a dragoon shot the colonel in the back, after his surrender.

Colonel van Cortlandt came up soon afterward to relieve Scammell and heard the story from the pickets. They knew only that their colonel had been wounded and hurried away roughly toward Yorktown, still alive; no one knew whether the British dragoon had shot Scammell in cold blood or by accident, unaware that he had already surrendered.

By eight o'clock it was clear that the British had evacuated all three commanding posts of the outer line, and the allied troops moved into them without opposition. Washington and Rochambeau could hardly believe their good fortune; once the big guns had come up, they would have a clear field of fire into Yorktown from the positions given up by Cornwallis. Washington wrote President John McKean of Congress, "We are in possession of very advantageous grounds, which command their line of works." Dr. Thacher, who was near headquarters throughout this Sunday, noted that the army was "agreeably surprised" to be presented these earthworks, "which might have cost us much labor and many lives to obtain by force." Rochambeau learned of the move from his night duty officer, Baron d'Èsebeck, and rode out with Count Deux-Ponts and other officers. They inspected the new line from end to end. Deux-Ponts recorded the French reaction: "The enemy ought to have kept these redoubts until they were forced to abondon them . . . it would have compelled us to feel our way, and would have held us in doubt; it would have retarded our works . . . instead of leaving us masters of all the approaches to the place. . . ."

The Frenchmen found that the earthworks were well placed and joined by covered approaches, so that they could be made impregnable. The redoubts were not solid and their sandy walls were so thin that Rochambeau thought they needed reinforcement. He sent a few picked men into the abandoned redoubts and moved up the bulk of his force behind the new line, where they were sheltered from British guns. The enemy fired eight or ten rounds on this front without a hit.

On the far left of the allied line, near the river, Saint-Simon's men fought the only skirmish of the day. These troops followed reconnoitering officers into a woodland near the river and drove out enemy pickets who had been sniping at them but came under a hail of bullets and grapeshot from the fort. A French hussar was killed, and ten men were wounded, one of them M. de Bouillet, an officer of the Agenais regiment, whose thigh was broken by a cannon ball.

By early afternoon men of the allied army were swarming over the new works, deepening trenches, and throwing up mounds of sand. Engineers began laying out positions for the artillery, which was still to come. In the distance they could see the British troops equally busy, strengthening the inner works of Yorktown. Colonel Richard Butler of the Pennsylvania troops reported high morale in his trenches, where "every thing goes on with spirit." Lieutenant Feltman of Butler's command made a bet of a beaver hat with his Captain that the British would not surrender by the next Sunday.

In the early afternoon Feltman and his friend Lieutenant Tilden walked out to see the new works and saw a redcoat walking across the open with a white flag. The Englishman had a letter from Colonel Scammell asking that his servant and some clothing be sent back to Williamsburg, where he was to go on parole after British surgeons had dressed his wound.

Washington was out reconnoitering again during the day. He rode first to an abandoned British redoubt under enormous poplar trees with several of his generals, an enticing target for enemy gunners. Philip van Cortlandt sat in this redoubt, studying the nearest British artillery position, which was about a mile away. He saw a puff of gray smoke; a cannon ball flew above the heads of Washington's party, showering van Cortlandt with poplar twigs. The generals did not move until a second shot plowed into the earth about fifty feet away, and then they spurred toward the rear, except for Washington who sat his horse in the open, calmly sweeping the distant front of the enemy with his spyglass. Though he remained there for some time, the British did not fire again.

Back at his headquarters Washington dealt with some of the day's problems: he ordered deserters halted at the front, especially those with smallpox, warned his men against wearing red coats on duty, and ordered twelve hundred men to gather materials for strengthening the earthworks.

There was also a message from Lafayette, who blithely asked Washington to put him in command of all American forces before Yorktown and to transfer General Lincoln to the Gloucester side of the river. He argued that Lincoln's reputation was already established and added with an air of confidence, "I am sure you will be so very kind to me as to adopt any plan consistent with propriety that may bring on an event so highly interesting to me. . . ."

Washington refused him gently but firmly, and Lincoln remained as second in command.

Lafayette also still feared that Cornwallis might escape inland up the York River: "I am far from laughing at the idea of the enemy's making a retreat. It is not very probable, but it is not impossible." This drew smiles from headquarters staff officers, but it was an accurate forecast of what Cornwallis was to attempt within a few days.

Sometime during the day Washington sent Marquis de Choisy by water to de Grasse's flagship to ask for six hundred or eight hundred marines to join the siege at Gloucester. They came immediately, but de Grasse was not always so cooperative. Once when asked for thirty pounds of artillery candles he refused, "Damn it! You have stretched the blanket too tight." He soon apologized to Rochambeau, "I am a Provençal, and a sailor, which is enough to entitle me to a quick temper and I acknowledge my fault and trust in your friendship."

In every camp of the army, sergeants called out Washington's exhortations in the orders of the day:

> The General . . . expects and requires the officers and soldiers . . . to pursue the duties of their respective departments . . . with the most unabating ardour. The present moment . . . will decide American independence . . . the passive conduct of the enemy argues his weakness . . . the liberties of America and the honour of the Allied Arms are in our hands.

Thirty men were killed or wounded in the British lines in the brief Sunday morning skirmish. Lieutenant James watched the French attack on the fusiliers' redoubt: "After a smart action of two hours they were repulsed with some loss, retreating into the woods with the utmost precipitance and confusion, our batteries having much galled them."

Stephan Popp, who watched from the trenches as three French charges were beaten back, recorded the victory in his diary, but added glumly, "This month we had hard work and poor provisions."

Washington neglected his diary during the first days of October, noting that "nothing of importance" happened on the lines. It was not so with men on the front, nearest the enemy.

At daybreak on October 1 the troops saw the first signs of the enemy's distress, scores of gaunt horses shambling about in the mist, driven from Yorktown, where they could no longer be fed. The starving animals stumbled weakly across the sand, heads down. British deserters who came into the lines soon afterward said that hundreds of horses had been slaughtered on the beach at Yorktown, and Surgeon Thacher often saw their bloated carcasses bobbing down the York—six hundred or seven hundred, he estimated, a pathetic end for the fine blooded animals Cornwallis had seized in his march through the South.

Other pitiable refugees from Yorktown lay in woods near the allied camp, bands of sick and starving Negroes no longer able to work, most of them dying of smallpox. Sergeant Martin saw them everywhere—dead and dying, with pieces of burnt Indian corn in their hands and mouths, even those who were already dead.

The American sector now became a vast labor camp. One third of the troops were sent to the woods, where they hacked down thousands of saplings and slashed branches from trees. Twigs were tied into thick bundles, known as fascines, for use in filling trenches and making earthworks. Saplings were driven into the earth in small circles and woven with branches to form bottomless wicker baskets—gabions—which were to be filled with soil in new fortifications. The work went on until the woods and roadsides were piled high with these materials for the trenches Washington planned to open nearer the enemy. Preparations for the parallel, from which the big guns would fire, occupied the army for more than a week. In some camps, workmen hammered away at heavy boards, building platforms for the artillery.

Long lines of men tugged at ropes, hauling the big guns into position by hand. They were relieved by herds of tiny oxen of the neighborhood, but the work was slow until October 4, when the huge workhorses of the army arrived from the North after a four-hundred-mile overland drive. Washington and other general officers sent their own horses and wagons to the rear to help move the guns and ammunition. The commander betrayed his restiveness in an order to the army: ". . . it is of the utmost importance that the Heavy Artillery should be brought up without a moment's loss of time."

While this work went on, strong parties of pickets filed out into no-man's land as darkness fell each night. Whole regiments moved away into the dusk, to lie all night on the plain between the armies, guarding those who worked on the line. Casualties were light, for the British fire dwindled after nightfall—a Pennsylvania officer lay awake during the night of October 1 and counted an average of ten rounds of cannon fire each hour. Men of Hazen's Canadian regiment went out to cut underbrush where an engineer had staked a new trench, but the enemy did not fire on them. Captain James Duncan was mystified by the British failure to fire: "I am at a loss to account for it, for the moon shone bright, and by the help of their night glasses they must certainly have discovered us." Duncan's men were relieved at daybreak, and just as they moved out of the position, enemy fire began falling there.

By day, any Allied officer who exposed himself drew fire

from Yorktown, and when generals and engineers rode in large parties, Tarleton's horsemen often galloped out after them. Washington kept up a constant reconnaissance, hiding his escorts behind small hills or in woods, hoping to entice the British into a trap. Ensign Denny, in Wayne's ranks, was amused by the chasing back and forth; it was like a boys' game of prisoner's base, he thought.

From the British trenches, Corporal Popp realized that hope of the army's escape was fading: "October 1 the enemy began to fortify heavily to really block us up. They threw no shots against us, because they had no cannon yet. But we fired steadily upon them and destroyed much of their labor again. We . . . had no rest day or night. . . ."

Near midnight of October 1, British sentries caught a Negro deserter as he tried to slip through the lines and took from him a letter sent out by a Yorktown merchant. The letter revealed the "state of the garrison's distress," Lieutenant James noted indignantly. The merchant was arrested at once.

British gunners kept up a steady fire to disrupt the placement of allied artillery; they often flashed powder charges at their gun muzzles to simulate fire, forcing the Americans to dive for cover. On October 2 the cannonade increased, and the enemy soon taught Washington's reckless troops to be more cautious. An American drummer who stood to watch the enemy artillery was struck by a cannon ball. A militiaman clambered atop a parapet and capered about for hours, growing bolder as he drew the attention of the army. He shouted defiance, "Damn my soul if I'll dodge for the buggers!" He shook his spade at every ball that flew nearby until at last he was hit, and his mangled body was flung into a trench.

Four men of a Pennsylvania regiment were killed by the same cannon ball; and Lieutenant Feltman saw one of his corporals die in anguish, the victim of a nine-pound iron shot that passed through his rump.

This heavy fire had no effect upon Washington's composure during his frequent visits to the front. An enemy ball once fell so close by as to cover a chaplain's hat with sand, and the frightened minister held out his hat to Washington. The general smiled. "Mr. Evans," he said, "you'd better carry that home, and show it to your wife and children."

Each day more deserters came out from the village—German and British, infantry and cavalry. Four dragoons slipped away from enemy lines and surrendered to American riflemen. But there were also American deserters. Lieutenant Feltman watched a ludicrous chase as a Maryland soldier fled across the open one afternoon, bound for the British lines. Feltman sent his servant in pursuit, but the Marylander was too fleet; he dropped his musket and other equipment but soon disappeared into the enemy lines.

A man who deserted from Captain James Duncan's regiment one night pointed out the Pennsylvanians' position to British gunners, but their aim was inaccurate, and they halted after a few rounds. Washington tried to halt his losses by issuing a stern general order: "Every Deserter from the American Troops after this public Notice is given who shall be found within the enemies lines at York, if the place falls into our hands, will be instantly Hanged."

At about 10:00 P.M. on October 2, British ships moored in the York opened a storm of fire, which soon died away. The mysterious cannonade covered the passage of British cavalrymen across the river to Gloucester, where they were to escort infantrymen of the outpost on a foraging party. The movement set the stage for a colorful clash on the Gloucester plain.

American militia led by General George Weedon had surrounded the British fort at Gloucester, but, as the Duke de

Lauzun said, at a distance of fifteen miles. The French hussar chief scorned Weedon as an officer "who detested fighting . . . terribly afraid of gunshot." The Frenchman did not realize that Washington had ordered Weedon, a brave veteran of northern campaigns, to keep his poorly trained infantry beyond the reach of British dragoons posted at Gloucester.

Lauzun was little more pleased with the Marquis de Choisy, who had arrived to command the infantry: "An excellent and worthy man, absurdly violent in temper, constantly in a rage, quarreling with everybody and without common sense."

This oddly matched trio—the titled Frenchmen Lauzun and Choisy, and the ex-innkeeper Weedon—was soon to meet Banastre Tarleton and his fearsome Legion.

The British marched out from their garrison on the morning of October 3, foraging toward the north, robbing Gloucester farmyards and filling wagons with their loot. The infantry turned back after a few hours, but Tarleton, eager for action, laid an ambush for a troop of Virginia cavalrymen hanging about the rear. He stumbled into the whole allied force, led by Lauzun and Choisy, and narrowly escaped.

Lauzun stopped to ask directions as he rode toward the scene:

I saw a very pretty woman at the door of a little farm house on the high road . . . and questioned her. She told me that Colonel Tarleton had left her house a moment before, that he was very anxious to shake hands with the French Duke. I assured her that I had come on purpose to gratify him. She seemed very sorry for me, judging from experience, I suppose, that Tarleton was irresistible. The American troops seemed to be of the same opinion.

The Frenchman was hardly a hundred yards from this house when he met the enemy:

I saw the English cavalry in force three times my own. I charged it without halting; we met hand to hand. Tarleton saw me and rode towards me with pistol raised. We were about to fight singlehanded between the two troops when his horse was thrown by one of his own dragoons pursued by one of my lancers. I rode up to capture him. A troop of English dragoons rode in between and covered his retreat; he left his horse with me.

After a brief, bloody clash in which the despised American militia shattered a charge by Tarleton, Lauzun drove the green-coated dragoons back into the Gloucester fort, taking a few prisoners. He estimated British losses at one officer and fifty men.

Tarleton explained that his retreat was the result of an accident—a flying French spear struck a dragoon's horse, which reared and plunged, threw Tarleton from his mount, and put the English rear guard to flight. The cavalry's retreat, Tarleton said, was ordered "to afford them the opportunity of recovering from their confusion." He reported that the French had sixteen casualties and admitted to twelve of his own.

It was the last British foraging party in Gloucester, and the final action of the campaign on the north shore of the river. As Tarleton said, "The next day General de Choisy, being reinforced by a detachment of marines, proceeded to cut off all land communication between the country and Gloucester."

On the same day, Cornwallis wrote Clinton from Yorktown, conceding that he was surrounded, and that the enemy had built threatening new fortifications:

I expect they will go on with their Work this night. From the time that the Enemy have given us, and in uncommon exertion of the Troops our works are in a better state of defence than we had reason to hope.

I can see no means of forming a junction with me but

by York river, and I do not think that any diversion would be of use to us. . . .

By October 5 Washington was almost ready for his first decisive move—to open a parallel, a new trench in advance of his line, much nearer the enemy. The long excavation must be done in one night. By now, as Jonathan Trumbull of the staff said, scores of big guns were ranked together in the rear and had begun to "look respectable." Still Washington refused to open with his artillery. Not an allied shell would be fired until all the guns were in place.

The seasons changed abruptly during the night. A cold wind swept in from the bay, bringing a wintry rain. Men in the camps at the rear huddled about their fires. There was an early dusk, and the night was stormy. Most of the troops lay miserably in the open lines, but at least one party went off into the dark toward the enemy—a few engineers and a squad of sappers and miners, Sergeant Martin among them. The engineers led the way to the site of the new line, and Martin's men went to work, laying strips of pine on the wet sand to mark the course of the trenches. An engineer officer halted them: "All right, men. Stop and hold your position. We're going up front—don't move a foot from this spot until we return."

While the engineers prowled about on their mysterious business, Martin and his mates waited in the blowing rain, almost motionless, staring out at the dim lights of Yorktown. They were interrupted. No one knew who he was, nor where he had come from, but a tall man was suddenly beside them, wrapped in heavy clothing. He wore a cape, Martin thought, but it was too dark to be sure.

"Where are the engineers?" the stranger said.

The soldiers explained, but Martin was becoming nervous; they were unarmed, without support, and the enemy trenches were little more than two hundred yards away. The big man was inquisitive; he asked what troops they were, talked familiarly with them for a few minutes, and went off in the direction the officers had gone.

As he left the stranger said, "If you're captured out here, be sure the enemy doesn't find out that you're sappers and miners." Martin grinned wryly after the tall man, but, as he soon wrote in his diary, the troops needed none of this advice —they were always uneasily aware that they would be given no quarter if captured but would be executed at once, as terrorists beyond the protection of "the laws of warfare."

Martin and his men identified the stranger when he returned with the engineers, who continually called him "Your Excellency." Martin realized that their companion was Washington: "Had we dared, we might have cautioned him for exposing himself so carelessly to danger at such a time, and doubtless he would have taken it in good part if we had."

But the enemy did not stir. Rain began to fall harder, whipped by a rising wind, and the engineers ordered Martin's men back to their camp. It was the end of the night's work. Tomorrow night, they would dig the parallel.

Far in front of the British lines, no more than five hundred paces from the allied trenches, Johann Doehla took his two-hour turn of duty. He lay on the ground until he was stiff and then rose cautiously to sit, watching the enemy; he did not stand for fear that the Americans would see him against the sky. When the rain lessened he could hear every relief of patrols and outposts of both armies, and the exchange of watchwords and countersigns in French, English, or German.

Doehla found this duty lonely and dangerous: "Everything must proceed quietly. One dares call out neither to sentry nor patrol except to give only the agreed signal. Nor does one dare to smoke tobacco nor make a fire. The men call it the 'lost post' with all justice."

11

THE LAST
CANNONADE

A steady southeast wind drove intermittent showers across the Yorktown peninsula and into the British lines in the cloudy dawn of October 6. It was allied weather; if it held, the night would be ideal for digging the new parallel line nearer the enemy.

Washington wrote President McKean of Congress confidently, "We shall this night open trenches." He ordered 4300 men to be ready for duty after dark—1500 of them to dig the new line and the others to stand guard over the workmen. The General spent most of the day with his engineers and artillery officers, watching the guns and trenching materials move toward the front. The American position was acrawl with columns of men bringing up wickerwork gabions and fascines, but Washington was not satisfied. Several regiments had been making more gabions since sunrise; they finished the task at noon and carried the huge baskets to the front, only 400 paces from the enemy.

Headquarters had depressing news from Williamsburg during the day—Alexander Scammell was dead of his wounds. Washington had lost one of his favorite staff officers, a renowned story teller who was said to be the only man who could make the commander laugh. The staff remembered Scammell as a young Harvard graduate who had volunteered at the beginning of the war, had become the army's adjutant general, but had insisted on the combat duty on which he had died. Headquarters officers could only mutter helplessly of British barbarity. Washington named John Laurens of South Carolina to take over Scammell's Light Infantry Regiment, an almost inevitable choice. Laurens, the son of a wealthy planter, was known as one of the bravest men in the army; in cavalry actions in the South he had fought so recklessly that some officers had resigned rather than ride with him.

The picked troops began to gather in mid-afternoon for the night's work, and despite optimism at headquarters, there was an air of tension in the camp. John Lamb, the artilleryman, told a friend, "You may depend on its being a night of business." Claude Blanchard feared that his little medical corps would be overwhelmed by casualties.

The troops moved out behind the engineers soon after nightfall, carrying fascines and gabions, muskets, pickaxes and spades, trailed by wagons loaded with sandbags. They halted in the open about eight hundred yards from the British. Sergeant Martin and his Sappers and Miners were on the line, at the spot where they had met Washington the night before—and Martin noted that the commander in chief had also returned. Washington struck a few blows with a pick axe, a mere ceremony the Sergeant noted, so "that it might be said 'Gen Washington with his own hands first broke ground at the siege of Yorktown.'"

When the General stopped, the men fell to the task. The gabions were placed in rows, and the soft, sandy soil from the ditch was thrown into them so that there was soon a four-foot trench behind a sturdy breastwork. For more than two hours there was only the steady rhythm of the picks and spades in the earth; the enemy was quiet.

The new trench was two thousand yards long, running from the head of Yorktown creek near the center, across the Hampton road, and thence in a long arc to the bluff above the York. The line was divided equally between French and American troops. The men also built four strong points on the line to prevent the trench from being overrun. On the northernmost end of the French front, a narrow support trench was cut, leading to a new battery position from which guns could reach British ships in the river.

The French had been ordered to divert British attention from American workmen with a false attack, but firing broke out prematurely at nine o'clock; Washington had a report that a French deserter had slipped away and alerted the enemy. Cannon and rocket fire was turned on the French from the

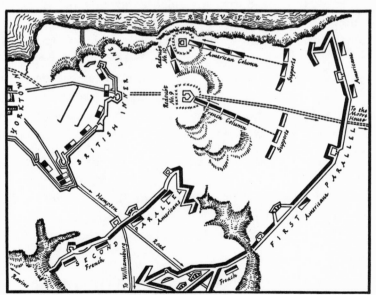

Attack on the Redoubts, October 14, 1781

fusiliers' redoubt, but there was only an occasional shot from other parts of the British line. The Americans had a ruse of their own—a detachment posted near a marsh built large camp-fires, and men passed back and forth before them, drawing British fire. All the while, Sergeant Martin said, "we were entrenching literally under their noses." The night-long rain, now a drizzle, now a downpour, hampered only the British gunners; the Americans were never halted in their work, and the line grew rapidly.

At dawn British sentries looked out across the plain to see an entire new allied trench just out of musket range, manned by troops already under cover. The British rolled out two field guns and fired a few rounds, providing an unexpected diversion for the Americans. A large English bulldog raced across the open and jumped the new trench in chase of the cannon balls. American officers ordered their men to catch the dog so that they could send a message into Yorktown, but the men refused. "He looked too formidable for any of us to encounter," Sergeant Martin said.

During the morning Lieutenant Colonel Alexander Hamilton led his light infantry into the new trench with drums beating and flags flying. Captain James Duncan, who marched with the color guard, was relieved when they had planted the flags on the parapet without losing a man. He was astonished by Hamilton's next move, which "wantonly exposed" his troops:

> We were ordered to mount the bank, front the enemy, and there by word of command go through all the ceremony of soldiery, ordering and grounding our arms; and although the enemy had been firing a little before, they did not now give us a single shot. I suppose their astonishment . . . must have prevented them. . . .

The occupation of the new trench was a brief pause for the working crews. For two more days the French and Americans

were driven to back-breaking labor, completing gun platforms and dragging massive artillery pieces into line—mortars, howitzers, and battering pieces. The gunners mounted
mortars on carriages invented by General Knox to elevate the
barrels so that shells could be lobbed high in the air and fall
into the town. The men still worked without returning a shot,
but as more guns became visible in the allied line, British fire
dwindled and, as Colonel Butler said, "The enemy seem embarrassed, confused, and indeterminate; their fire seems feeble
... and although we have not as yet fired one shot from a piece
of artillery, they are as cautious as if the heaviest fire was
kept up."

The sun came out on October 9. By noon big American and
French batteries were complete and ammunition had been
brought up. Knox had installed huge guns in the American
works—three twenty-four pounders, three eighteen pounders,
a pair of eight-inch howitzers, and half a dozen mortars. A
deserter had come into the lines early in the morning with a
story that amused the Pennsylvania troops—Cornwallis had
told his men that they should not fear the Americans, who had
no heavy guns, and that the French fleet had come into the
Chesapeake only to load tobacco and was afraid to attack.

French guns opened the Allied barrage at three o'clock in
the afternoon, and the first rounds drove the British frigate
Guadeloupe across the York.

Two hours later the Americans opened fire. The signal
for the opening gun on this sector was the raising of the flag
on the front line, and the troops watched impatiently until it
fluttered up the flagpole. Sergeant Martin was shaken by emotion as the flag rose, the guns rolled and cheering swept the
trenches: "I felt a secret pride swell my heart when I saw 'the
Star Spangled Banner' waving majestically in the faces of our
implacable adversaries; it appeared like an omen of success."
Dr. Thacher said, "His excellency Gen. Washington put the

match to the first gun, and a furious discharge of cannon and mortars immediately followed."

Colonel Philip van Cortlandt, who was on the front nearest Yorktown, heard this first American shot plunge into the village: "I could hear the ball strike from house to house, and I was afterwards informed that it went through the one where many of the officers were at dinner, and over the tables, discomposing the dishes and either killed or wounded the one at the head of the table. . . ." Van Cortlandt did not see Washington fire this shot but was soon told that he had done so.

The next few howitzer shells fell short of the enemy trenches, but the gunners found the range and their shot began to tear apart the British works. Cannon that had been firing against the new line gradually disappeared. It was only the beginning. Washington ordered the guns to fire all night so that the British could not make repairs, and while the plain trembled under the bombardment, his crews were hauling still more guns into position. Colonel Butler watched for hours as "the shot and shells flew incessantly through the night, dismounted the guns of the enemy, and destroyed many of their embrasures.'" By the next day four more batteries joined the cannonade; about fifty guns now showered their metal on Yorktown.

Lieutenant James, who huddled with his gunners under this rain of fire, wrote in his diary that night, "It will be impossible to account for the number killed and wounded . . . I must content myself with observing that the slaughter was great, and that among the killed on this day was the Commissary General, who with some other officers was killed at dinner."

Cornwallis reported, "The fire continued incessant from heavy cannon . . . until all our guns on the left were silenced, our work much damaged and our loss of men considerable."

Corporal Popp and his companions, driven to cover by this

bombardment, were forced to pitch their tents in the trenches. Throughout the ranks, men "began to desert in large numbers, and left the commands, watches and posts. Why? Out of fear!"

Johann Doehla said,

> They threw bombs in here from 100, 150 pounds and also some of 200 pounds; and their howitzer and cannon balls ... One could therefore not avoid the horribly many cannon balls either inside or outside the city. Most of the inhabitants who were still to be found here fled with their best possessions eastward to the bank of the York river, and dug in among the sand cliffs, but . . . many were badly injured and mortally wounded by the fragments of bombs which exploded partly in the air and partly on the ground, their arms and legs severed or themselves struck dead.
>
> The ships in the harbour also suffered great damage because the cannon balls flew across the whole river to the Gloucester shore.

Feeding the troops under the bombardment was increasingly difficult, but though the men had little else to eat, they feasted incongruously on chocolate, which had come from a captured Dutch ship. The Germans drank chocolate four or five times a day and also ate it with sugar on bread but still could not use it all. Now that they saw that surrender was near: "We greatly enjoyed ourselves after the great loss of sleep, the work and hardships which we had experienced day and night with the greatest danger to our lives."

Washington rode out early the next morning, October 10, to admire the skill of the French gunners, who blasted targets in the village with great accuracy. These crews boasted that they could fire six consecutive shots into a narrow embrasure. Blanchard explained that the French guns were new and "the balls perfectly suited to their calibre." The artillery of Henry Knox was the elite service of Washington's army, but it could not match the French. American ammunition was faulty, and many of the shells flung into the town failed to explode.

Lafayette, who often favored the Americans over the French, would not concede the superiority of his countrymen. He once watched some of the gunners of Knox at work and said, "You fire better than the French!" Knox's aide, Major Sam Shaw, smiled and shook his head, but Lafayette burst out passionately, "On my honor, it's the truth. Everyone knows the progress of your artillery is one of the wonders of the Revolution."

Allied guns halted for a few minutes at noon, when a white flag appeared on the enemy's works, and a striking party came slowly toward the allied lines—an infirm old man helped along by two soldiers and followed by a servant with a large bundle of family silver. He was the Governor's uncle, Thomas Nelson. Cornwallis had sent the old man out to safety after American cannon had battered his handsome house and forced a move of British headquarters. The secretary had news for Washington.

Cornwallis and his staff now lived "burrowed in the ground," in a grotto below Nelson's garden. A dispatch boat, just in from New York, had brought a promise that a British fleet would come south to attack Admiral de Grasse. The cavalrymen, Tarleton and Simcoe, were both ill of fever. More than a thousand horses had been slaughtered. The shelling was ruining the town and its defenses; many Negroes had died "in the most miserable manner," and several officers had been killed. The old man told St. George Tucker, the Virginia militiaman, "The British are a good deal dispirited, but they pretend to have no apprehensions of the garrison's falling."

Gunners of Captain Thomas Machin's Second Artillery found a new target during the afternoon—a tall brick house whose massive chimneys towered above Yorktown. Men in the trenches turned to watch, and excitedly passed along the story of the big house.

Lafayette, the general officer of the day, had invited Governor Thomas Nelson, Jr., to see the Second Artillery open fire and asked his advice:

"Is there some spot in the town we should hit?"

Nelson pointed to the tall house. "Now that they've knocked Uncle Tom's house to pieces, that's the best one in town. Cornwallis may be there. Have them fire there. It's my house." Admiring infantrymen were soon repeating the Governor's challenge to hesitant gunners, "I'll give five guineas to the first man to hit it." Solid shot began to strike the house, plunging through its roof and shattering the walls.

There was a new air of confidence at headquarters as the bombardment went on, systematically destroying the enemy's works. Steuben amused the command with a show of bravado in the afternoon. Baron Viomenil, who held the French sector, sent Deux-Ponts to warn Steuben of a threatened British attack at night and offered to send five hundred to eight hundred men to bolster Steuben's front. The Prussian bristled, "I think I want no reinforcements. If I am attacked, I will hold until support can come—and you may say to Baron Viomenil that if he is attacked, I will send *him* 800 men."

When Deux-Ponts had gone, Anthony Wayne badgered Steuben: "You know you have only 1000 men in the whole division."

"Yes, yes, but I will leave 200 to defend the battery, and attack with all the rest—and if I have boasted a little, Wayne, it was only for the honor of your country."

Wayne pumped his hand and grinned at the officers of the division staff, "Now, gentlemen, it's up to us to make good the Baron's exaggeration, and to support him as if he had twice his strength."

The old drill master was still in distress and without a copper in his pocket. He was living only from army rations served in camp and was forced to beg a loan from Henry Knox, who gave him five half-Joes, Portuguese coins worth only a few dollars.

There were signs of growing British distress on the river front. Cornwallis sank more than a dozen of his own vessels near the shore on the first day of allied fire, and after dark the French began lobbing red-hot shot into the river, splashing them among the crowded shipping. They scored a spectacular hit. Dr. Thacher had a clear view of the blaze—a hot shot struck the forty-four-gun British *Charon*, which burned and set two or three other ships afire:

> The ships were enwrapped in a torrent of fire, which spread with vivid brightness among the combustible rigging, and running with amazing rapidity to the tops of the several masts, while all around was thunder and lightning from our numerous cannon and mortars . . . one of the most sublime and magnificent spectacles which can be imagined. Some of our shells, overreaching the town, are seen to fall in the river, and bursting, throw up columns of water like the spouting of the monsters of the deep.

From Yorktown, Lieutenant James watched the death of his ship, one of the finest of her class in the navy. The *Charon* broke her moorings and crashed into a transport and set it afire, and the two blazing ships drifted across the black river to the Gloucester shore, where they burned to the water's edge. Allied shells now fell rapidly in the town. The night passed "in dreadful slaughter," James said. He and his gun crew worked desperately to shore up works knocked down by shells. Much of the garrison was set afire, "a view awful and tremendous."

Johann Doehla, who sat on the beach during the shelling, said "it felt like the shocks of an earthquake"; more than 3600 shot had fallen on the town and harbor in twenty-four hours, with terrible effect:

> One saw men lying everywhere who were mortally wounded and whose heads, arms and legs had been shot off . . . enemy cannon balls of 24 and more pounds flew over our whole line and city into the river, where they often struck through 1 and 2 ships.

Doehla saw the shot skip across the water to Gloucester, where they wounded soldiers on the beach.

A small open boat moved into the harbor's carnage during the cannonade of October 10, passed unharmed to the beach, and put ashore Major Charles Cochrane, who had a dispatch for Cornwallis. Cochrane had made an epic passage of seven days from New York, through rough coastal waters in a twelve-oared whaleboat, past the French blockade, and up the bay to the York. The message he brought from Henry Clinton was tortured and contradictory and under the allied barrage had an odd irrelevance:

> . . . I am doing every thing in my power to relieve you by a direct move, and I have reason to hope, from the assurances given me this day by Admiral Graves, that we may pass the bar by the 12th of October, if the winds permit, and no unforeseen accident happens: this, however, is subject to disappointment, wherefore, if I hear from you, your wishes will of course direct me and I shall persist in the idea of a direct move, even to the middle of November, should it be your Lordship's opinion that

you can hold out so long; but if, when I hear from you, you tell me that you cannot, and I am without hopes of arriving in time . . . I will immediately make an attempt by Philadelphia. . . .

Cornwallis replied by repeating his warning that "nothing but a direct move to York River which includes a Successful Naval Action can save us." The enemy guns had already cost him seventy men, and his works were badly damaged. He added a warning, "With such works on disadvantageous ground against so powerful an attack, we cannot hope to make a very long Resistance."

The Earl held the letter for five hours, as the shells continued to fall, and added a postscript, "Since the above was written we have lost Thirty Men."

The following day, October 12, Cornwallis lost his dispatch bearer, Major Cochrane. As the two stood on a parapet to watch British guns fire at the enemy, a cannon ball tore Cochrane's head from his body.

Washington's troops dug a second parallel on the night of October 11, opening a new trench about four hundred yards closer to the enemy line. This work could not be extended to the river on the right because of two large British redoubts which were far in front of the defense line, and allied engineers agreed that the two outposts must be captured before the parallel could become effective.

American and French troops once more dug all night with little interference from the enemy; British fire continued to fall on the old line in the rear, as if Cornwallis did not suspect that a new parallel was being dug. By morning of the twelfth the troops were in position in the new line. Washington was puzzled by the lack of opposition: "Lord Cornwallis' conduct has hitherto been passive beyond conception; he either has not the means of defence, or he intends to reserve his strength until we approach very near him." And Trumbull said that unless the British made stronger resistance, "the town must soon be too hot for his Lordship and his troops."

Two days later, on October 14, Washington ordered all guns within range to begin blasting the redoubts in an effort to soften them up for an attack, and at 2:00 P.M., when Washington saw that the two posts were so badly damaged that they could be stormed, the orders went out: the redoubts would be taken in a night attack by two 400-man columns, one French, one American. The French would take the nearest work, lying beside the road that led from Yorktown to the nearby Moore House—a post held by 120 British and Hessians. Lafayette's Americans were to take the Rock Redoubt, nearest the river, which was held by seventy men.

The troops of Saint-Simon were to open musket fire at 6:30 P.M., a feint to draw enemy attention. Half an hour later, six mortar rounds from another battery would signal the attack. The ground was to be reconnoitered in the afternoon, the troops fed early, and the columns ready by dusk. As men hurried through the lines to prepare the assault, a squabble raged in the high command. Lafayette had named his aide, the Chevalier de Gimat, to lead the American attack, but Alexander Hamilton protested. Since he was the senior officer, Hamilton said, he should lead the party. Washington called Lafayette to headquarters and dealt swiftly with the matter, as if determined that his old quarrel with his former aide, Hamilton, should be forgotten. He reviewed the seniority of the officers and placed Hamilton in command.

Lafayette's command was soon ready. Under Hamilton's direction, de Gimat and Major Nicholas Fish of New York would lead battalions, supported by a detachment of the explosives experts, the sappers and miners. John Laurens would take his men to the rear of the redoubt to cut off the enemy retreat.

The French chose Count William Deux-Ponts to lead their column, and a veteran of forty years in the army, Baron l'Estrade, as his second in command. The troops of both columns lay in the trenches for a few hours, smoking or sleeping. Washington visited both camps and made one of his rare battlefield speeches to Lafayette's officers and men. It was a simple plea— they must be brave and firm since the success of the attack rested with them alone. The troops watched him closely. One officer wrote, "I thought then that His Excellency's knees rather shook, but I have since doubted whether it was not mine."

Army gossips were slow in learning the secret of this assault. Lieutenant Feltman could write only, "This evening it is reported that there is something grand to be done by our Infantry." Sergeant Martin saw officers fixing bayonets on long staves and thought that the army was to make a general assault on Yorktown. He was told of the plan only when axes were passed out to the sappers and miners, who were to cut paths through the sharp branches protecting the British works. The detachment moved into the open field at dusk and lay down to wait. Martin saw the planets Jupiter and Venus, close together in the sky, and once started to jump to his feet, thinking that the signal had been fired. The watchword for the night passed through the ranks: "Rochambeau." The Americans were told to empty their muskets. They were to take their redoubt with the bayonet.

Rochambeau was in the trench as the Frenchmen went forward, calling to the men of his old regiment, "My children, I have great need of you tonight. I trust you will not forget that we have served together in the brave Regiment of the Auvergne—*Auvergne sans tache,* the spotless." One of the young men answered, "We will fight like lions . . . until the last man is killed."

As they emerged from the trench, Count Deux-Ponts was

surrounded by volunteers who had been refused by Rochambeau and Washington, among them the Chevalier de Lameth
and two counts, de Damas and de Vauban. "I tried to turn
them back," Deux-Ponts said, "but they would not pay heed."
The French column was led by fifty men carrying fascines to
throw into enemy trenches; behind them were eight men with
ladders.

From the left, Saint-Simon's muskets opened in the false
attack, and British guns replied. At seven o'clock a mortar
shell soared up from the big French battery, quickly followed
by five more shells. The two assault columns moved out into
the fog toward the enemy.

"Up, up," the American sergeants called, and Hamilton
led them off. Captain Stephen Olney, an old Rhode Islander,
was none too sure of some of his company, and he whispered
to them, "I know you'll be brave men, come what will. If
you lose your gun, don't fall back—take the gun of the first
man killed." Olney knew what his companions were thinking—in less than a quarter of a mile, their days on earth
would come to an end.

The column was halted halfway to the redoubt, and one
man was chosen from each company to form the "forlorn
hope," which would climb over the enemy wall. The twenty
men crept off after their commander, Lieutenant John Mansfield of the Fourth Connecticut, and John Laurens and his
men also left the column, circling toward the rear of the
redoubt.

Martin and his companions reached the enemy's abatis
and fumbled among the sharp branches—the barrier had
hardly been damaged by artillery fire. They began chopping
with their axes.

A sentry called a challenge, and when there was no reply
the British fired a volley. Impulsively, the exposed Americans
shouted. "Our men broke silence and huzzaed," Olney said.

The captain called to reassure his men, "They're scared to death—firing right into the air." Olney did not realize that the British pickets were signaling to their army, which now blazed away along the entire line.

Lieutenant Mansfield and his suicide squad overran the sappers and miners as they hacked at the abatis, squirming through the thicket, crossing a ditch, and climbing the parapet into the redoubt. Mansfield was slashed by a bayonet, but his men were at his heels, and several fought their way into the work. There was a furious scramble to reach the wall. Sergeant Martin saw men falling on every side and thought British fire was wiping out the column—until he saw that they were tumbling into enormous shell holes, clambering out, and rushing forward, only to fall again. Fire from above was so heavy that Martin could recognize his companions in the yellow light of powder flashes.

Old Captain Olney led the way through the palisade and called to his men, "Olney's company form here!" Half a dozen bayonets lunged down at him, and Olney tried to beat them off with his long spear. The bayonets slashed his fingers and stabbed into his thigh and abdomen, but Olney felled one of the enemy with a blow to the forehead. The captain's life was saved by two of his men who had loaded their muskets in defiance of orders and now drove off the redcoat party with their fire.

Someone in the front shouted, "Rush on boys! The fort's ours!"

The British threw small hand grenades, which crackled in the trench—so many of them that the Americans thought they were fire crackers.

Men in the trench below stood on the shoulders of their companions to climb up, but the tiny Hamilton, too short to reach the top, commanded a nearby soldier to kneel, stepped on his back, and vaulted into the redoubt. A brief bayonet fight soon cleared the redoubt, and the British began to leap away into the darkness; Martin saw one of them jump from the bluff, land thirty or forty feet below, and run desperately into Yorktown. The remaining redcoats surrendered. John Laurens and his men cut off retreat at the rear and soon appeared with the redoubt's commander, Major Campbell, and several of his men as prisoners.

The post had hardly fallen when Dr. Thacher was led through the darkness to treat the wounded, "even before the balls had ceased whistling about my ears." He saw a sergeant and eight men lying dead in a ditch, and when he had climbed inside, found many wounded, including the captured Campbell, and de Gimat, who had a slight wound in a foot.

When the fort was cleared Lafayette came up, chattering excitedly. He sent an aide to Viomenil with a message: "I am in my redoubt. Where are you?" The Baron was under fire, waiting for his men to clear the British barricade, and replied, "Tell the Marquis I am not in mine, but will be in five minutes."

The American loss in the attack was nine dead and twenty-five wounded. One of the wounded was Sergeant William Brown of the Fifth Connecticut, who founded an American tradition: he was decorated with the Purple Heart, the first U.S. military award for valor* without regard for rank.

The French assault had begun at the same moment, but there was an agonizing delay. The vanguard had gone only five hundred or six hundred yards when it was halted by the abatis, undamaged by the shell fire. Deux-Ponts whispered orders for his axemen to clear the way.

---

* The Purple Heart originally corresponded to the modern Medal of Honor; only when it was revived in 1932 was it awarded for wounds received in action.

A Hessian sentry called from above, *"Wer da?"*—"who's there?" The French column crowded closer, and the enemy fired. Carpenters chopped at the abatis and the men stood calmly in ranks for five minutes, firing upward at the Germans on the parapet—they were the veterans of the Bose Regiment. Deux-Ponts lost many men in the waiting, and then, the young Colonel said, "We threw ourselves into the ditch . . . and each one sought to break through the fraises and to mount the parapet."

The Chevalier de Lameth, the first man up, fell with a musket ball through both knees, and Baron l'Estrade, who was just behind him, was tumbled back into the ditch by a soldier who yanked at his coattails; he was then trampled by those who came after him. The Baron struggled up, cursing the troops with the seasoned vocabulary of a veteran.

The Germans charged the handful of Frenchmen on the wall but were driven off by a volley; they huddled behind a stack of barrels, a protective barrier which had been raised against shell fragments, and the French poured fire on them from above. Deux-Ponts was ordering a bayonet charge when the Hessians threw down their muskets and surrendered. Deux-Ponts and his men yelled, "Vive le Roi!" and those in the rear trenches echoed the cry. As if in retaliation for the loss of the redoubts, the enemy fired all the guns of their main line at once. "I never saw a sight more beautiful or more majestic," Deux-Ponts said.

The French had lagged behind the Americans but, once they had broken through the outer defenses, had taken the post in seven minutes, taking fifty prisoners and killing eighteen of the enemy. Deux-Ponts had lost fifteen dead and seventy-seven wounded. Reinforcements were called up to help hold the redoubt. The delighted Rochambeau rewarded the courage of his troops with two days' extra pay and gave the carpenters a bonus of two louis each; Baron Viomenil invited two of his sergeants to dine at headquarters, seated them in places of honor at his right, and "treated them with the highest Respect and Attention."

There was only one disappointment for the French. Count Custine, whose men were to fire from their flank at seven-thirty to help distract the enemy, waited until an hour later, fifteen minutes after the redoubts had fallen, before breaking into volleys. Closen was disgusted; he suspected his friend was drunk. Rochambeau put Custine under arrest for twenty-four hours, and the Count was the butt of army jokes until the siege had ended.*

When quiet had fallen in redoubt No. 9, a sentry heard an enemy patrol outside and called to Deux-Ponts. As the Colonel looked over the parapet, a ricocheting cannon ball struck within inches of his head, blasting his face with gravel and wounding him so painfully that he was led away to a waiting ambulance wagon.

Workmen began digging new trenches to link the redoubts to the second parallel before prisoners had been led to the rear. Enemy fire flew harmlessly overhead on the American sector, but the French had heavy casualties—more than one hundred men were struck in one blast, twenty-seven of them dead; Claude Blanchard's hospital soon had more than five hundred patients.

When enemy fire dwindled, allied officers staged a false attack to see whether Cornwallis could still resist an assault with his batteries. A column was sent into the open, and an officer bellowed in German: "Brigade! Forward March! Halt! Cannon to the front!" The Americans fired a few rounds, but the redcoat response was faint.

Washington, Lincoln, and Knox had dismounted in the open during the hottest of the fighting and stood in a group

---

* Custine became an army commander in the French Revolution ten years later and died on the guillotine.

with a dozen or more aides. Colonel David Cobb of the staff was alarmed.

"Sir, you're too much exposed here. Hadn't you better step back a little?"

Washington replied shortly, "Colonel Cobb, if you are afraid, you have the liberty to step back." The group continued to stand there despite heavy enemy fire, peering anxiously across the field to where the handful of men fought for the redoubts which would command the Yorktown position.

When the fire died away, Washington said quietly to his officers, "The work is done, and well done," then turned to Billy Lee: "Billy, hand me my horse." He rode to headquarters to deal with the paper work of the army. By morning, his troops had moved their own guns into the two big redoubts, facing the enemy; workmen had also completed the second parallel, and the deep trench ran all the way to the river bank. The general wrote to President McKean, "The works we have carried are of vast importance to us. From them we shall enfilade the enemy's whole line."

The next day increased British fire fell upon the new allied line, which was only 250 yards away. Knox and Hamilton, who were in the Rock Redoubt, were arguing over Washington's order that men should yell warnings when they heard a shell coming in. Hamilton was scornful. It was unsoldierly and cowardly to shout under fire. Knox insisted that the order saved lives. A Connecticut soldier standing nearby watched as two shells dropped into the work, and the bulky Knox and his tiny friend leapt for safety:

Instantly the cry broke out on all sides, "A shell! A shell!" and [there was] such a scrambling and jumping to reach the blinds and get behind them for defense. Knox and Hamilton . . . both got behind the blinds, and

Hamilton to be yet more secure held on behind Knox
. . . Upon this, Knox struggled and threw Hamilton off
and in the effort himself . . . rolled over and threw
Hamilton off toward the shells. Hamilton, however,
scrambled back again behind the blinds. In two minutes
the shells burst and threw their deadly missiles in all
directions. It was now safe and soldierly to stand out.

"Now," says Knox, "now what do you think, Mr.
Hamilton, about crying 'shell'? But let me tell you not
to make a breastwork of me again!"

Sounds of the attacks on the redoubts rolled into the British lines with chilling clarity. A Hessian soldier wrote, "They
made such a terrible yell and loud cheering that one believed
nothing but that the whole 'Wild Hunt' had broken out.
There must have been 3000 men . . . who undertook this
assault . . . the alarm was sounded throughout our entire
camp." Even in the night the troops in Yorktown saw that
the white French flag with its Bourbon lilies now flew over
a fort. Desertions increased during the night.

Corporal Popp watched helplessly as German and English
survivors, fleeing from the redoubts, ran in front of the lines
and were killed by their own men: "Some of them were
even shot by us with grapeshot . . . A Hessian was found
in three pieces."

The Earl sent out a message in cipher to Clinton on October 15, acknowledging for the first time that it was hopeless
to attempt a rescue of his army:

My situation now becomes very critical. We dare not
show a gun to their old batteries, and I expect their
new ones will open To-Morrow Morning . . . we shall
soon be exposed to an assault in ruined Works, in a bad
position and with weakened Numbers.

I cannot recommend that the Fleet and Army should run great Risque in endeavouring to save us.

Cornwallis made a final effort to check the enemy. Late at night he turned all of his guns and mortars on the nearest allied positions and soon afterward sent a storming party of 350 men to slip into enemy lines and spike guns. At 3:00 A.M. Lieutenant Colonel Robert Abercromby assembled the troops, a picked band of guardsmen and light infantry. They filed out of the trenches in two parties, and by four o'clock had moved undetected to the weakest point of the allied lines, where the French and American sectors joined.

Washington's weary troops had relaxed after seizing the two British redoubts; men were asleep at their posts, and others did not have their arms at hand. The British entered the second parallel between two unfinished redoubts whose workmen had been sent to another part of the line. One of the redcoat columns turned westward along an empty trench and came upon a work occupied by an officer and fifty men of the Agenais Regiment. Most of the French were asleep, and few sentries were out. Abercromby's men deceived a sentry by pretending to be an American relief party, scaled the walls, stabbed several of the sleepy Frenchmen, drove off the rest, and hurriedly broke their bayonets in the touchholes of the cannon.

The second British band filed toward the allied rear and came upon Savage's battery of Colonel Henry Skipwith's Virginia militia; one hundred men occupied the position, but had left their arms in a trench just behind them.

"What troops?" a British officer called.

"French," someone shouted.

There was a shout from the redcoat. "Push on, boys, and skin the bastards!"

Many of the unarmed militiamen fled into the darkness.

The British spiked the guns of the redoubt. The Viscount de Noailles, who was nearby with some troops, shouted and led a charge. The French skewered eight of the attackers and drove the others back to their lines, carrying the Agenais officer and one or two other prisoners with them.

The assault party took exaggerated reports of its victory into British lines: in five minutes it had spiked eleven guns and bayonetted more than one hundred Frenchmen, at the cost of only a dozen dead and wounded.

Allied field officers admired the "secrecy and spirit" of the attack, but Washington reported that it was "small and ineffective and of little consequence to either party." His casualties were seventeen killed and wounded; the British had lost eight men dead and six as prisoners.

Six allied guns had been spiked, but d'Aboville's crewmen had extracted the bayonet tips within six hours, and the guns rejoined the bombardment. Many new cannon had also come into line.

The increased fire stunned those still on duty in the Yorktown trenches; they had not imagined that the cannonading could become more intense. One young Hessian said, ". . . with the dawn the enemy began to fire heavily, as he had not done before . . . so fiercely as though the heavens should split . . . this afternoon the enemy firing was almost unendurable. Now we saw what was to happen to us."

Cornwallis assembled small boats on the beach in the afternoon of October 16, and the sick and wounded were loaded and rowed across the river to Gloucester. Johann Doehla noted in his diary, "Everybody easily saw that we could not hold out much longer in this place if we did not get help soon."

For several days the British staff had wrangled over a desperate plan of escape, and many officers had urged an immediate evacuation. Cornwallis hesitated, but the council was persuasive—the army must move or be destroyed; two thousand of the infantry could cross the river by night, destroy the boats on the north shore, drive back Choisy's weak force, mount captured horses, and march one hundred miles inland before Washington could start in pursuit. They might then march to New York to join Clinton, or south, to regain the Carolinas. It was dangerous, but there was no alternative.

The Virginia countryside between the York and Rappahannock rivers was "as rich and plentiful as any part of America," not yet plundered, its harvests gathered and ready for seizure. Most of the troops were hardened to long, hungry marches and accustomed to light travel—the French, who could not march without their baking ovens, would never overtake them. In any event, Washington would spend three or four days in occupying vacated Yorktown and communicating with de Grasse. Even if the attempt to escape failed, it would prolong the end. The younger officers pressed Cornwallis hard, reminding him that it would soon be too late; bad weather and further allied advances would halt them.

Cornwallis delayed while Washington opened his second parallel, stormed the redoubts, and pushed his guns nearer the town. The Earl succumbed only on October 16, when hope had all but vanished. As Tarleton wrote, "A retreat by Gloucester was the only expedient . . . to avert the mortification of a surrender . . . though this plan appeared less practicable than when first proposed, and was adopted at this crisis, as the last resource, it yet afforded some hopes of success."

The move began at 11:00 P.M., when British regulars were relieved by Germans of the Anspach Regiment, a skeleton force, to man the trenches while Navy gunners kept up a fire to deceive the enemy. A thousand men went across the river in the first wave—the English light infantry, most of the crack Brigade of Guards, and several companies of the Twenty-third Regiment. Cornwallis was to follow with the second wave when he had finished a letter to Washington, asking mercy for the few men he was leaving behind. The first boats had hardly returned from the north bank for more troops when a vicious York River squall swept down from the west, marooning those on the north shore, scattering the boats, and lashing the water of the narrows into whitecaps. Two boatloads of troops were blown downstream and captured by the Americans. A rainstorm pelted Yorktown until 2:00 A.M. without abating.

Guns fired slowly in the village trenches, without response from the Allies. A few British troops returned from the beach, but the men from the north bank were not brought back until noon of the next day, under heavy fire from the French. Cornwallis abandoned the attempt to break away. Tarleton wrote, "Thus expired the last hope of the British army."

Dawn brought a chilling sight to men in the front line. Johann Doehla, who was in the strongest redoubt, now understood the enemy's night-long silence: "Toward morning they brought a trench and a strong battery of 14 guns so close to our hornwork that one could nearly throw stones into it."

When the British troops returned to the earthworks from Gloucester they told the Germans glumly, "We'll never break through there. They have trenches around our whole garrison—and behind them a cordon of the French hussars, as far as you can see. Nothing passes in or out."

The allied guns then opened once more, nearer than ever.

THIRTEEN
COUNCILS OF WAR

In New York, the coming of autumn found Henry Clinton more perplexed than ever. For two weeks after Graves had sailed southward with the fleet, Sir Henry and his staff did not realize the full extent of the danger, but there was uneasiness at headquarters. While the officers bickered over plans for aiding Cornwallis, four thousand weary troops waited aboard transports in the harbor. Clinton had sent them there late in August when he planned an attack on Rhode Island, disembarked them when Graves left, but had re-embarked them on September 6, so that they would be ready to sail in an emergency.

It was not clear how these troops were to be landed in Virginia, but they had a long wait aboard the sweltering ships during the days when there was only silence from the south.

On September 13, before he had heard from Graves and was still unaware that the fleet had been driven from the Chesapeake, Clinton called a council of war—the first of thirteen he was to hold in little over a month. Old General

Robertson made an impassioned plea for action: they should crowd all possible reinforcements aboard the transports under convoy of only one warship and hurry them to the Chesapeake. Clinton refused to listen to the reckless plan. Even if the troops got through to Cornwallis, they would have no provisions and would merely add to the Earl's burdens. Clinton proposed instead his old scheme of a counter-attack against Philadelphia. After some debate the council decided to wait for Admiral Robert Digby, who was expected from England.

Robertson persisted. He wrote Clinton the next day, outlining his desperate plan at length. He conceded that odds were against it, but said that the alternative was to do nothing: ". . . the destruction of the whole is certain if the army in Virginia be destroyed. One chance is for us; we give up the game if we do not try to risk it."

Almost at the moment that Robertson's letter reached him, Clinton had a dispatch from Graves with the distressing news that the French force in the Chesapeake was so large that, "they are absolute masters of its navigation." Clinton replied to Graves, saying confidently that Cornwallis had provisions to last him until November and could be in no immediate danger. But the news from the Chesapeake prompted him to call another council of war to reconsider Robertson's plan.

Robertson gave a notable performance in behalf of his scheme: "The old General enforced his opinion with great earnestness and all his abilities, which were great . . . but not an officer concurred with him, but rather laughed at his extravagant zeal." Clinton called in officers who had recently returned from Yorktown, who assured the council that even after a siege had begun Cornwallis could hold out for three weeks against an army of twenty thousand. The officers were so cocksure that even Robertson was convinced, and the council voted once more to await the arrival of Digby.

In the midst of these concerns Clinton succumbed to his penchant for petty quarreling. General Robertson, as Lieutenant Mackenzie had noticed, was by now "a mixture of good sense and inconsistency, and seems to be inclining to dotage," but Clinton turned upon the old man as if he suspected him of treachery, as if all his distrust of Robertson was aroused by this proposal to relieve Cornwallis. The version read to the council was not similar in all details to the one Robertson had written to Clinton, and Sir Henry demanded an explanation. When Robertson responded with a new and still different version, Clinton turned aside from his duties to write a long, querulous memorandum, comparing the three versions and emphasizing their differences, phrase by phrase. This activity occupied Sir Henry for many hours when he should have been considering a course of decisive action.

On September 17 Clinton had his first news of the battle off the Virginia coast, a somber dispatch from Graves saying that the "shattered" fleet was limping back toward New York, and that the French had sealed the Chesapeake so tightly that Cornwallis could be reached only by small boats slipping through the blockade at night. Even this report failed to arouse Clinton. He called another council of war, which decided that Cornwallis must be sent reinforcements at the first opportunity, certainly before the end of October.

Sir Henry wrote to Graves almost blithely, directing that the fleet open the way to Yorktown and then stand by to land and protect the troops. "We must stand or fall together," Clinton wrote, as if he did not comprehend that the fleet returning to him was badly damaged and that its Admiral was a beaten man.

Graves and the fleet reached New York on September 19, and, at first sight of the battered ships, army officers removed the waiting troops from the transports and put them ashore.

The navy could give no estimate as to how long the fleet must be in harbor for repairs and refitting. Alarm spread through the city, and some families moved away. Judge Smith recorded the popular fear: "Poor Cornwallis! is the general lamentation."

For a few days Graves had a vision of returning to Virginia with a fleet large enough to challenge de Grasse on something like equal terms. He had lost the *Terrible,* but two other ships in the harbor had been repaired in his absence, two others were due from Jamaica, and Admiral Digby was coming with three more—to bring the fleet to a total of twenty-five ships of the line. But on September 23, Cornwallis sent news of thirty-six French ships in the bay; the superiority of the enemy was overwhelming, after all. The Earl also finally told Clinton the truth of his situation: the defenses could not be held for long, he could be rescued only by a naval force sailing directly into the York River, and "If you cannot relieve me very soon, you must be prepared to hear the worst." The effects of British bungling and the bold moves of de Grasse, Washington, and Rochambeau had now become apparent. Rescue of Cornwallis was probably impossible; it must be attempted at once, if at all, and in face of staggering odds.

It was a busy day at headquarters when this news came in from Cornwallis: Graves finally sent ten damaged ships to the yards—after a delay of four days to ascertain what repairs were needed; Clinton held another council of war, without the navy; and Admiral Digby arrived at last, bringing as a passenger the sixteen-year-old Prince William Henry, the King's third son, who was to become William IV.

The prince occupied the attention of the command and the city for several days. Clinton escorted the boy on a walk to inspect some of the New York defenses and to review troops and entertained him with a dinner and concert at headquarters. Lieutenant Mackenzie admired the young man: "The graceful appearance and the manner of The Prince, with his liveliness and affability, gives universal satisfaction." The Prince was entertained by parties, reviews, carriage rides, dinners, and parades, and one day he was taken to the front lines at Kingsbridge, to the posts of the outermost sentries, where he could get a glimpse of the enemy. Some of his bedazzled subjects behaved as if a royal visit were a worthy substitute for a naval squadron. "All well," Judge Smith wrote, "the presence of the Prince may supply our deficiency."

Bemused rebel spies reported the feting of the Prince, and the *Pennsylvania Packet* taunted the British:

> Sir Henry Clinton remains quiet in New York notwithstanding the imminent danger now hanging over the head of his colleague in wickedness, Lord Cornwallis, but it is presumed the presence of his *"Young Master"* will at once dissipate his fears.

Admiral Digby's arrival might have precipitated a struggle for naval command, since he was senior to Graves, but the newcomer, perhaps because he foresaw catastrophe, insisted that Graves retain the fleet. Samuel Hood muttered, none too discreetly, that Graves should sail at once to the West Indies, for the good of the cause.

Within a day after he had the ominous news from Cornwallis, Clinton had convinced himself that the Earl merely intended to abandon Yorktown and retreat to safety, but a council of officers disagreed sharply—to be prepared to hear "the worst," they said, meant "something more serious than a retreat." The Admirals agreed, for the first time, to send Cornwallis a definite promise of relief and set the date of sailing for October 5.

The Admirals explained to Clinton that they would turn French superiority of numbers and position to advantage—

the anchorage of de Grasse was swept by violent tides, which would permit the British to slip past before the French could maneuver. Graves could then sail to the mouth of the York, where the narrowing bay would permit the enemy little room to come in pursuit. Clinton consoled himself with this dubious plan, noting that the naval captains with Cornwallis had also urged the fleet to come to the mouth of the York; hence the scheme must be feasible.

Digby and Hood scorned this plan. If by some miracle the ships, heavily laden with troops, got through the narrow opening of the Chesapeake and found de Grasse so sound asleep as to be at the mercy of the tides, what then? Taking fresh troops to Cornwallis would not save the army; Washington would not submissively retreat nor would the French fleet return to the Indies. Instead, the allies had only to remain in place, and the army and its reinforcements would be trapped in the bay.

Digby did not relish the thought of entering the bay, but in any case, he said, the fleet could do no more than land the troops.

"The Army will be lost unless you remain," Clinton said. "The council is already committed to keeping the fleet in the bay."

"What will the Army do, once it has landed?" Digby asked.

Clinton said that would depend upon circumstances, and added, "I suppose of course that there will be no more difficulty getting off than going in." Sir Henry saw that his arguments were unconvincing: "The Admiral's countenance seemed to express some doubt."

The council ended inconclusively, saying that if the date of sailing must be postponed, Cornwallis should be advised to use his own judgment.

But it was September 25, almost a week after his arrival,

before it was reported to Graves that the dockyards had no lumber to repair his ships, after all. Clinton offered him some lumber he had stockpiled to build barracks in the West Indies. Graves then discovered a shortage of combustibles for his fireships and called on Clinton to provide them, as well.

There was an air of desperation at headquarters as September came to an end. Delays in the dockyards were interminable; each session of the council was more gloomy than the last, and plans were even more unrealistic. Graves wanted to reopen the entire question—and now reported that he could not sail before October 8.

Clinton called another council with the navy on September 30. The generals and admirals agreed once more that they must sail, even though the entire French navy had surrounded Cornwallis, but postponed the date once again, to October 12. When this decision had been made, the naval officers withdrew. The generals held a private conference and agreed to notify Cornwallis of the further postponement at once—but refused to tell the Navy that they had done so.

Clinton wrote on the day of this council, "I see this in so serious a light, so horrible, that I dare not look at it," but a day or so later he told Judge Smith that all was well, that the admirals were willing to sail and were confident of success. Sir Henry brushed aside Smith's warning that the navy would continue to delay.

The army and the city's civilians had begun to despair. Lieutenant Mackenzie wrote in his diary:

Sept. 27 . . . Altho' the Navy are now hard at work in refitting the ships, and are preparing every thing for Sea with great diligence, yet I greatly fear that something decisive will take place against Lord Cornwallis before we can possibly be ready to go from hence.

Captain William Cornwallis, of the seventy-four-gun *Canada*, stormed in and out of headquarters, cursing about delays in the rescue of his brother, and Major Daner, a friend of Lord Germain, who had been embarked, disembarked, and reembarked until he was weary, was openly hostile in his criticism of Clinton. Robertson and Hood fumed with impatience—the old governor seeking relief from tension on evenings "abandoned to Frivolity—he has Parties of Girls in the Fort Garden, in the Midst of his own Fears, and the Anxieties of this Hour."

New York's Loyalists, now alarmed, joined the effort to help launch the expedition; the city's leading businessmen gave money to help enlist volunteers for the ships, and civilians joined the hunt for reluctant sailors who had gone into hiding. Judge Smith wrote, "The populace raves at the Navy."

Work on the ships continued while the Americans were drawing their lines more tightly around Yorktown. On October 5, when Washington was preparing to open his first parallel, Admiral Graves discovered that there was no gunpowder fit for use aboard the flagship *London*. Without complaint, Clinton sent him a new supply from army magazines. The next day Graves reopened an old quarrel with Clinton over the control of the Sixty-ninth Regiment, as to whether it belonged to the army or to the navy's fleet marine force. Graves carried on other squabbles—on October 8 he refused to attend a council called by Clinton, since he planned a meeting of his own, and wrote a stiffly formal note to Sir Henry, saying in effect, "Don't hold the meeting for me, as I shall not be there."

Samuel Hood was thunderstruck by the behavior of Graves at the navy's meeting on this day. When his officers assembled, Graves asked them to consider a question: "Is it practicable to relieve Lord Cornwallis in the Chesapeake?"

Hood could hardly believe his ears. He saw that Graves was deliberately trying to reverse the plan unanimously adopted weeks before.

"That appears to me a very unnecessary and improper question," Hood said. "It has been maturely discussed and we have decided to make the attempt as soon as possible. It is my opinion—and I will give it in writing—that we must try to reach Cornwallis at every risk, and if possible, we must attack the French fleet."

Sir Samuel expressed his angry resentment in letters to fellow officers:

I flattered myself when we came in that we should ere this have been in the Chesapeake, but the repairs of the squadron have gone on unaccountably tedious, which has filled me with apprehensions that we shall be too late to give relief to Lord Cornwallis. I pray God grant my fears may prove abortive.

And of Graves he wrote, "I think very meanly of the ability of our present commanding officer. I know he is a *cunning* man, he may be a good theoretical man, but he is certainly a bad practical one."

A freak storm added to the troubles of the navy on October 13, when hail pelted the city and a violent wind swept the harbor, driving some ships aground. The *Alcide* collided with the *Shrewsbury,* and both were again in need of repairs.

Graves himself blamed the British plight on bad luck and indolent workmen who were making repairs to his "crazy and shattered Squadron." He despaired of the ships ever being made ready for sea.

They are not quite ready—They are now very short of bread, and all the ovens will not keep up the daily consumption—Several Ships have parted their cables, others broke their anchors and three have been driven on shore; I see no end to disappointments.

Robertson said that Graves acted like a man who "considers himself as ruined already." The admiral, it was said, had written friends in England that he "will not fight if he can avoid it."

At last, when they had postponed the sailing of the fleet to October 17, the commanders again sent the troops and crews aboard the ships for the voyage. Prince William Henry went to the beach and watched as the troops were loaded into boats. The boy seemed especially pleased with the tall Grenadiers, who were "in high spirits." The days slipped by with more indecisive councils; on October 9 Clinton held a meeting to determine where they would land troops, in case the French barred the way to Yorktown. The officers chose implausible landings at Newport News on the James and Monday's Point, on the north bank of the York, without explanation as to how they would pass de Grasse's big ships to reach these places.

As late as October 14, Clinton spent hours writing to Cornwallis on his landing plans and to Lord Germain, assuring him that the relief army was already aboard the ships. The fleet was wind bound for another day—and the next day, October 16, another council of war reversed the decision on the landing plan and proposed to land instead on the Rappahannock River, far up the Chesapeake, north of the York River.

Lieutenant Mackenzie, the headquarters critic, had almost lost hope by now: "If the Navy are not a little more active, they will not get a sight of the Capes of Virginia before the end of this Month, and then it will be too late. They do not seem to be so hearty in the business." Mackenzie overheard one captain say that the rescue of the army in Virginia was not worth the loss of two ships. Only Samuel Hood, the Lieutenant thought, was "urgent about the matter." Hood seemed to others the only vigorous officer in the command, "a native of Shropshire but the image of a Yankee colonel both in person and stiff behavior."

Clinton signed two copies of his will, gave one to his mistress, Mrs. Baddeley, and sent the other to England. He told friends that the expedition was risky, but necessary to save British control in America. He had his last word from Yorktown on the seventeenth, a doleful recounting of the weakness of the defenses and the vigor of the allied attack: "The safety of the place is, therefore, so precarious, that I cannot recommend that the fleet and army should run great risque in endeavouring to save us." Almost as he received this dispatch from Cornwallis, Clinton saw some of the ships begin straggling out of New York harbor toward the sea.

Two days later, on October 19, the fleet finally left Sandy Hook, beating southward before a brisk wind. Clinton, aboard the *London,* wrote Germain that he would be in time to save Cornwallis. Sir Henry seemed to have convinced himself that all was well and that his trials had come to an end: "The stake is great . . . the two services start in perfect good humor with each other, and determined to do their best."

13

SURRENDER

It was very cold when Washington's guns opened at sunrise on October 17. New pieces had joined the line, and at least one hundred cannon pounded the village from close range. Johann Doehla was in the hornwork, where the shells came in "more horribly than ever before . . . without a stopping. Our detachment . . . could scarcely avoid the enemy's bombs." Every British embrasure was closed, and the only response to the allies was light mortar fire.

Just as the bugles called reveille Cornwallis entered the hornwork. His troops read his intentions in the Earl's bleak face as he studied the allied line and looked about at his own battered works. He had scarcely left the outpost for his headquarters when English infantrymen began slashing their new tents and smashing all the valuables in the place. "It looked as though there would be an early surrender," Corporal Popp said, "and we were heartily glad."

Cornwallis went back to his headquarters and talked glumly with a few staff officers; they agreed that their situation was hopeless. The works, the Earl said, "were in many places assailable in the forenoon." If the barrage continued a few hours, all would be destroyed. He could not fire a single large gun—only one eight-inch shell and one hundred mortar shells remained. More men were wounded daily, hundreds were ill of fever, and the 3200 still fit for duty were exhausted. Cornwallis expected the French fleet to join the attack on the town at any time. "Under all these circumstances, I thought it would have been wanton and inhuman to . . . sacrifice the lives of this small body of gallant soldiers."

At about nine o'clock a redcoat drummer boy clambered upon a British parapet and began a steady roll. He went unheard in the shelling until he was seen by allied infantrymen, then by the gunners. The batteries fell silent one by one.

Ebenezer Denny of the Pennsylvanians had seen the boy at once. "He might have beat away till Doomsday," Denny said, "if he had not been sighted by men in the front lines. The constant firing was too much for the sound of the single drum; but when the firing ceased, I thought I had never heard a drum equal to it—the most delightful music to us all."

An English officer came out of the works, holding a white handkerchief over his head, and the drummer scrambled down to join him, still furiously beating the call for a parley. An American officer crossed the open between the lines, which shells had torn until it was like a ploughed field. He blindfolded the British officer with his handkerchief, led him back into the allied line and into a house in the rear. The infantry and the gun crews stared after them. It was the anniversary of the American victory at Saratoga, four years before.

Washington opened a message from Cornwallis:

Sir, I propose a cessation of hostilities for twenty-four hours, and that two officers may be appointed by each side, to meet at Mr. Moore's house, to settle terms for the surrender of the posts at York and Gloucester.

It had come much sooner than Washington and Rochambeau had expected, but despite the air of exhilaration at headquarters, there was hesitation. The General did not intend to suspend the siege for a day, however remote the chances of the British fleet storming its way into the Bay. He would grant no more than an hour or so. It was noon before Washington sent the redcoat messenger back into his lines; men of both armies watched him closely as he crossed the open: "The soldiers were all standing on their works and in Yorktown the merchants were getting all their things on shore, as the shipping were to be given up to the French."

As soon as the officer stepped into his lines, allied guns opened once more and fired briefly—but at 3:00 P.M. there was another silence. Washington sent out an officer with a reply to Cornwallis.

Once more, with the passing of the flag, the bizarre pattern was repeated; the messenger disappeared, men atop the earthworks dropped from sight, and a few more guns fired. Johann Doehla left the front about this time: "We marched from our position back to our camp. The enemy cannon balls accompanied us on our march back."

Cornwallis and his staff read Washington's message:

An Ardent Desire to spare the further Effusion of Blood, will readily incline me to listen to such Terms for the Surrender of your Posts. . . .

I wish . . . that your Lordship's proposals in writing, may be sent to the American Lines: for which Purpose a Suspension of hostilities during two Hours from the Delivery of this Letter will be granted.

Washington was so sure that Cornwallis was ready to surrender on almost any terms that he wrote to de Grasse asking him to come ashore for the signing of a treaty, which he thought would "shortly take place." The General was not concerned even when he had Cornwallis' reply an hour or so later. The Earl coolly asked that his army be set free:

> . . . the time limited for sending my answer will not admit of entering into . . . detail . . . but the basis of my proposals will be . . . that the British shall be sent to Britain and the Germans to Germany . . . not to serve against France, America or their allies until released or regularly exchanged. . . .

Cornwallis offered to surrender his arms and supplies, but proposed that his troops keep their private property.

Washington smiled grimly at the suggestion that he send the enemy troops on parole to Europe, but he agreed to suspend hostilities until the next day to work out a settlement.

Flags continued to pass and firing halted for the night at about five o'clock. In Yorktown, men destroyed more equipment to keep it from allied hands, as if the surrender had already been signed. The navy scuttled the *Guadeloupe* and towed the *Fowey* into shallow water, where carpenters sank her by boring holes in her hull. A British powder magazine blew up during the night, killing thirteen men. Some of these, Doehla said, were "flying in pieces into the air . . . blown to bits and covered with earth."

But in the American camp the beauty of the night moved St. George Tucker, the Virginia militiaman, to poetic phrases:

A solemn stillness prevailed—the night was remarkably

clear and the sky decorated with 10,000 stars—numberless
Meteors gleaming thro' the Atmosphere afforded a
pleasing resemblance to the Bombs which had exhibited
a noble Firework the night before. . . .

The next morning, British bagpipers serenaded the Allies
and were answered by musicians of the Deux-Ponts Regiment. In the first light of the sun, Tucker watched a striking
scene:

From the . . . Rock Battery on our side our Lines completely mann'd and our Works crowded with soldiers . . .
opposite these at the Distance of two hundred yards . . .
The British Works; their parapets crowded with officers
looking at those who were assembled at the top of our
Works—the Secretary's house with one of the Corners
broke off, and many large holes through the Roof and
Walls part of which seem'd tottering with their weight.
On the Beach of York . . . hundreds of busy people
might be seen moving to and fro—At a small distance
from the Shore were seen ships sunk down to the Waters
Edge—further out in the Channel the Masts, Yards and
even the top gallant Masts of some might be seen. . . .

Eastward, through mists aglow in the light of the rising
sun, Tucker saw two French ships coming up the river
under full sail. By noon these ships had nosed in among the
British wrecks in Yorktown harbor and dropped anchor.

Trumbull's draft of the allied proposal was ready by the
morning of the eighteenth, and Washington sent it off to
Cornwallis at once:

Head Quarters before York, October 18, 1781
MY LORD: To avoid unnecessary Discussions and Delays, I shall at Once . . . declare the general Basis upon

which a Definitive Treaty and Capitulation must take place. The Garrisons of York and Gloucester, including the Seamen . . . will be received Prisoners of War. The Condition annexed, of sending the British and German troops . . . to Europe . . . is inadmissible. Instead of this, they will be marched to such parts of the Country as can most conveniently provide for their Subsistence . . . the same Honors will be granted to the Surrendering Army as were granted to the Garrison of Charles Town . . .

The Artillery, Arms, Accoutrements, Military Chest and Public Stores of every denomination, shall be delivered unimpaired. . . .

Your Lordship will be pleased to . . . accept or reject. . . . In the Course of Two Hours from the Delivery of this Letter, that Commissioners may be appointed to digest the Articles of Capitulation or a renewal of hostilities may take place.

Washington agreed that British troops could keep their personal property—but he would not grant immunity to Tories and deserters in the British lines.

Cornwallis abandoned his effort to have his army sent home, but he again requested protection for Loyalists in Yorktown and asked permission to send off to New York one boat which would sail without allied inspection. The Earl said he would appoint two field officers to meet with Washington's representatives at the Moore House, which was half a mile behind the American first parallel, near the river. Rochambeau chose Viscount de Noailles, Lafayette's brother-in-law, as his commissioner, and Washington named John Laurens.

Flags now passed back and forth so frequently that messengers crossed the lines without the formality of drum beats, and this traffic continued while the Commissioners met during the day. Noailles and Laurens went to the Moore House and waited until two British officers joined them—Lieutenant Colonel Thomas Dundas and Major Alexander Ross.

Washington expected a settlement within a few hours and sent two detachments of French and American troops to the front, ready to occupy British defenses. The men were ready to move by mid-afternoon, but there was only silence from the Moore House. The afternoon passed and night came as the armies waited. The picket troops went back into the lines.

Inside the Moore House the four officers haggled over every article of the surrender. Ross and Laurens argued hotly the question of American deserters now in British uniform, and though Laurens finally agreed to leave the article protecting the Loyalists in the agreement, he warned the British that Washington would not approve.

After a long debate the British agreed to march out their troops with furled flags and with their band playing one of their own marches. Ross protested this article—surrendering troops traditionally gave up their arms while flying their colors and playing enemy tunes as a gesture of derision.

"This is a harsh article," Ross said.

Laurens reminded Ross that these terms had been forced upon the American garrison at Charleston where he himself had surrendered. "This remains an article," Laurens said, "or I cease to be a commissioner."

There was also a squabble over captured silver. The British had little money, so little that during the debate over terms of surrender Noailles had demanded that Cornwallis state on his honor the value of his military chest—it was a mere 1800 pounds sterling, and Noailles said that so trifling an amount should be omitted from the settlement. It was only at the insistence of John Laurens that Cornwallis was forced to give up this money. The South Carolinian challenged Noailles, "A subject of one of the world's great monarchs may think 1800 pounds inconsiderable, but in our new country with its poor currency, this means a great deal indeed."

It was about midnight when Laurens and Noailles returned to headquarters, weary and exasperated, but they brought the rough draft of a surrender document, which the staff worked over during the night. Washington read the articles one by one, and after ten of the fourteen articles he wrote, "granted." He refused to approve immunity for Tories and deserters who had joined the British, insisted that merchants with the British army should be prisoners of war, and that the British care for their own sick and wounded.

Washington notified the British of the final changes, had the articles copied, and sent word to Cornwallis that he expected to have them signed at eleven o'clock. The garrison would march out and surrender its arms at 2:00 P.M.

Just before eleven Washington and Rochambeau rode with a party of general officers to the Rock Redoubt captured by the Americans; Admiral de Barras joined them as representative of de Grasse, who was confined to his cabin with an attack of asthma. The documents came back from the British lines a few minutes later, bearing the signatures of Cornwallis and Captain Thomas Symonds, his chief naval officer.

Washington had Trumbull add a line: "Done in the trenches before Yorktown in Virginia, October 19, 1781."

He signed himself, "G. Washington," and de Barras signed for de Grasse. There was no ceremony, and no stir among the troops.

In New York at this hour the British rescue fleet at last shook out its sails and passed over the bar, bound southward for the Chesapeake.

At noon, as the British and Germans left their posts, allied pickets marched into the enemy lines, occupying trenches, magazines, and storehouses, and barring the road into Yorktown.

Corporal Popp, the Anspacher, reported the orderly transfer in the trenches: "We were not harmed in the least . . . we were treated with justice and military usage. We had no complaints to make."

Johann Doehla was thankful that it was over without a final assault: "I . . . had indeed just cause to thank my God . . . who had so graciously preserved my life throughout the siege . . . Oh! how many thousand cannon balls I have escaped, with danger of my life hanging before my eyes!"

The only outbreak of hostilities during the occupation of British works was between Steuben and the Pennsylvanians. The tall, strong figure of Ebenezer Denny, the youngest of Richard Butler's ensigns, marched at the head of the American file, carrying the regimental flag—but once Denny was in the British works, ready to plant the colors in the parapet, Steuben seized the staff and ceremoniously stuck it atop the works. Men cheered at the sight, but the plump little Colonel Butler, who watched from the rear, trembled with rage, cursing Steuben as an arrogant, ignorant, knavish foreigner. Butler sent Steuben an insulting message later in the day, and only the diplomacy of Washington and Rochambeau prevented a duel.

Other Pennsylvania troops with spades on their shoulders followed the picket party and within less than an hour had levelled the trenches which crossed the road to Yorktown. Washington and Rochambeau led their armies into the great field across the road, where the men fell into ranks—two files facing each other a few yards apart. Bands played to pass the time as they waited; the British were late.

News of the victory had spread rapidly, and an enormous

crowd of civilians pressed close behind the troops, anxious to watch the surrender. They had come in carriages and wagons and on horseback, and seemed almost as numerous as the allied army. The Swede, Axel Fersen, was fascinated by the natives:

> It really seems as if the Virginians belonged to a totally different race of people . . . No white man ever labors, but all the work is done by black slaves, guarded by white men who in their turn are under an overseer . . . Business men, of course, are considered quite an inferior order of being by the lordly planters who, not looking on them as gentlemen, preclude them from their society.

These Virginians were much like aristocrats the world over, Fersen thought. "The only wonder is how they were ever induced to accept a government founded on perfect equality of rights."

The French troops were splendid in their white linen and pastel silk facings, in striking contrast to the scarecrow Americans—but many Frenchmen looked admiringly at their allies, as Baron von Closen did at this moment: ". . . most of these unfortunate persons were clad in small jackets of white cloth, dirty and ragged, and a number of them were almost barefoot . . . What does it matter! . . . These people are much more praise-worthy to fight as they do, when they are so poorly supplied with everything."

At last there was a roll of drums from the town, and the enemy came, their color guard carrying furled flags and their bands playing "The World Turned Upside Down," a melancholy, unmilitary tune. As the column moved toward the lines of the allied troops, men craned for a glimpse of Cornwallis, but he was not there. The British were led by General O'Hara, stiffly erect in his saddle, a baroque figure in enormous jackboots. Double rows of curls hung like tiny sausages about his temples, in the mode of earlier generations.

Count Dumas rode out to guide the column to the surrender field, and O'Hara flashed him a dazzling smile, his face "ruddy and black."

"Where is General Rochambeau?" O'Hara said. Dumas nodded to the head of the French line. O'Hara urged his horse toward the Frenchman, but Dumas, guessing that he intended to surrender to Rochambeau, spurred ahead to block his path.

O'Hara held out his sword to Rochambeau, but the old man shook his head and pointed to Washington in the opposite line: "We are subordinate to the Americans. General Washington will give you orders."

O'Hara swung his horse and reined before Washington. Dumas watched closely as he tried to surrender his sword: "General Washington, anticipating him, said, 'Never from such a good hand.' "

Commodore Richard Taylor of the American navy, who was a few feet away, overheard O'Hara speak to the allied commander: "O'Hara apologized for Cornwallis not coming out; that he was sick (heart-sick, no doubt)."

Washington passed O'Hara to Benjamin Lincoln, his deputy commander, and Lincoln pointed to the field just beyond Washington and his staff, where Lauzun's hussars sat their horses in a large circle; the British would enter the circle, each regiment in turn, put down their arms and march back between the allied lines. The troops came on.

Light-horse Harry Lee, who was near the head of the American line, was struck by the "universal silence" of the motionless allied troops and the civilians, who stared in fascination as the enemy soldiers gave up their arms. Lee thought the crowd was gripped by "an awful sense of the vicissitudes of human life, mingled with commiseration for the unhappy."

The enemy soldiers were spruce in new uniforms, but otherwise, Dr. Thacher thought, they were "disorderly and unsoldierly . . . their step was irregular, and their ranks frequently broken." A Virginia colonel had the same impression. The Earl's men were so overcome by the numbers of the allies "that their knees seemed to tremble, and you could not see a platoon that marched in any order." The English seemed more weary and "much less heroic" than the Germans.

A New Jersey officer had a more touching view of the enemy: "The British officers in general behaved like boys who had been whipped at school. Some bit their lips; some pouted, others cried. Their round, broad-brimmed hats were well adapted to the occasion, hiding those faces they were ashamed to show."

Lieutenant Feltman said, "The British prisoners all appeared to be much in liquor."

The British could no longer hide their mortification when they came to the field where they were to stack their muskets. They went slowly into the circle of hussars to give up the weapons. Thacher wrote:

> Some of the platoon officers appeared to be exceedingly chagrined when giving the word 'ground arms', and . . . they performed this duty in a very unofficer-like manner . . . many of the soldiers manifested a sullen temper, throwing their arms on the pile with violence, as if determined to render them useless.

General Lincoln sent a brusque order, and the British began stacking arms with care.

A veteran Scot corporal of the Seventy-first Highland Regiment hugged his musket to his chest before throwing it down, wailing, "You can never have as good a master as I was."

From the ranks of the surrendering army, Johann Doehla looked "with wonder on the great force of the enemy." Most of the men in Doehla's regiment were sobbing as they marched. The Colonel, von Seybothen, gave commands with tears streaming down his cheeks:

"Present arms!

"Lay . . . down . . . arms!

"Put off swords and cartridge boxes!"

The enemy, one German officer thought, could never understand the grief and rage that shook them—to be here on this field, surrendering to a pack of farmers and shopkeepers. He was cheered somewhat by expressions of warmth on the faces of the Americans; the French were more soldierly but also noisier and more vain.

In nearby ranks, Corporal Popp was even more astonished than Doehla as he marched between the lines of the allies, hearing the fine music of their bands: "We . . . were staggered by the multitude of those who had besieged us. We were just a guard-mounting in comparison with them, and they could have eaten us up with their power."

Popp especially admired the French: "They were mostly fine young men and looked very good. Their generals were in front and had aides who were beautifully attired in silver." These officers did not conceal their pleasure at the plight of the conquered army: "All drew much satisfaction and joy from the sight of our troops."

The British and Germans marched off at last, when all the shrunken regiments had given up their arms. The column seemed shorter as the men passed, empty-handed, between the French and Americans—about 3500 troops had come out to surrender; as many more waited in Yorktown, mostly the sick and wounded.

The dignity of the scene was marred only by a mishap of Admiral de Barras. The admiral was a poor horseman, but he had said resolutely that he would sit in his saddle for forty-eight hours, if need be, to see British prisoners file past. Now, in the midst of the ceremony, de Barras amused bystanders with a yelp of alarm as his mount stretched beneath him to relieve himself, "Good heavens! I believe my horse is sinking!"

Across the river, at almost the same hour, the Marquis de Choisy presided over a similar surrender in miniature, as the British gave up their arms and turned over the post at Gloucester Point.

The troops of Cornwallis had no sooner returned to Yorktown than Washington's headquarters was thronged by officers of the defeated army, chattering with the French and Americans as if they had never been enemies. O'Hara had come to dinner, in place of Cornwallis, and the Irishman amazed his hosts by his poise. The occasion was remarkably free of tension. Trumbull thought the meal was "very social and easy"—it was as if the war had ended long ago, its hatreds forgotten. Some American officers were outraged by the new spirit of brotherhood; they could not forget British atrocities—murder, arson, and the inhuman treatment of civilians.

Washington had an added burden as he dealt with the avalanche of army affairs that evening. Jacky Custis, who was ill with fever, had insisted upon watching the surrender, despite the advice of doctors. Custis had gone in a carriage, bright-eyed and gaunt, to see the enemy give up their arms. A few hours later Dr. Craik told Washington that Jacky was in danger and should be carried away. He was sent westward in a carriage.

After dark a belated reinforcement arrived in the British

camp, seventeen men from the Bayreuth Regiment, survivors of a band of one thousand who had marched up from South Carolina, only to blunder into allied lines near Williamsburg, where the unit was scattered and most of the men killed, wounded, or captured. The survivors found protection in Yorktown that night, despite the chaos reigning there—the French formed a ring about them to keep the Americans from stripping them.

Ensign Denny of Wayne's troops, who was on guard duty in the village on the night of October 19, found that the enemy had thrown off all discipline: "Much confusion and riot among the British through the day; many of the soldiers were intoxicated; several attempts in the course of the night to break into stores . . . our patrols kept busy."

Denny reported the last battle casualty of the Yorktown campaign—an American sentinel killed by a British soldier with a bayonet.

EPILOGUE

In the strange aftermath of the surrender, allied headquarters entertained the urbane British commanders as if they had never been enemies. Rochambeau had a dinner party for General O'Hara on October 20. The handsome Irishman was the only man of Cornwallis' staff who spoke French perfectly, but he was garrulous at table, and some of the allied staff found him a braggart, apparently unaffected by the disaster of Yorktown. The Irishman told French officers, in stage whispers, that he was glad he had not been captured by the Americans alone. Lafayette overheard him and snapped, "It's obvious that General O'Hara does not like encores"—O'Hara had been taken at Saratoga also, that time by Americans fighting alone.

Baron von Closen thought O'Hara was "very self-centered and interested in serving . . . as much for profit as for glory." Some Americans noted bitterly that the French and English fell into companionable discussions of other times and other wars, much as if the campaign just ended had been only a diversion.

Rochambeau left the table to visit Cornwallis in Yorktown, accompanied by several aides. Closen was astonished by the Earl's air of serenity: "His appearance gave the impression of nobility of soul, magnanimity, and strength of character; his manner seemed to say, 'I have nothing with which to reproach myself, I have done my duty, and I held out as long as possible.'"

Cornwallis talked pleasantly for half an hour, explaining the failure of the river crossing, and repeating much of the anguished letter he had written to Sir Henry Clinton that day; the question of fixing the blame for the disaster preyed on the Earl's mind. He had spent hours composing his dispatch:

> Yorktown, October 20, 1781
> I have the mortification to inform your Excellency that I have been forced to give up the posts of York and Gloucester, and to surrender the troops under my command. . . .
>
> I never saw this post in a very favourable light . . . nothing but the hopes of relief would have induced me to attempt its defense. . . .

Cornwallis added a summary of the siege, of the steady constriction of his lines, and of the ruin showered on the village by allied artillery, until his situation had become hopeless. He ended with phrases which had become familiar to him during the gloomy councils of war under the marl bluff:

> Under all these circumstances, I thought it would have been wanton and inhuman to the last degree to sacri-

fice the lives of this small body of gallant soldiers . . .
I therefore proposed to capitulate.

On the same day Lafayette called on Cornwallis at the
latter's request; the Earl was eager to meet the young Frenchman with whom he had dueled all summer and to explain
why he had surrendered. Cornwallis greeted the marquis
with a map of Virginia in hand, pointing out how he had
planned to escape from Gloucester before the storm had
struck, scattering his boats. Lafayette smilingly explained
the moves the army had made to cut off the British retreat
even if he had successfully crossed the river.

The Earl received other French visitors the day after the
surrender—Rochambeau sent an officer with £150,000 in
silver, a loan to Cornwallis, who said that he and his staff
were impoverished. The Earl wrote Rochambeau that the
Americans had treated him well, but that "the kindness and
attention that has been shown to us by the French officers
in particular—their delicate sensibility of our situation, their
generous and pressing offers of money, both public and private, to any amount—has really gone beyond what I can
possibly describe."

Yorktown itself was a landscape of horrors, Closen noted,
"One could not take three steps without running into some
great holes made by bombs . . . half covered trenches, with
scattered white or Negro arms or legs, some bits of uniforms." The houses were riddled by shot, and window panes
were blown out. Most striking of all, Closen thought, was
the terror of the few inhabitants, now that the Americans
had come to pillage.

The fears of Yorktown merchants were justified; Closen
passed shops where "the deputy quarter-masters acted shame-
fully." The surrender terms provided that all merchandise

should be paid for, but Closen thought, "surely half of it must have been taken *gratis*."

When merchants closed their stores in self-defense against American looters, speculators moved in to sell goods to the troops at high prices; the newcomers were farmers and watermen of the neighborhood, anxious to sell food to the prisoners in return for hard cash. Colonel Butler blamed the enemy for setting the example: "I observe the greatest villainy practiced by the British; they don't appear to have an idea of honor . . . They have completely plundered everything in their power, and do not pay the least regard to any treaty." Dr. Thacher agreed; he estimated that British looting in the six months before Yorktown amounted to three million pounds sterling.

Thacher spent much of the day in the battered village:

> It contains about sixty houses . . . many of them greatly damaged and some totally ruined, being shot through in a thousand places and honey-combed, ready to crumble to pieces. Rich furniture and books were scattered over the ground, and the carcases of men and horses half-covered with earth . . . The earth in many places is thrown up into mounds by the force of our shells, and it is difficult to point to a spot where a man could have resorted for safety.

Ensign Ebenezer Denny saw other casualties: "Negroes lie about, sick and dying, in every stage of the small pox. Never was in so filthy a place." Denny also found evidence of defective American ammunition: "Vast heaps of shot and shells lying about . . . which came from our works. The shells did not burst as expected."

The allies found mountains of arms and supplies in the village. Despite the earlier reports of Cornwallis that his stocks were depleted, there was actually much artillery and ammunition, including 144 cannon and mortars, about 1500 round shot, 500 shells, thousands of cartridges for the big guns, 600 hand grenades, and 120 barrels of powder. Other equipment was almost beyond counting: tools and leather, fuses and powder horns, carts and harness, nails and sheet iron, and all the apparatus of a large artillery park. Ordnance officers found eleven blunderbusses and twenty-six toma- hawks.

Small arms were also plentiful: about 800 muskets, 3400 flints, 266,000 musket cartridges, and more than 2000 swords and sabers.

Almost a hundred stands of colors were captured, includ- ing eighteen German and six British regimental flags.

The quartermasters took over a bewildering variety of stores: about 300 horses, 43 wagons, 400 saddles, three tons of hemp, three tons of iron, 1000 sand bags, four tons of coal, 500 bushels of corn, 836 sheets, 450 tents, 613 gross of buttons, more than 1000 uniforms, 1300 pairs of shoes, 1100 pairs of hose, and thousands of yards of cloth and ribbon.

The bountiful stocks of food in the larder would have infuriated soldiers who had gone hungry during the siege: 73,000 pounds of flour, 60,000 pounds of bread, 20,000 pounds of pickled beef, 75,000 pounds of pork, 20,000 pounds of butter, 1200 pounds of oatmeal, 30,000 bushels of peas, 3000 pounds of sugar, 1500 pounds of rice, 3000 pounds of cocoa, 2500 pounds of coffee, and 1250 gallons of liquor.

British casualty reports revealed lighter losses than sur- vivors of the bombardment had indicated. Official returns set redcoat strength at 7247 men; an estimated 309 were killed during the siege, and 44 had deserted. In addition there were 840 naval prisoners.

Washington sent out an order of congratulations to the

army and was busy with the endless details of completing the occupation and surrender. It was nightfall before he found time to consider a victory dispatch to Congress. He asked Trumbull to write it, discussed it with the staff, and made revisions. His secretary, David Humphreys, made a final copy. The message was brief and self-effacing, almost casual in tone:

> Sir: I have the Honor to inform Congress, that a Reduction of the British Army under the Command of Lord Cornwallis, is most happily effected. The unremitting Ardour which actuated every Officer and Soldier in the combined Army in this Occasion, has principally led to this Important Event, at an earlier period than my most sanguine Hope had induced me to expect. . . .

There were a few more lines, all in praise of others who had helped to win this campaign.

Washington chose his messenger without hesitation—Lieutenant Colonel Tench Tilghman, Jr., a handsome Marylander who had spent five years on the staff, usually without pay. Tilghman was one of Washington's intimates who had shared command secrets almost from the start, soon after he had closed his business in Philadelphia to become a militia captain. The colonel was thirty-six, a slender, gray-eyed man of deep reserve, earnest and sensible, celebrated even on the close-knit staff for his complete loyalty to Washington.

Tilghman carried a letter to Thomas McKean, the president of Congress, asking that the veteran who bore the message "be honored by the notice of your excellency and Congress." He hurried off toward Philadelphia with the news for which the country had waited so long; it was a singular journey.

The colonel had recently suffered from fever, probably malaria, and was still weak and flushed as he left camp. He went down the York in a tiny Chesapeake sailboat and at the mouth of the river turned northward, up the long reach of the bay. Winds were favorable at first, and the home-made craft scudded swiftly past the tidal flats of the Mobjack country. Even this brisk wind was too light for the impatient Tilghman; he was two days late in a race to carry the news to the capital—Admiral de Grasse had written of the surrender of Cornwallis on October 18, the day before the British had given up their arms.

The courier's luck soon worsened. "By the stupidity of the skipper," the boat ran aground near Tangier Island, far out in the Bay; they spent a night waiting to be freed by the tide, while Tilghman fumed. The wind died to a whisper the next morning, and they sailed no more than twenty miles during the day. Then, as the exasperated Tilghman reported to Washington, "The wind left us entirely on Sunday evening thirty miles below Annapolis."

Tilghman's anxiety grew; he realized that if de Grasse's news had reached Philadelphia, Congress would be uneasy because it had not heard from Washington. There would be doubts in the capital, so often deluded by false tidings from the army. Tilghman also became ill with his "intermittent fever," but there was no time for rest. He went ashore at Rock Hall, on Maryland's eastern shore, persuaded someone to lend him a horse, and galloped off on the final leg of the journey. He halted often to change horses, shouting to astonished farmers and householders in the Maryland and Pennsylvania countryside, "Cornwallis is taken! A horse for the Congress!"

It was after midnight of October 23 when he rode into Philadelphia, shaking with chills and fever. At last, with the aid of a night watchman, he aroused President McKean at his home and gave him the dispatch announcing the final and decisive victory of the war. The old German watchman returned to his rounds, bellowing in the empty streets, "Past dree o'clock—und Corn-val-lis is ta-gen!" The bell at the State House—Independence Hall—tolled until daybreak. Congress held an early morning session to discuss the news from Virginia.

Tilghman was now so ill that he was put to bed—but since he was penniless, among the first business of Congress, as celebrations rocked the city, was to find money for the messenger. There was none in the Treasury, and Congressmen dug into their own pockets and gave one dollar apiece to pay Tilghman's room and board.

The victory message also stirred trouble in Independence Hall, where there were angry shouts that Cornwallis should be hanged in revenge for his atrocities in the South. Several members demanded that Washington be ordered to execute the Earl at once; and despite protests that Cornwallis had surrendered in good faith and that Washington's reputation was at stake, Congress defeated the resolution for vengeance only by a small majority.

Congress declared a day of national thanksgiving and voted Tilghman a horse, saddle, bridle, and "an elegant sword"; Congress also sent a vote of thanks to the forces at Yorktown, gave Washington some captured British flags, and two cannon to Rochambeau. Tilghman spent several days in bed before he could return to the army.

Philadelphia celebrated with a grand illumination of the city the night after the colonel's arrival, and a patriot posse marched out to see that all citizens took part. Mobs attacked houses whose windows were not lit with candles. It was a long night for the peace-loving Quakers of the city. The mobs hung about the darkened houses, throwing rocks and shouting insults, giving vent to their long-standing resentment at the antiwar stand of the Quakers.

Elizabeth Drinker, the wife of a Quaker shipper, who was ill in her house on Front Street, recorded the violence:

> Scarcely one Friend's house escaped. We had nearly 70 panes of glass broken ... the door crashed and violently burst open; when they threw stones into the house for some time, but did not enter . . . some houses, after breaking the door, they entered and destroyed the furniture. Many women and children were frightened into fits.

The allied armies at Yorktown hurried to move the troops of Cornwallis to safety, and early on Sunday morning, October 21, the second day after the surrender, the prisoners were herded into the road toward Williamsburg. The French commissary, Claude Blanchard, watched them admiringly: the British and Hessians were "very fine-looking men," especially the tall, handsome Grenadiers. "The remainder of the English were small; there were some Scotch troops, strong and good soldiers."

These men, privates and non-commissioned officers, trudged off westward under guard of General Lawson's Virginia militia; the six thousand were to be divided between prison camps at Winchester, Virginia, and Frederick, Maryland. Except for 180 unfortunate officers assigned to stay behind with their men, it was only the rank and file that ended as prisoners of war. Most officers were already on parole, having agreed not to fight again until exchanged —they were free to leave for England or for any British port in America.

Blanchard rode into the camp of the prisoners, a few miles out on the road to Williamsburg, inspecting them with the eye of a commissary officer; he saw men going about routine tasks, gathering wood, pitching tents, and making soup. Blanchard noted a sharp contrast between British and German troops even now: "The Germans preserved order and a certain discipline; on the contrary, there was very little order among the English, who were proud and arrogant."

Blanchard was indignant over the scornful attitude of the British toward their captors: "There was no call for this; they had not even made a handsome defense, and, at this very moment, were beaten and disarmed by peasants who were almost naked, whom they pretended to despise and who, nevertheless, were their conquerors."

Not all of these men were to reach their prison pens. Many escaped to start new lives in backwoods America, and some plunged across country on the four-hundred-mile journey toward safety in New York; a handful got through. In early November five Germans of the Anspach Regiment reached Manhattan, having posed as deserters as they passed through American territory. About twenty British escapees were caught in New Jersey and imprisoned at Morristown.

Washington was impatient to leave Yorktown. On the day the prisoners left he sent General Choiseul across the York to supervise the disarming of the Gloucester garrison. The commander himself went out to the fleet to thank de Grasse for his part in the victory; it was only after Cornwallis had surrendered that Washington fully appreciated the decisiveness of the September battle at sea. As he wrote General Heath, "The naval engagement appears to have been of much greater importance than was at first estimated."

Washington gave other signs that he foresaw the coming of peace and independence. In an unprecedented move, he opened the army's stockades and freed all prisoners, without regard to their offenses. But a few hours later, deserters caught in Yorktown—men who had once served with him but had changed uniforms—were hanged from gibbets; other Americans who had followed their conscience to serve with the British throughout the war were set free. The French praised his sense of justice.

Virginia civilians also came to settle accounts with the British. One of them was a Mr. Day, the overseer of Sir Peyton Skipwith's distant plantation, Prestwould, in southwestern Virginia, who came into camp in search of a stolen horse. After a ride of more than 150 miles he was in no mood to be denied.

The overseer saw Banastre Tarleton on the stolen horse and announced to American officers, "That's our horse that that damned Tarleton's riding. He's worth 500 pounds and I'm going to get him—I didn't come all the way from Dan River for nothing." Day cut a sweetgum sapling, making a cudgel about as thick as his wrist, and strode off toward the town.

A few minutes later Tarleton and a servant came out from Yorktown, "riding in high style." Day stepped into the road with his club, seized the horse's bridle and drawled softly, "Good morning, Col. Tarleton. This is my horse. Dismount." The colonel hesitated briefly, and Day raised his cudgel. An officer who watched the scene reported, "Colonel Tarleton jumped off quicker than I ever saw a man in my life." Day leapt into the saddle and trotted away westward on the blooded stallion. Tarleton went to a nearby tavern, took his servant's horse, and rode back to headquarters, followed by the hoots of the Americans. One onlooker, Daniel Trabue, never forgot the scene:

Oh! how we did laugh to think how the mighty man who had caused so much terror and alarm in Virginia had been made to jump off the wrong side of his horse so quickly, with nothing but a sweet gum stick and a chunky little man against him, while he, who was a tall, large likely man had a fine sword by his side.

Other overseers and planters came to the camp in search of slaves. Troops were hired to hunt down the Negroes in the woods. Sergeant Martin and his friends chased down some slaves for a Colonel Banister for a price of one guinea per head, but the soldiers refused to deliver until Banister promised not to punish the slaves. Banister gave the Negroes their choice of remaining or returning to his plantation without punishment, and the half-starved blacks went off with him, wild with joy. Martin's share in catching one of these pathetic men was twelve hundred dollars in paper money. He spent it all on a quart of rum.

The British sloop *Bonetta* left Yorktown on October 23 under the terms of the surrender, without allied inspection. Colonel Butler, the choleric Pennsylvanian, suspected British treachery and watched sourly as the little ship fell down the river, "with her iniquitous cargo of deserters, stolen Negroes, and public stores that the British officers had secreted, in violation of treaty and in breach of honor."

As Butler suspected, the *Bonetta* had saved the necks of about 250 deserters and Tories; these men arrived in New York, more than a week later, "so extremely riotous" that the exasperated skipper risked his ship to put them ashore in the midst of a storm.

A ragged line of lights appeared off the Virginia coast in the windy darkness of October 24, bobbing dimly above the turbulent sea. It was the British fleet. From Smith's Island, a few miles north of Cape Charles, three men who had escaped from Yorktown put to sea in a tiny schooner, fighting their way outward through tall waves, guiding on the ghostly lamps of the warships. By 4:00 A.M. they were taken aboard the flagship *London*, cold and drenched. They told Graves and Clinton a grim story that had the ring of truth: Cornwallis had given up. Silence had fallen on Yorktown.

The leader of the three was a Negro, James Robinson, who had been pilot of HMS *Charon*. They had fled Yorktown on October 18 when they heard rumors of a surrender, Robinson said; there had been no firing for a day before they left—and they had heard none since. Another refugee, Robert Moyse, a quartermaster's clerk, said that others had already fled Yorktown and that the army had been low on ammunition for many days.

The fleet sailed on to the South and the next day met the forty-gun frigate *Nymphe*, which had slipped away from Yorktown with Cornwallis' dispatch of October 15. The final words of the message confirmed the story of the escapees: "I cannot recommend that the Fleet and Army should run great Risque in endeavouring to save us."

On the twenty-sixth, when the fleet was within plain sight of the opening between the Chesapeake Capes, Admiral Graves sent a whale boat to the beach and brought off some Tories who told the same tale: the Yorktown garrison had surrendered. For two days the fleet cruised in heavy weather as Graves probed gingerly for the enemy.

He sent two frigates between the Capes to look for the French, and at about sunset of Saturday, October 27, Captain G. K. Elphinstone of the *Warwick* climbed his mast and counted forty-five sail in Hampton Roads. Two big French ships chased the frigates briefly the next day and fired a couple of wild shots.

It was Sunday evening before Washington, ashore at Yorktown, got word from de Grasse that the French had sighted thirty-six British ships. The Frenchman called his shore parties aboard, but the wind was so strong from the northeast that he could not leave his anchorage. By the next day de Grasse reported forty-four British sail—but the enemy gave no sign of wanting to fight his way into the bay.

There were now seventy-two ships of the line and heavy frigates in the waters near the Capes, but no other shots were fired. It was October 29 when Graves gave up. He pushed his fleet very near the Middle Ground Shoal at the entrance of the bay and once more grilled the three escapees who had come from Yorktown. They clung to their story so convincingly and were corroborated in such detail by the Loyalists aboard that Graves sent the *Rattlesnake* to London and the *Nymphe* to New York with the news.

They did not openly challenge his decision, but Hood and Clinton did not agree with Graves. As the ships bobbed in the whitecaps a few fathoms off shore, Hood went to his cabin and wrote disdainfully:

> Mr. Graves has just sent me word he is about to send a ship to England. His messenger brings the most melancholy news Great Britain ever received . . . a most heartbreaking business, and the more so to my mind, as I shall ever think his Lordship ought to have been succoured or brought off . . . which Mr. Graves had in his power to effect at his pleasure . . . my mind is too greatly depressed with the sense I have of my country's calamities to dwell longer upon the painful subject.

Graves had come to the end of his resources: "There appeared nothing so proper as to return with the Fleet to New York."

The approaches to the Chesapeake were soon empty, and French shore parties put out for the land once more.

In the allied camp at Yorktown it was clear that the campaign had ended with the disappearance of the British fleet. Closen said that the fleet had come "after the pot had boiled." Lafayette said, "the play is over."

The round of dinner parties continued, with French and American commanders entertaining Cornwallis and his staff, night after night. When all other major generals had played host, Steuben was overcome with embarrassment. He sold his favorite horse and asked a friend for a loan so that he could give a banquet himself. He protested even more bitterly his obligations to the Frenchmen. "We are constantly feasted by the French without giving them a bit of *bratwurst,*" he told one of his aides. "I will give one grand dinner to our allies, should I eat my soup with a wooden spoon forever after."

Steuben was apparently penniless when he was ready to leave Yorktown and was so distressed that he swallowed his pride, asking Washington for a loan. The commander seemed strongly moved; he insisted that Steuben take twenty guineas, but as to whether the Government would ever pay the Prussian what he was due, Washington could give him "no hopes of any future alteration."

About November 1 the Prussian veteran left for Philadelphia, hoping to settle his accounts with Congress; he left one of his sick aides his carriage and half the money remaining from Washington's loan, setting off for the North with a single gold coin in his pocket.*

Allied entertainments of the enemy continued in Yorktown. On November 2 Rochambeau again invited all the ranking English and German officers to dinner, and this time the earl accepted. The French were impressed by Corn-

* An audit showed that the U.S. owed Steuben $8500 in hard cash, but he was given only $1700—the balance of $6800 was paid in the form of a Treasury Certificate at 6 percent interest—which the Baron later tried in vain to sell for ten cents on the dollar.

wallis and his "reflective, mild, and noble bearing." The Earl spoke of his Carolinas campaign and conceded that even his victories there had contributed to defeat.

The Earl repaid Lafayette's visit about this time and was shocked to find in the Frenchman's headquarters a Negro he had hired to spy on the Americans—he had been spying on the British instead.

The chief actors in the drama were soon gone. On November 3 a nondescript fleet of scows and work boats sailed up the bay, carrying American troops. Many trenches had been filled in, but the French strengthened the inner wall about Yorktown and placed guns to defend the port. Rochambeau and his men settled for the winter in Yorktown, Hampton, and Williamsburg.

Two days later Cornwallis and O'Hara sailed for New York, and Washington rode westward with his staff, stopping in Williamsburg to visit patients in the hospital. By evening he reached Eltham at the head of the York River, the home of his brother-in-law, Burwell Bassett, where he came upon a family tragedy—Jacky Custis was in his last hours. The young man died during the night, leaving four young children. It was a week later when Washington and his grieving wife finally reached Mount Vernon.

Rumors of the Yorktown disaster had first reached British headquarters in New York on October 24, about twelve hours after Tench Tilghman had reached Philadelphia. The redcoats heard cannon fire in New Jersey during the day, and as it rolled on into the night, they concluded that the rebels were celebrating. Lieutenant Frederick Mackenzie, the headquarters diarist, noted casually, "It is supposed that the Enemy would have taken Yorktown." At night a courier came in with a captured letter announcing the surrender of

Cornwallis and his army, but many at headquarters were skeptical of the report.

General Robertson was almost alone in believing that Cornwallis had surrendered, and the senile old officer rambled about the affair until staff officers were sick of him. Mackenzie wrote, "He appears displeased with those who differ in opinion with him . . . He now begins to talk much of the delays made by our fleet in refitting, and says they might have been out five days sooner, which would have saved Cornwallis."

Mackenzie said that Robertson "cannot keep any secret," and regaled a crowd at a public dinner party with details of the most recent letter from Cornwallis. It was obvious, Robertson said, that the army at Yorktown was doomed.

On October 26 "a confidential person from Philadelphia" brought more detailed news: Cornwallis had defiantly refused to surrender to Washington, saying that he would make terms only with the French and not the American rabble. Washington had then sent Anthony Wayne and his men storming into the village, forcing the capitulation.

The spy from Philadelphia had more ominous news: he had it from a man who had seen a letter from de Grasse that "Mons. Clinton was the Count de Grasse's next object."

Mackenzie thought there were "too many improbabilities in this account"—but headquarters ordered New York harbor blocked by sunken ships to keep out the French, just in case.

It was October 27 when New York had final confirmation: "The fate of the army under Lord Cornwallis is no longer doubted." Details of the surrender agreement were read at headquarters during the day.

The British fleet returned to New York on November 7, and Sir Henry Clinton went back to his headquarters.

Lieutenant Mackenzie detected no signs of despair. The staff still indulged in daydreams that the fleet would turn about, sweep down on Yorktown once more, and yet save the day. But behind the scenes at headquarters, as Judge Smith saw, there was only gloom and despair. Clinton obviously realized that the battle for America had been lost.

Sir Henry now bitterly and openly denounced everyone concerned with the loss at Yorktown, an incessant flood of protest that others were to blame, not he. Lord Germain was "the falsest man alive," he told Smith.

"If I could have ended the war in half an hour, he would have prevented it," Clinton said.

Sir Henry's conversation was now a monologue, "a desultory justification of his own conduct and censure of everybody else—Lord Amherst, the Secretary of State, Sir George Rodney, Lord Cornwallis, General Robertson, General Knyphausen, General Tryon, Admiral Arbuthnot, Mr. Graves, the fleet, etc." "He is a distressed man," Smith concluded, "looking for friends and suspicious of all mankind, and complains of the number of his enemies . . . The man is wild . . . I pity him in his disgrace."

Clinton had only begun to protest his innocence. Years later, he was to buttonhole everyone in England who would listen, petulantly disclaiming blame for Yorktown. "I may say with Macbeth," he often cried, " 'Thou canst not say I did it.' "

The gloom that settled over New York was slow in reaching London. George III was at first optimistic: "I have no doubt when men are a little recovered of the shock felt by the bad news . . . that they will then find the necessity of carrying on the war . . ."

The king said firmly that Yorktown would not make the "smallest alteration in those principles of my conduct which have directed me in past time." A few months later, when the meaning of Yorktown had become clearer and North's administration had fallen, the king said bitterly to his resigning minister, "It is you who desert me, not I you."

George III had by then become so despondent that he drafted a message of abdication rather than accept American independence, but thought better of it and struggled through the final months of the war with a new government. There was to be no end to the war for two years, until the treaty of Paris in 1783, but though strong British armies still occupied New York and Charleston, and though Washington feared that the country would compromise the victory at Yorktown by falling into "a state of Languor and Relaxation," the fighting in America was over.

No one had seen more clearly the meaning of Yorktown than the Minister, Lord North, who had learned of the defeat in the distant Virginia tobacco port from the blundering Germain. North took the news "as one might a ball in the breast. He reeled, threw out his arms, exclaiming wildly, as he paced up and down . . . 'Oh, God! It's all over!' "

Chapter Notes

Chapter 1
The Vanishing Army

The opening incident is drawn from Joseph Plumb Martin's *A Narrative of Some of the Adventures, Dangers and Sufferings of a Revolutionary Soldier . . .* (Hallowell, Me., 1830). Other details are from contemporary sources, the temperature of July 6, for example, from vol. 2 of *The Diary of Frederick Mackenzie* (Cambridge, 1930).

The description of the French troops and their movements is based on *The Revolutionary Journal of Baron Ludwig von Closen* (Chapel Hill, N.C., 1958); *My Campaigns in America,* by Count William de Deux-Ponts (Boston, 1868); the journals of Axel Fersen in vol. 3, of Count Cromot du Bourg (listed as "anonymous") in vol. 4, and of the Duke de Lauzun in vol. 6, *Magazine of American History; New Voyage in America . . .* by Abbé Claude Robin (Philadelphia, 1782); and the *Journal of Claude Blanchard,* edited by Thomas Balch (Albany, 1876).

Chapter Notes

A helpful general account is Stephen Bonsal's *When the French Were Here* (New York, 1945), which presents previously unpublished documents. The description of Washington is drawn largely from observations of the French officers cited, which are conveniently summarized in Gilbert Chinard's *George Washington As the French Knew Him* (Princeton, 1940). The reconnaissance of Washington and Rochambeau is described in Rochambeau's *Memoires Militaires Historiques et Politiques* (Paris, 1809) and Washington's *Diaries*, vol. 2 (Boston, 1925). The correspondence between Washington, Rochambeau and de Grasse, and Washington and Lafayette, is in vols. 22 and 23 of John C. Fitzpatrick's familiar and comprehensive *The Writings of George Washington . . .* (hereafter designated as *GW*) (Washington, D.C., 1931–44). Blanchard's *Journal* describes the scene at the crossing of the Hudson and the French observers cited above added numerous details.

Timothy Pickering's account of Washington's angry outburst has been neglected by historians because it does not fit into the accepted version of the general's personality and of the campaign's strategic development. The astute Pickering, however, left a persuasive account and his glimpse of Washington in the moment of crisis is one of the most telling on record. It is found in vol. 2 of Charles W. Upham's *Life of Timothy Pickering* (Boston, 1873), pp. 54–55. This instance is illustrative of the difficulty of reconstructing every step in the process of decision in this campaign.

The sketch of Knox is drawn from North Callahan's biography, *Henry Knox—General Washington's General* (New York, 1958).

The remainder of this brief summary of the opening moves of the campaign by land is based upon such sources as the *Minutes* of Jonathan Trumbull, Jr. (in Massachusetts Historical Society *Papers*, April, 1876); the recollections of Col. Philip van Cortlandt (in *Magazine of American History*, vol. 2); and of Count Mathieu Dumas (. . . *Memoirs of His*

Own Time, Philadelphia, 1839) and other Frenchmen already cited; the *Journal* of Elias Boudinot (Philadelphia, 1894) and the invaluable journal of the young surgeon Dr. James Thacher (Hartford, 1861).

Details of the route of the march are taken from W. S. Baker's *Itinerary of General Washington* (Philadelphia, 1892). The order of August 29, Lincoln-Lamb, is from the Lamb MSS, New York Historical Society. Washington to Governor Lee, dated 28 August, is in vol. 23, p. 58, of the *George Washington Papers,* Library of Congress, and the intelligence report from Forman to Washington is in 36 *GW* 183. The comment which ends the chapter is from vol. 2 of Washington's *Diaries,* page 258, under the date of 30 August.

Chapter 2
A Perplexed Onlooker

This chapter owes much to Sir Henry Clinton's exhaustive account of his role in the war, *The American Rebellion,* edited by William B. Willcox (New Haven, 1954), and even more to Willcox's *Portrait of a General . . .* (New York, 1964), a biography of Clinton based largely on the Clinton Papers in the Clements Library, University of Michigan, and on the Newcastle Papers at Nottingham, England. Also of great importance were two diarists, Lt. Frederick Mackenzie and Judge William Smith, the latter still largely unpublished. The picture of corruption and high living at British headquarters is based on Thomas Jones's *History of New York During the Revolutionary War . . .* (New York, 1879).

The cited correspondence between Clinton and Cornwallis here and in later chapters comes from vol. 2 of *Clinton-Cornwallis Controversy,* edited by B. F. Stevens (London, 1888). Of special interest are the voluminous spy reports, detailing Washington's movements, received and disregarded by Clinton. These are still in the Clements Library; copies of more than a dozen are in the author's collection.

The sketch of Admiral Hood is based on Dorothy Hood's work, *The Admirals Hood* (London, 1911), and on *Letters Written by Sir Samuel Hood,* edited by David Hannay (London, 1895).

Chapter 3
The Great Ships Gather

The description of de Grasse and his preliminary movements toward the Chesapeake are based on Harold A. Larrabee's *Decision at the Chesapeake* (New York, 1964), and upon the major sources of that work, especially *Admiral de Grasse and American Independence,* by Charles Lewis (Annapolis, 1945), *The Naval Campaigns of Count de Grasse* by Karl G. Tornquist (Philadelphia, 1942), *The Graves Papers . . . ,* edited by French E. Chadwick (New York, 1916), *The British Navy in Adversity . . .* by William M. James (London, 1926), and the *Journal* of Rear Admiral Bartholomew James (London, 1896). Other important sources were *Lafayette and the Close of the American Revolution,* by Louis Gottschalk (Chicago, 1942), and *Brigadier-General Louis Lebègue Duportail,* by Elizabeth S. Kite (Baltimore, 1933).

Chapter 4
The Long March

The chief sources for the Philadelphia scene, in addition to Washington and the French diarists, are *The French in America During the War of Independence* . . . by Thomas Balch (Philadelphia, 1891); *Philadelphia, A History* . . . by Ellis P. Oberholtzer, vol. 1 (Philadelphia, 1912); *The History of Philadelphia*, by J. Thomas Scharff and Thompson Westcott, vol. 1 (Philadelphia, 1884); "The Route of the Allies From King's Ferry" by John Austin Stevens, in the *Magazine of American History*, vol. 5, pp. 13 ff; and biographies of Robert Morris by Ellis Oberholtzer (*Robert Morris, Patriot and Financier*, New York, 1903) and Howard Swiggett (*The Extraordinary Mr. Morris*, New York, 1952).

Details of the desperate efforts to pay the troops are found in Oberholtzer's *Morris*, p. 86, and the engaging scene in which Washington expresses his joy over the news from de Grasse is based largely on the accounts of Deux-Ponts and von Closen. The news as announced to the troops, as cited in "Lt. Sanderson's MSS Diary," is found in Henry P. Johnston's *Yorktown Campaign* (New York, 1881); a slightly different version is in 23 *GW* 94. Baker's *Itinerary* is again used for the routes of the troops and Balch, vol. 1, describes the movements by water.

The defacement of the Washington portrait in Philadelphia is reported in the *Freeman's Journal* of September 12, 1781. The description of Washington's appearance at Mt. Vernon is from Benson Lossing's *Mary and Martha* . . . (New York, 1886). Trumbull's comment on Mt. Vernon is in

3 *GW* 333; Washington's urgent message to Lincoln is in Jared Sparks's *Writings of George Washington,* vol. 8 (Boston, 1834), p. 159; Washington's dispatch to Lafayette from Mt. Vernon is from Washington's *Diaries,* vol. 2, p. 260.

Chapter 5
War In The Backwoods

The summary of Cornwallis' campaign in the Carolinas is based generally upon Willcox's life of Clinton; the *Clinton-Cornwallis Controversy,* vol. 1; Clinton's *American Rebellion*; lives of Nathanael Greene by George Washington Greene (New York, 1871) and Theodore Thayer (New York, 1960); North Callahan's *Life of Daniel Morgan* (New York, 1961); histories of the Revolution by Christopher Ward (*The War of the Revolution,* New York, 1952) and John R. Alden (*The American Revolution, 1775–1783,* New York, 1954); "A View of Cornwallis' Surrender at Yorktown" by Randolph G. Adams in *American Historical Review,* vol. 36; Henry B. Carrington's *Washington the Soldier* (Boston, 1898); Rupert Hughes's *George Washington* (New York, 1930); *The Cowpens-Guilford Courthouse Campaign,* by Burke Davis (Philadelphia, 1960); Hugh F. Rankin's *The American Revolution* (New York, 1964) and *The Spirit of Seventy-Six,* edited by Henry Steele Commager and Richard B. Morris (Indianapolis, 1958).

The graphic view of the battlefield at King's Mountain after the combat is given by a participant, James P. Collins, in *Autobiography of a Revolutionary Soldier* (Clinton, La.,

1859) and that of the battle of Cowpens is drawn from "Memoir of Thomas Young . . ." in *The Orion,* vol. 3, p. 88. The stern orders of Cornwallis in his attempt to discipline unruly camp followers are found in "A British Orderly Book" edited by A. R. Newsome, *North Carolina Historical Review,* vol. 9, 1932. St. George Tucker's letter to his wife describing the flight of Virginia troops at Guilford Courthouse is in *Magazine of American History,* vol. 7.

Chapter 6
The Boy General

Basic secondary sources are Gottschalk's *Lafayette and the Close of the American Revolution; Lafayette in Virginia,* by Gilbert Chinard (Baltimore, 1928); Carrington's *Washington the Soldier;* lives of Steuben by Friedrich Kapp (*The Life of Frederick William von Steuben,* New York, 1859) and John Palmer (*General von Steuben,* New Haven, 1937); and the biographies of Anthony Wayne by Harry Emerson Wildes (New York, 1941) and Charles J. Stillé (Philadelphia, 1893).

Most of the Lafayette letters in this chapter are cited by Gottschalk and many of them are in the Washington papers in the Library of Congress. Numerous others have been published by Gottschalk in *The Letters of Lafayette to Washington, 1777–1779* (New York, 1944).

Several Pennsylvania participants left valuable accounts, among them Richard Butler in vol. 7 of *Historical Magazine* (1864, p. 110); and William Feltman in vol. 2 and John Bell

Tilden in vol. 19 of *Pennsylvania Magazine*. Lt. Feltman's journal is especially revealing. For example, there is his unique description of naked Negroes by the roadside and the sexual endowments of these young men—a passage deleted in all published versions of the journal until the appearance of Winthrop D. Jordan's *White Over Black* (Chapel Hill, 1968).

The early protest by Cornwallis after being ordered to Yorktown was dated 8 July 1781 and is in the *Clinton-Cornwallis Controversy*. Washington's unstinted praise of Lafayette's generalship in the campaign was written to Joseph Jones on July 10 and is in 22 *GW* 353. Lafayette's expressed awe of the abilities of Cornwallis was written to Henry Knox on August 18 and appears in *Historical Magazine*, vol. 8, p. 73.

Chapter 7
Into The Trap

The movement of Cornwallis to Yorktown is made clear in vol. 2 of the *Clinton-Cornwallis Controversy* and analyzed in Willcox's life of Clinton in much greater detail than was possible in this narrative. Naval aspects of this, especially Cornwallis' reconnaissance of an alternative post at Old Point Comfort, are documented in *The Graves Papers*.

Historians are fortunate that several perceptive diarists shared Cornwallis' fate at Yorktown, among them Cols. John Simcoe (*A Military Journal*, New York, 1844) and Banastre Tarleton (*A History of the Campaigns of 1780–1781 . . .*,

Dublin, 1781) of the cavalry, Johann Doehla and Stephan Popp of the German infantry, and Lt. Bartholomew James of the Navy. Their premonitions of impending disaster are in striking contrast to the dispatches of Cornwallis. Further details concerning the Germans are in *The German Allied Troops in the North American War . . .* by Max von Eelking, (Albany, 1893).

Doehla's "Journal" is in the *William & Mary Quarterly*, 2nd series, vol. 12, 1942; Popp's is excerpted in *American Heritage*, October, 1961.

Chapter 8
Decision At Sea

Despite the passage of time and voluminous publication, the all-important naval battle preceding Yorktown remains little known to laymen, and no comprehensive study has yet resolved conflicting details. As D. S. Freeman pointed out, there has been a need for an exhaustive study of the action.

The guide for this chapter was Larrabee's *Decision at the Chesapeake*, the only extensive published account of the battle. A summary of the literature is in Freeman's *George Washington*, vol. 5, pp. 511 ff. Essential primary sources on the British side were Chadwick's *The Graves Papers* and Hannay's *Letters Written by . . . Hood*. Of lesser importance was *Two Letters Respecting the Conduct of Rear Admiral Graves . . .* by William Graves (Morristown, N.J., 1865). The French sources included de Grasse's own *Account of the Campaign of Naval Armament . . .*, which was printed aboard his flagship soon after the action; *Journal of "The Chevalier de Goosencourt"*, by a participant writing under a pseudonym; *Journal of An Officer In the Naval Army . . . ,* published in Amsterdam in 1783; and Tornquist's *The Naval Campaigns of de Grasse*. Important reports and dispatches of de Grasse are found in *Correspondence of General Washington and Comte de Grasse* (Washington, 1931).

Two British journals of value were left by Lt. Bartholomew James and by Capt. Henry Duncan, in the *Naval Miscellany,* vol. 1 (London, 1902).

Useful secondary sources are Beatson's *Naval and Military Memoirs of Great Britain* (London, 1804); Thomas White's *Naval Researches* (London, 1830); J. C. Shea's *The Operations of the French Fleet . . .* (New York, 1864); W. M. James's *The British Navy in Adversity* and Alfred T. Mahan's *The Major Operations of the Navies in the War of American Independence* (Boston, 1913); Balch's *The French in America . . .* vol. 2; and James B. Scott, *De Grasse at Yorktown* (Baltimore, 1931).

Chapter 9
"Every Door Is Shut"

The Virginia campaign before Washington's arrival in Williamsburg in mid-September is ably set forth in Gottschalk's *Lafayette and the Close of the American Revolution* and his *Letters of Lafayette to Washington*. The role of the French reinforcements from the West Indies is described in

Chapter Notes

Harold A. Larrabee's story of Marquis de Saint-Simon, *A Neglected French Collaborator in the Victory of Yorktown* (Paris, 1932). Firsthand accounts are in diaries and journals of previously cited witnesses—Feltman, Butler, Ebenezer Denny ("A Military Journal, . . ." in *Memoirs of the Pennsylvania Historical Society*, vol. 7), Thacher, Blanchard and Martin. There is some uncertainty about Feltman's testimony, since he is said to have been captured during the skirmish at Greenspring; someone, in any event, continued the diary to the end of the campaign, and this narrative assumes that Feltman made the later entries.

Another witness is the anonymous author of "Journal of the Siege of York in Virginia by a Chaplain of the American Army," in vol. 9 of *Massachusetts Historical Collections* (1st series). One of Lafayette's staff officers, James McHenry, wrote copiously to Governor Thomas Sim Lee of Maryland, and these published letters shed considerable light on events. The incident of the murder and mutilation of a Virginia woman is recounted in Tornquist, pp. 56–57.

The amusing incident of Lafayette's embrace of Washington at their reunion in Williamsburg was written by Judge St. George Tucker in his old age, but it varied from his contemporary version of the incident only in minor detail. The version cited here is found in W. C. Bruce's *John Randolph of Roanoke*, vol. 1 (New York, 1922).

The graphic sketch of the French latrine at the College of William & Mary is from James Tilton's *Economical Observations on Military Hospitals* (Wilmington, 1813), pp. 63–64. Washington's voyages to and from the *Ville de Paris* are recounted in Trumbull's *Minutes*. The unavoidably stilted account of the dialogue between Washington and de Grasse traces to important documents prepared by a staff officer, published in . . . *Washington and . . . de Grasse;* the original text of Washington's queries is in 23 *GW* 122–25. The traditional anecdote of de Grasse's greeting to Washington is from G. W. P. Custis' *Recollections and Private Memoirs of Washington* (New York, 1860), a source that must be used with caution.

The quoted orders to American troops at the close of the chapter are from *The Orderly Book, Continental Army, Siege of Yorktown, Sept. 26–Nov. 2, 1781* (Philadelphia, 1865).

Chapters *10 & 11*
"The Liberties Of America . . . Are In Our Hands."

The narrative of the siege is based on Henry P. Johnston, D. S. Freeman's account in vol. 5 of his *George Washington*, Rupert Hughes's biography of Washington, and Thomas J. Fleming's *Beat the Last Drum* (New York, 1963). Throughout this work, however, the fullest possible use of the accounts of participants has been made and witnesses frequently cited heretofore are of especial importance during the siege. The Americans were: Feltman, Butler, "An American Chaplain," Trumbull, Martin, Thacher, Tench Tilghman, Van Cortlandt, Capt. James Duncan (*Pennsylvania Archives*, 2d series, vol. 15), Capt. John Davis of the Pennsylvania Line (in *Virginia Magazine*, vol. 1, no. 1), Major David Cobb (*Massachusetts Historical Society Papers*, 1881–1882), Elias Dayton (in *New Jersey Historical Society Papers*, 1st series, vol. 9), and, most important, the diary of St. George

Tucker, edited by E. M. Riley (*William & Mary Quarterly,* July 1948). The French included: Blanchard, Deux-Ponts, Lauzun, Dumas, von Closen. The English were: Tarleton, Simcoe and James. The German witnesses cited were Doehla and Popp. The narrative does not pause for comment when these come into conflict—as in the case of Tarleton *vs.* Cornwallis. The cavalryman's later criticism of the Earl gained much from hindsight. Other important sources include *The Orderly Book* and Washington's *Diaries,* vol. 2, for the American side, and *Clinton-Cornwallis Controversy* for the British.

Both Washington's worn headquarters tents and his horse "Nelson" are described by G. W. P. Custis; Washington Irving's biography is the authority for placing the commander's first camp under a mulberry tree.

Joseph Martin's story of his night encounter with Washington between the lines and of Washington breaking ground with a pick are among the rare unstudied views of the commander during the war.

An example of the unresolved puzzles existing in documents on the siege is the timing of the opening of allied artillery. This narrative accepts Washington's version—3 P.M. of October 9. Feltman, Butler, Duncan and Trumbull say 4 P.M. and St. George Tucker, 5 P.M. There is some question as to whether Washington actually fired the first American gun, but Dr. Thacher, usually a reliable witness, is taken as authority here; van Cortlandt's secondhand testimony to this effect adds substance to this version.

Another incident that cannot be approached with assurance by historians is Governor Nelson's offer of his own house as a target to American gunners. Johnston, pp. 139–40, offers this story, citing G. W. P. Custis as a source, and Hugh Rankin in *The American Revolution,* p. 333, presents as traditional Nelson's offer of a cash reward to the first gunner to hit the house.

The story of Steuben's bravado in his exchange with

Viomenil is from Kapp's *Steuben*, p. 458. The story of Knox and Hamilton and their narrow escape from a bursting shell is from Callahan's biography of Knox, citing a witness, Aeneas Monson.

Chapter 12
Thirteen Councils Of War

The almost incredible tale of procrastination, bungling and ineptitude at British headquarters in New York as the noose was drawn about Cornwallis emerges clearly from the pages of Willcox's biography of Clinton. The story is buttressed by Clinton's own narrative in *The American Rebellion,* and by the Clinton Papers at the Clements Library, especially the minutes of the various councils.

Randolph G. Adams in "A View of Cornwallis' Surrender . . ." offers further details, and once again the inveterate diarists, Judge William Smith and Lt. Frederick Mackenzie, are most effective witnesses. The correspondence cited is from *Clinton-Cornwallis Controversy,* or from *Facsimilies of Manuscripts in European Archives Relating to America,* edited by B. F. Stevens (London, 1889).

Despite the picture of Clinton, Robertson, and the British admirals as incompetent and negligent agents of royal power in America, it is probable that any course of action, however vigorously pursued, would have been futile at this stage. Once the French fleet had won control of the Chesapeake, and Washington and Rochambeau had invested Yorktown, the British army there was doomed, and the pathetic efforts of Clinton and his staff to meet the crisis were merely an epilogue.

Chapter *13*
Surrender

But for the diarists—many of them obscure men in the ranks—we would know very little of the surrender. Only Ebenezer Denny recorded fully the dramatic moment when the British drummer leapt to a parapet under heavy fire and beat a call for a truce—and there was only Denny to describe the planting of the American flag on the captured works. Once more, Doehla, Popp and James told what it was like in the camp of Cornwallis. St. George Tucker's poetic description preserved a vivid view of Yorktown and its harbor on the day the guns fell silent. J. B. Tilden, Joseph P. Martin, Thacher, Pickering, Dumas and others, when their accounts are combined, offer a satisfying view of events.

As is so often the case, there is conflicting testimony as to details—even as to the hour the redcoat drummer appeared. The diarists Denny and Ebenezer Wild saw him at 9 A.M.; but Washington (who was not a witness) said he began his beat at ten o'clock.

The documents exchanged between Cornwallis and Washington, frequently published, are here taken from Tarleton and Henry Johnston.

The ceremony of surrender was remarkably described by von Closen and by Doehla and Popp from the German ranks. Numerous others left more limited accounts. Two major controversies have vexed historians: did the British bands actually play "The World Turned Upside Down"? And did Gen. O'Hara attempt to surrender his sword to the French? The musical tradition stems from Alexander Garden's *Anecdotes of the Revolutionary War,* vol. 2 (Charleston, S.C., 1822), but though corroboration is lacking, the story is plausible. Several versions of the tune were well known at the time and the most popular was a somewhat melancholy dirge. Freeman, in vol. 5 of *Washington,* pp. 388 ff., and Commager and Morris, in vol. 2 of *The Spirit of Seventy-Six,* p. 1245, offer exhaustive commentary on this point. As to O'Hara's role, this narrative accepts the persuasive account by Dumas, who was most intimately involved; the testimony of other nearby witnesses, such as Richard Taylor, appears to support the version of Dumas.

The distress of Admiral de Barras during the ceremony was reported by von Closen.

Epilogue

The sketch of O'Hara at dinner is by von Closen, and his humorous exchange with Lafayette was reported by Lafayette in vol. 1 of his *Memoires,* p. 281 n. Lafayette's meeting with Cornwallis is described by Gottschalk in *Lafayette and the Close of the American Revolution,* pp. 329–30, citing "Sparks MSS."

Estimates of the casualties and relative strengths of the opposing forces at Yorktown vary as widely today as in the eighteenth century. By Freeman's estimate in 1952, the allies outnumbered Cornwallis by about two to one—20,000 to

10,000—but these figures are admittedly only approximations. No accurate reports were made by either side. The official report on arms and ammunition found in Yorktown was made by Henry Knox, and the Quartermaster General's report by Timothy Pickering; they are reprinted in Tarleton.

The sketch of Tench Tilghman and his ride to Philadelphia is based on *Memoir of Lt. Col. Tench Tilghman,* by Oswald Tilghman (Albany, 1876); *Sidelights of Maryland History,* by Hester D. Richardson (Baltimore, 1903); and on an unpublished article "Tench Tilghman—The Courier From Yorktown," by Lee Crutchfield, Jr., in the Maryland Historical Society. Efforts in Congress to hang Cornwallis were reported by Elias Boudinot in his *Journal,* p. 59; approval of the awards to Tilghman and Rochambeau are found in *Journals of the Continental Congress, 1774–1789* (Washington, D.C., 1904–1937), vol. 21, edited by Gaillard Hunt, p. 108. Miss Drinker's account of violence against Quakers by celebrating patriots is from *Extracts From the Journal of Elizabeth Drinker,* edited by Henry D. Biddle, (Philadelphia, 1889), p. 137.

Claude Blanchard was evidently the only witness to take special note of the prisoners from Yorktown; his observations are the basis of this sketch. The freeing of all prisoners in American hands is mentioned by Thacher, p. 291, and Washtington's hanging of some deserters found in Yorktown by Shea in his *Operations,* pp. 86–88—but no first-hand account is cited.

The humiliation of Col. Tarleton by Sir Peyton Skipwith's overseer, recorded by several witnesses, is here drawn from the Journal of Col. Daniel Trabue, in *Colonial Men and Times . . . ,* edited by Lillie Du Puy Harper (Philadelphia, 1916).

A more detailed account of the roundup of slaves by bounty-seeking soldiers is in Joseph P. Martin's *Memoir,* pp. 174–5.

Chapter Notes

The belated arrival of the British fleet is depicted in *The Graves Papers,* pp. 137 ff.; Hood's somber letter on the British disaster is on p. 145 of this source.

Von Steuben's poverty, and his entertainment of brother officers, is reported by his aide, William North, in vol. 8 of *Magazine of American History;* by Steuben in a letter to Nathanael Greene, November 5, 1781 (cited in Palmer's biography of Steuben); and by Alexander Garden in his *Anecdotes of the Revolutionary War,* vol. 1.

The Washington-Cornwallis anecdote is given by Thacher, p. 292, and should be accepted as traditional.

Reception of the news of the surrender in New York is described by Mackenzie, vol. 2, pp. 694 ff; Willcox tells the story well, with frequent citations from Mackenzie and from William Smith's *Diary.*

The quotation from King George is cited by Johnston, p. 160, as "Correspondence with Lord North . . ."—Donne.

Washington's fears of American overconfidence were expressed in a letter to Nathanael Greene, cited by Hughes, p. 686.

The final quotation of Lord North, in the brief final scene, is from vol. 2 of *The Historical and Posthumous Memoirs of Sir Nathaniel Wraxall . . . ,* edited by Henry B. Wheatley (New York, 1884).

INDEX

Index

Index